OPEN ROAD

A MIDLIFE MEMOIR OF TRAVEL THROUGH THE NATIONAL PARKS

T W NEAL

This book could only be dedicated to the love of my life, my partner around every curve of the road: Michael Ray Neal.

Oh, these vast, calm, measureless mountain days, days in whose light everything seems equally divine, opening a thousand windows to show us God . . . The mountains are calling, and I must go. ~ John Muir

CHAPTER ONE
THE ABYSS

Change only happens, especially in midlife, when we are uncomfortable or want something badly enough; and I had reached that tipping point. My heart rate hadn't calmed since the ranger's station where we'd checked in—*were we really doing this?*

I sat on the sidewalk near the Keonehe'ehe'e (Sliding Sands) Trailhead, waiting beside our full backpacks, at the summit of Haleakalā National Park on Maui. At ten thousand feet of elevation, the air was thin, cold, and unfamiliarly bracing. I dug a parka out of my pack and put it on.

Just yesterday I'd been in the chiropractor's office for the lower back pain generated by our training hikes. I had a bad hip from years of toting babies back in my twenties, ankles prone to sprains from running in my thirties, and a lower back injury from doing capoeira in my forties. Now, at almost fifty, I was thirty pounds overweight.

My husband, Mike, wasn't in much better shape. In addition to being eleven years older, he'd recently undergone multiple surgeries, and he'd lost most of his colon to a severe bout of diverticulitis that had almost made me a widow. His new titanium shoulder was about to be carrying a forty-pound pack for strenuous miles, and his arthritic knees, recently shot full of cortisone, would be strained by the deep sand leading down into the depths.

We were about to launch ourselves into a *No Service* zone. No one would be able to help or communicate with us, and few even knew we were attempting a strenuous, three-day hike in the crater.

I surveyed the area around me to distract my anxious thoughts.

The astronomy observation buildings that crowned Haleakalā's summit clustered nearby like a hen surrounded by round white eggs. Off in the distance to my right the ocean glimmered, a hammered bluish mirror. Popcorn puffs of cloud raced by below, casting shadows across the water's surface.

To my left, the crater itself swooped down—a vast swath of rusty, tiny cinders in shades of umber and burnt sienna. Cinder cones deep in the great bowl below looked like peaks churned up during child's play in a giant's bathtub. A chilly wind whipped up from the long gray sand path and smacked my cheeks.

Mike finally returned, panting from the effort of walking part of the way uphill from where he'd been dropped off from parking our truck at the trailhead where we'd exit in a few days. Even without the packs, the ten-thousand-foot elevation was having an effect. "You ready?" he asked.

"As I'll never be." An old joke. We'd been married close to thirty years, long enough to have many of those.

Getting the backpack on was daunting. I couldn't lift it. I eventually set the big metal frame on a large boulder, sidled back into it, and hoisted it up, leaning over to secure the belt. Hopefully the thirty pounds of extra weight resting on my tricky hip was a good thing.

"Let me see if I can strap yours onto mine." Mike hovered, adjusting my shoulder straps and testing the weight by lifting it from behind. "If push comes to shove, I can carry them both."

He was worried about my recent chiropractor visit, though neither of us mentioned it. Carrying my pack also had a precedent: way back when we were first engaged, we'd hiked in Yosemite's

Tuolumne Meadows. Flush with first love and in the prime of his considerable strength at thirty-one years old, he'd carried both our packs when I got tired.

I'd loved him for that back then, and I loved him for his concern right now; but I was tired of being a wimp. I'd decided that had to change. "I got this."

I pushed out in front of him and set off down the trail.

The truth was simple: *If I think about this adventure any longer, I'll chicken out.*

Little poufs of grayish cinder sand rose beneath my boots as I crunched downhill into the crater, avoiding looking anywhere but directly ahead. The trail, while fairly wide, plunged hundreds of feet off to one side in a slippery scree of rough cinder.

Mike soon caught up to me with his much longer legs.

I mentally reviewed today's plan: go down a total of four miles on the Sliding Sands trail to the caldera floor, then two more miles across the crater's floor to the Park Service cabin called Kapalaoa Cabin (the Whale's Tooth.) We'd spend the first night there, then hike the roughly four miles across the crater floor to the Hōlua cabin, spend another night, then hike out another four miles the next day up the infamous "Switchbacks" (Halemau'u) Trail to exit.

"We can do it," I muttered, though I had a persistent pain in my hip and my toes were being slowly crushed by the tightness of too-thick socks and my forward-leaning weight with thirty extra pounds on my back as we headed downhill through deep sand.

We moved slowly but steadily, stopping occasionally to take a vista photo or a shot of the velvety pincushions of gray green silver-swords dotting the colorful expanse of boulder-strewn lava. These gems of Haleakalā live only in this barren and remote setting; the unusual plants vary in size from that of a teacup to a barrel. Silver-swords grow in a rosette pouf of velvety, pointed succulent leaves that resemble a sea urchin, and they looked lovely against the harsh, unbroken cinder soil. Each plant may grow from five to twenty years before flowering in a great spire and dying.

Mike had kept his DSLR camera handy, and as we went, he captured images of those currently flowering. The tall spires looked like brussels sprouts shooting up from a candleholder base—unlike any flower I'd ever seen.

About halfway down into the crater, Mike stumbled behind me and emitted a rare curse. Stumbling wasn't good—I turned in fright, still trying to avoid thinking about how far we'd fall, were one of us to slip off the trail. "Are you okay?"

Breathing hard, Mike backed up against the nearest rock outcrop, rested his pack on it, and shook his head. "I think my boot blew out." With the weight of the pack temporarily lifted, he was able to raise one foot. Sure enough, his stockinged foot wiggled comically in a large crack between the boot's toe and the flap of the sole.

"We didn't even make it to the bottom before catastrophe!" I leaned over and put my hands on my knees to rest the weight on my back. "What do you want to do?"

"I brought some duct tape in case of emergencies. I'll fix it right here." My husband never went anywhere without duct tape. Mike wriggled out of his pack and lowered it to lean against the rock, then dug in a side pocket.

I backed up to a boulder, rested the weight of my pack on it, and finally looked down into the abyss. *Such a long way to fall.* My imagination supplied a vivid scene of me flopping ass over teakettle thousands of yards to the bottom, pulverized by my backpack. I shivered and looked away, remembering the moment that had started us on this journey—a trip for which this hike was only the first step.

The madness had started when, approaching my fiftieth birthday, I went to the doctor's office for my annual physical, always a time for reflection and hangdog glances at the scale.

The news wasn't good. Clearly, the marathon of overwork and stress I'd been on for the last thirty years had taken a toll on my health: my hair was falling out in clumps, my cuticles bled from biting, my weight and cholesterol had skyrocketed, and my hands were peppered with itchy red hives.

A calendar of the United States National Parks was pinned to the wall across from my position of surrender on the table. I turned my head on the crinkling paper pillow to stare at it, eager for any distraction from my upcoming pelvic exam.

Bryce Canyon National Park met my gaze, glowing with the hypersaturated color of cheap printing on a calendar whose pages curled back from the thumbtack holding it to the wall.

Mystical crenellated shapes of sandstone hoodoos, massed columns of eroded sandstone, filled a deep valley, a vast army of melting stone warriors in shades of russet and gold, setting forth in the purple light of dawn—a magical, compelling image, so beautiful that it was hard to believe it was real.

"I want to see that with my own eyes," I said aloud. "I want to be healthy enough to travel and hike, and I want to experience the National Parks."

I'D BARELY TURNED TWENTY-ONE WHEN MIKE NEAL AND I WERE married in Hanalei, Kauai, at the landmark green Waiʻoli Huiʻia Church, the site of childhood memories both good and ugly.

Three years later, we had children: a boy and a girl.

Eventually, we both completed college degrees and settled on Maui, raising our family and doing work we enjoyed: I as a counselor/therapist and Mike as a woodwork artist, photographer, and social worker. But we'd sacrificed for a long time to get to the comfortable middle-class existence we eventually achieved, and the gaunt wolf of age was chewing at the backs of our legs.

Mike had a terrible year as he approached sixty. He was in and out of the hospital, unable to work, while I held down three jobs to keep the family boat afloat. Eventually, the crisis subsided, and now I was making a big transition in my career: leaving my full-time work as a child/adolescent therapist and embarking on a new, risk-filled adventure as a writer.

But somewhere along the way, I'd given up my health and—myself. I no longer recognized the girl I'd once been. Maybe she could be found, somewhere along the road to the National Parks.

"Seeing the National Parks is how I want to celebrate turning fifty," I told Mike when I got home from the doctor's office. "Let's take a road trip, just the two of us."

Mike's smile was my reward as he lit up—he'd always been more adventurous than I. "Sounds like a plan!"

"A *long* road trip," I said. "Let's go for at least a month and see what parks we can visit in that time."

"Wow, you're really ready to let rip," he said dubiously.

After a tumultuous childhood filled with changes and moving, I'd settled into being an adult who liked to rule out surprises: buying insurance, studying *Consumer Reports*, and conducting heavy research into anything new. As a reaction to my hippie upbringing, I was deeply committed to being "normal."

Safe. Predictable. Padded.

Our family of four ate three square meals a day that followed the Recommended Food Pyramid. We drove a newish, reliable Honda sedan in a color designed to hide dirt, following the Suggested Maintenance Schedule of oil changes, and avoiding even a whiff of misbehavior in the form of parking tickets. Our kids had no idea how I'd been raised, running wild and semi-clothed in the jungle on Kauai, until they read my first memoir, *Freckled*—because they'd grown up *normal*.

I liked sensible clothing built for longevity and wore shoes with orthotics to protect my arches. My powerful imagination could be an enemy, creating worst-case scenarios and serial killers under every doorknob—so I was friendly, but socially cautious.

I wasn't a sanguine traveler, either. Prone to highlighter-marking map routes, I made Byzantine checklists, overpacked to anticipate every possible scenario, and experienced sleepless, tension-filled nights before any trip. I hyperventilated in heavy traffic, clutched the armrests on bumpy flights, got dizzy when confronted by heights, squealed at the sight of rodents, and sweated nervously in crowds.

I had a very narrow temperature comfort window (65 to 85 degrees) and cried at the mere idea of the dentist's drill.

I didn't recognize myself anymore: not only the crow's feet and pudgy silhouette in the mirror, but the anxious, timid, conventional woman I'd become. I'd been a brave and resilient young person, but somewhere along the strenuous trek to reach "normal," I'd lost the brave, tough, outdoorsy girl I used to be.

If we were going on a road trip for a month to see the National Parks, I needed to get in shape for it: not only physically but mentally and emotionally.

We sat down to figure out how to allot enough time and money for the trip. My birthday was in January, and winter wasn't a great time on the mainland for road trips, so we planned to leave on our expedition in May, beginning our trip in California and then heading to the Southwest parks.

"But it makes no sense to fly and drive all the way to the Southwest to see the other parks when we haven't even fully explored the one right in our backyard," Mike said. He had a point: in all the years we'd lived on Haleakalā, despite visiting the National Park in all its moods, we'd never hiked the Crater.

"You're right." I firmed my chubby chin. "I just finished Cheryl Strayed's *Wild* memoir. If that ill-prepared lady could hike the Pacific Crest Trail alone, surely I can hike Haleakalā with you!"

Haleakalā is Hawaiian for "house of the sun," and according to legend, the demigod Maui lassoed the sun from its peak to lengthen the day for his beloved mother. Back in 1916, Haleakalā National Park was created as part of one large Hawaii National Park, which included the volcanoes of Mauna Loa and Kīlauea on the island of Hawaii.

Hawaii Volcanoes National Park on the Big Island broke off into a separate entity in 1961, and the name *Haleakalā* was chosen for the Maui park, though the park also encompasses a large area of coastline along the eastern shore of the island, past the area of Hana at Kipahulu. This portion of the park is popularly known as "Seven Sacred Pools" (officially, the Pools of 'Ohe'o), nicknamed for a series of waterfalls pouring from one to the next, down from the summit to the sea.

Maui's national park covers 33,265 acres, approximately 52 square miles, of which 19,270 acres is officially designated wilderness area—and it was into that wilderness that we were hiking.

Looking back up the trail was disconcerting; what had seemed like miles as we progressed now appeared to be only a couple of hundred yards. "Distances are deceiving in the crater," I muttered, repeating something I'd heard hikers in Haleakalā say.

Mike finished his duct tape repairs, got his boot back on, and hoisted his pack. "Just remember, when this hurts tomorrow—it was all your fault."

"Totally my fault. Thus, the journey of a thousand miles begins with a single step," I quoted, taking a theatrical lunge forward—and we got moving again.

CHAPTER TWO
HALEAKALĀ NATIONAL PARK

Mike's boot repair held up, and we eventually reached the crater's floor, joining a group of visitors who'd taken our route on horseback. The mules and horses munched from nose bags and drank water at a hitch rail while the tourists roamed about, loud and annoyingly energetic.

Mike and I slogged over to sit under a large, hospitable *mamane*, a large native plant with bright yellow flowers which cast a welcome umbrella of shade. We unslung our packs and sat on the ground under the big bush, whose nectar-laden blossoms are one of the few sources of food for endangered native Hawaiian honey-creeper birds.

The relief of taking off the packs was akin to pleasure. We ate sandwiches I'd packed for easy access as we fended off the bold overtures of non-native *chukar* grouse, colorful birds from India that resemble quail. The *chukars* liked the look of our lunch and circled us, begging for scraps in soft, piping chirps.

Seated there, chewing on my sandwich and washing it down with gulps of water, I eyed the terrain. The crater floor was peppered with sunblasted ferns and hardy *Pukiawe* shrubs, a small, juniperlike bush. These plants were slowly conquering the raw new rock, filling in and breaking down soil around gigantic boulders. The force needed to hurl those rocks through the air to where they'd landed must have been tremendous. I pictured them belching forth from the caldera like a giant's spitwads.

We didn't realize how strained our bodies were until it was time to put the packs back on and hit the trail again for the last two miles. My feet were swollen and bruised, and my toes throbbed from being pushed into the toes of my boots by miles of downhill hiking in deep sand, carrying significant weight. Every part of my body complained in a symphony of aches and twinges, but I didn't say a word. As Mike had pointed out, this was all my fault.

Trudging at least twenty feet behind Mike's tall form, I mentally designed a retroactive fitness preparation program: to train, we should have picked the longest beach on Maui, loaded up our packs with thirty pounds of rocks, and hiked six miles in the hot sun through the deep sand—then we might have had an idea what we were committing to.

The last two miles through the cinder dust on the floor of the crater assumed a sort of distorted, nightmarish quality. The air was so thin that I had to breathe twice as hard to get half as much oxygen. My heart pounded in my ears—why hadn't I brought some music to keep me moving?

There's a certain point in hiking where nothing exists but your breath, the trail directly ahead, and setting one boot in front of the other in a kind of existential moving Zen.

Surely, the cabin's just ahead, I kept thinking. *Distances are deceiving in the crater.*

I fell farther and farther behind Mike as I periodically paused to rest, leaning the pack on a boulder every hundred yards or so to catch my breath.

As the sun was beginning its descent into the west, we reached Kapalaoa Cabin, a surprisingly tidy and well-maintained building nestled in the shadow of the volcano's steep walls. Set on a velvety scrap of lawn, the small square cabin beckoned like an oasis.

I staggered forward to sit on the top step and loosened the straps of my pack so that it fell over backwards. Mike worked the number code on the locked front door and opened our quarters for the night.

I then discovered that the greatest joy of hiking, next to dropping the pack for the day, is taking off your boots. I stripped off sweaty socks and dug my bare toes into the silky grass, rubbing them around and moaning in bliss. *We made it!*

A part of me, that part that loved comfort, hated surprises, and was deeply committed to "normal," could hardly believe it.

When I had recuperated enough to stand again, I shuffled over to the water pump and soaked my feet in clear, cold water I'd pumped up from the earth. Nothing had ever felt as good as that cold water did on my hot, swollen feet.

The cabin was tidy on the outside, rugged on the inside. Equipped with triple-decker homemade wooden bunks of Naugahyde nailed over foam, the place was set up to sleep twelve Boy Scouts or *Menehune* (legendary Hawaiian "little people"). A wood-burning, potbellied heat stove and a couple of long picnic tables with built-in benches, scorched by cigarettes and decorated with graffiti, completed the furnishings.

Mike figured out how to light the kitchen burners, and we set a big pot of water from the outdoor pump on to boil for drinking and coffee.

Next, I set out to explore the joys of the rustic, splintery outhouse. Weathered gray cedar boards defined a narrow, coffin-shaped outbuilding with a bench inside crowned by a plastic toilet seat. Hectoring placards on the walls reminded me to *Pack out what you pack in!* and *Do not dispose of feminine products here!*

There was no toilet paper, but a couple of paper napkins, abandoned by previous hikers and anchored on the bench under a rock, worked fine. I peeked into the pit and saw that not everyone had heeded the Park's *Leave No Footprint* video we'd watched at the ranger station as part of our cabin use permit process. Fortunately, I'd carried one of the sandwich bags from lunch to the outhouse with me and was able to dispose of my wastepaper in that.

After a simple meal of Top Ramen noodles, Mike staked out a nearby cinder cone to plan the night's star photography projects, and I walked out onto the plain and lay on my back to watch the sunset.

The crater was quiet under the open sky, with the kind of silence that comes from emptiness—unbroken by anything for miles but the hum of wind in the sparse shrubs and the far-off honking of nene geese flying by. I soaked in the experience, smelling the dust of earth and stars, watching the red stain of dying day give way to indigo, then purple, then black, pierced by the light of distant suns.

I felt the vastness of space around me, as well as a quiver of the anxiety I battled on and off when faced with the extreme beauty and starkness of pure, undiluted nature. I was utterly drawn to experience it, and yet all too aware, in solitary moments, that what defined 'myself' was only a slightly different charting of atoms than what surrounded me.

CHAPTER THREE
HALEAKALĀ DAY TWO

Snuggled deep in my down sleeping bag on one of the bottom bunks inside the cabin, I was woken by the unearthly golden glow of the sunrise.

The temperature had fallen into the thirties during the night, but as I stuck my head out like a gopher from its burrow, I smelled the wood-burning stove, crackling with a warming fire, and the distinct aroma of fresh coffee. "Bless you, honey."

Mike wasn't there to hear. He'd always been an early riser, up before the sun to "dawn run" surfing, fishing, and now, to chase the light with his camera. On his way out, he often did some thoughtful thing to make the day more comfortable for me.

I unzipped the sleeping bag and helped myself to the hot brew on the stove. Mug in hand, I stepped out into the morning in Haleakalā Crater. I sat down on the top step and gazed around, my sleeping bag draped around my shoulders against the cold. I spotted Mike, a dark knob on one of the nearby cinder cones.

The silence was as thick as a presence. I heard nothing in the openness but the echoing clicks of one of Mike's cameras on a tripod beside the door, set for a time-lapse and aimed at a morning-streaked ridge.

I fetched my notebook and pen, looking up to feast my eyes on the wild display of highly pigmented colors as each section of rock was lit by the dawn. I sipped my luxurious coffee, wrote in my journal, and watched the sun slide up into the sky and pour light down, honey filling a bowl.

The knob on the crest wasn't Mike.

My husband walked toward me from a different direction entirely once the sunrise had spent its glory. Even after thirty years, watching him come toward me with that long-legged stride still made my heart thump in the best way. He moved with a gait that told me he was a little too tall for the bunk bed last night, and that all that hiking in sand was having an effect.

I wasn't the only one moving slowly this morning.

I got up and brought him a fresh cup of coffee when he reached the porch. "How're you doing?"

"Not bad." Mike held up his foot. The boot that had died yesterday was still held together around the insole with a couple of wraps of silver tape. "Long as this holds up."

I grinned. Mike is the original MacGyver; I've seen him fix everything from a kitchen sink to our kid's bike tire with that everuseful adhesive.

As the sun rose higher, we packed and donned our gear; we had four miles to hike across the crater floor to reach Holua Cabin, our next destination.

I'd hoped the trail would be fairly flat, but it wasn't. Up and down we went, over and around ash cones like huge sandcastles. We tracked ridges of lacy, brittle a'a lava. We crossed mountains of gray, powdered sand, and edged our way along cinder cliffs in the rainbow shades of melted crayons.

Every hundred yards or so arose some completely new, spectacular combination of vivid colors or arc of space and sky. No plants grew to distract from a land rendered in the purest forms of virgin rock. What no photo managed to convey, what looking from the rim at the tourist viewpoints couldn't show, was the mammoth scale of this setting: an ever-changing kaleidoscope of dramatic views impossible to see except by hiking. The walk across the floor of the crater was a revelation. What other miracles had I been missing by staying on the well-worn path of easy?

As we progressed, silverswords popped up again along the trail, punctuation marks of irreverent perfection, each one both random and symmetrical. Nearer our destination, rugged vegetation covered an older section of the crater: yellow *mamane* bushes and *Pukiawe* bloomed out of the harsh soil, along with hardy grasses. Clouds rolled up this easternmost side of the mountain every afternoon, and the mist provided enough moisture for the gradual process of taming the rock into dirt.

My calves were not happy by the time we arrived at our destination, but I was distracted from the stabs of pain by a pair of endangered native nene geese, tame as housecats, that walked up to greet us with soft, whuffling honks. Their sounds, like little swallowed snorts, were oddly conversational. The geese wore lovely colors—a buff like an English soldier's waistcoat with black and cream barring that contrasted with pearly, dawn-gray backs.

I sat down, immobilized by fatigue, on the plushy green grass in front of Holua cabin. The lawn was as neatly trimmed as a golf course, and I saw why as the birds chortled and grazed within inches of me, nibbling the grass with their delicate beaks.

Mike unpacked his camera to take their picture. I took my boots off, got up and walked to the water pump to splash my feet, face, and hands.

The geese followed. They waited for me to pump the water, then drank the falling drops straight from the tap, blinking their chocolate eyes and making soft commentary in their sweet voices. My chest tightened with joy at this evidence that these birds were fighting their way back from extinction, that they shared the space and water with us in such a friendly fashion.

"I'd love hiking if it weren't for the backpacks," I said later, as we unpacked in the cabin.

"I'd love it if it weren't for the hiking," he replied.

We were too tired to laugh.

Mike had packed a surprise romantic meal for our last night in the crater: steaks and broccoli, and a good bottle of Cabernet that must have added a couple of pounds of weight to his pack. Peacefully frying the steaks on the stove, the door open to the soft evening light and the wine breathing on the cabin's picnic table, we were startled by an aggressive hail.

"Hey!" an athletic-looking blonde woman yelled at us as she led a group of hikers in our direction. "That's our cabin!"

"What?" My heart lurched in alarm. At five p.m., it was way too late for us to hike to some other destination, and we had no other tent or shelter with us. The two approaching couples were younger, thinner, and much better dressed and equipped than we were, wearing Columbia and carrying fancy gear.

"We have permits," Mike said mildly. I turned off the stove, where the steaks, loudly crackling, were emitting mouthwatering smells.

"I'd like to see those," the blonde said, hands on her hips. "We're booked in here tonight." Her voice was so loud, and she was so confrontational, that I withdrew to the kitchen to perform cowardly mock dishwashing.

"Let's all look at the permits, together," Mike said, still calm. "Sort this out."

Everyone rustled around. Comparing the permits, it turned out that the two couples were supposed to be here the following night, not tonight. Our permit was the correct one.

The blonde woman stormed out, stomping around in front of the cabin, trying to call the Park Service with a phone that had no signal. Her boyfriend followed her out and tried to calm her down.

The quieter couple shuffled their feet, looking awkward. "Well, since it's so late—can we all bunk together?"

"Sure," Mike said.

There wasn't a lot of choice—we could just as easily have been the ones who'd made the mistake. Still, there went our romantic dinner. I tried to hide my disappointment and apprehension by cleaning the kitchen.

Social awkwardness fell upon us as a group as we all tried to adjust to the snafu.

The couples made their beds on the set of triple bunks furthest from ours, as Mike and I wolfed down our steaks in silence at the graffiti-scarred table adorned with stubs of candles puddled in their own wax.

Sunset was coming; we hurried outdoors with Mike's cameras and the bottle of wine, hoping to get some photos and adjust to the idea of close, shared quarters with strangers instead of the romantic togetherness we'd been hoping for.

"This is the perfect setting and situation for a crime," I told Mike as we sat, leaning against a boulder and sipping the wine from plastic cups. "I'm going to use this in a book. Picture this scenario: some poor hiker's in the cabin alone, trying to have a personal getaway, and someone arrives who shouldn't be there and takes her captive. There's no escape, no cell service. It's a perfect setup."

"Not so perfect," Mike said. "But we'll be fine. Nobody's taking *us* captive."

I had to smile at that, and so did he. I propped my head on his shoulder and we held hands as his cameras clicked away, set on auto. The sunset bathed us in golden-yellow, as if we'd been dipped in pollen, and gradually contentment returned as we watched the bonfire of day's end fade into the frozen star-glory that was night in the crater.

We returned to the cabin well after dark to find the group drinking and arguing politics around the picnic table. The blonde was a lawyer, and she and her boyfriend were on one side of the political fence from the others, with the upcoming Presidential election in much debate.

Mike fled into the night with his sleeping bag to watch over his cameras, as I lay on my tiny bunk, trying to read. Even with earplugs, I could hear the arguing go on and on. What ring of hell had I fallen into with these people?

An endless night proceeded. One of the men snored like a hibernating bear; someone else talked in her sleep. Innumerable openings and shuttings of the squeaky front door occurred as six people went to the outhouse to pee. In the wee hours, one of the hikers fell off his bunk trying to climb down, waking everyone.

These elements combined to drive Mike and me out of the cabin at the first hint of dawn. We had four hard miles to climb the infamous Switchbacks uphill trail out of the crater, so we figured we might as well get an early start since we had no desire for further interaction with our bunkmates. We hoisted our packs with nothing in our stomachs but coffee and determination and set out—but at least the backpacks were lighter sans a bottle of wine, steaks, and the frozen water bottles Mike had used to keep the food fresh.

Even so, at some point we hadn't boiled our water enough, or I'd eaten something not quite right, or I was feeling the altitude—but about halfway up the endless ascension from the floor of the crater, I got sick.

From both ends.

Hell did indeed have another ring besides politics.

I squatted just off the trail with uncontrollable diarrhea, fighting nausea and holding onto a bush just to stay upright, while worrying that some other hiker would catch me polluting the wilderness.

The mortification of a rescue drama was the only thing that kept me putting one boot in front of the other, in between bouts of being sick. At one point I considered crawling, and if the path had been any longer, I would have had to.

Mike returned to meet me as I sat miserably on the trail beside my backpack after another episode. "Still not feeling well, eh?"

I just squinted my eyes at him. Stringing words together to confirm the obvious didn't seem worth the effort.

Mike unslung his pack and set it on the ground. My hero was wearing an old pair of blue jeans, a duct-taped boot, and a battered leather hat that made him look like Indiana Jones. He retrieved a piece of rope from a side pocket and lashed my backpack onto his. "Last chance to call for help."

"No. I can do it. But I can't believe you have to carry my pack," I sniffled, dashing tears of self-pity off my cheeks. "Again."

"We'll make it. Take your time, and I'll take mine." He hoisted the ridiculously huge pile of gear onto a rock and strapped it on. "It's not far now. Come on, honey. Let me know when you need to take a break in the bushes."

"It's farther than it looks, and it's all uphill," I moaned.

"Well, what else have we got to do? Just put one boot in front of the other until you get there."

I hauled myself to my feet. We staggered along, and then stopped again. But even as sick as I was, whenever I would stop to rest or use the bushes, I marveled at the view.

The best vistas of the entire hike were on the Switchbacks trail ending at Halemau'u: grand views of the whole crater, down over the jungle-covered green Hana coast, all the way to the ocean. One spectacular part of the path was a narrow spine of ridge, with thousands of feet of drop on either side—truly breathtaking.

Of all the terrain we traversed, this section of the journey would be best to return to for a day visit, and what I'd recommend to visitors looking for a manageable but spectacular hike at Haleakalā Crater.

We kept going, slow but sure, pausing over and over until we reached the parking lot at last. Mike's old green truck, parked and waiting for us, looked like the Promised Land shimmering in the distance.

Mike helped me into the vehicle, threw the packs in the back, and got into the driver's seat. I sucked down lukewarm water from a jug we'd left in the truck, and we drove down the winding road toward home. I rested my head on the doorframe, keeping the window down and air moving across my face, hoping not to be sick again.

"How're you doing?" Mike asked.

"Distances are deceiving in the crater," I said. We both smiled. "I'll be fine."

I'd learned a few things, too: difficult challenges were still worth doing, and best taken one step at a time. Surprises could be wonderful (like the nene) or terrible (like the hikers) but should not be avoided; they're the spice of adventure—and might just be creative fuel, too.

Unsound, my psychological suspense novel, was inspired by our encounter with the hikers.

CHAPTER FOUR
VOLCANOES NATIONAL PARK

Mike had to fly to the Big Island of Hawaii to buy koa wood for a commissioned furniture project sometime after our Haleakalā hike. I had business to take care of there too, delivering books to my marketing rep in Hilo. The 125-mile drive from Kona to Hilo and back across the island and a few nights in lodgings would give me a little writing retreat, and seemed like a great practice run for our big trip. Mike and I could "road test" our ability to travel together as we got ready for the month in May, when we were planning to set out to see the Southwestern National Parks.

We flew into Kona from Maui, just a short half hour of bumpy wind over the 'Alenuihāhā Channel and rented a car. We enjoyed the drive from dry Kona all the way around the vast, sloping southern side of Hawaii, traversing the village of Captain Cook and passing through coffee farms and Miloli'i, a fishing village where we owned some land we'd bought years ago.

I enjoyed the arid but beautiful undulations, the tawny gold of a lion's pelt, flowing by thousands of feet below us and ending at a rugged line of new black lava rock and the cobalt, wind-whipped sea. I put my hand out the window and pretended it was a bird, soaring over all I saw. Sometimes I'd play one of my favorite imaginations from when I was a kid on Kauai with no TV or radio: I was driving a team of horses hell-for-leather on the road before us. I heard their pounding hooves, snorting breaths and creaking harnesses, felt the wind of their speed on my face, and watched their heaving manes and pricked ears as they galloped.

"Toby can have fun in a paper bag!" my wonderful hippie godmother Catherine used to say, and time hadn't changed that part of me, at least.

At four thousand and twenty-eight square miles in size, the Big Island is larger than the rest of the Hawaiian Islands combined. Many people don't know that Hawaii Island contains *eight* of the thirteen climate zones in the world, encompassing a variety of terrain from the snow-topped peaks of Mauna Loa to the desert areas of Kailua-Kona, contrasting with the tropical Hāmākua jungle and the temperate grasslands of Waimea.

We continued our scenic drive past Miloli'i to the barren protrusion of South Point, the southernmost tip of the United States. Mike and I once went scuba diving off the rocks at Ka Lae (as it's called in Hawaiian), a tricky and dangerous place to navigate as the wave surge is heavy against the boulders there, and scuba equipment doesn't exactly make you graceful. Still, once we made it into the water, the ocean's crystal clarity, the many colorful corals, and the abundance of fish and manta rays made the hazards of entry and exit worth it.

The South Point land area above the ocean is rugged, cut up by dirt roads made by four-wheel drive vehicles and laddered by a row of gigantic rusting windmills scoured by high wind, abandoned when the ravages of salt air exposed them as too expensive for proper maintenance. Continuing, the highway leading to Hilo runs right through Volcanoes National Park, and ready for a pit stop, we pulled in for an overnight at the park.

I fell in love immediately with Volcano House, the lodge built on the rim of Kīlauea Crater. It's truly a historic national treasure, every room infused with old-fashioned charm and a sense of history. The first version of Volcano House was an open-sided hut built of grass and *ohia* wood poles on the edge of Kīlauea Crater in 1846. In 1866 a fully functional inn was built, prompting a mention by Mark Twain in his memoir, *Roughing It:* "A neat, roomy, well-furnished and well-kept hotel. The surprise of finding such a hotel in such an outlandish place startled me, considerably more than the volcano did."

Over a hundred years later, I shared Twain's sentiment as we settled into a small but comfortable room decked out with vintage koa wood furniture and windows that overlooked the steaming caldera. I sat on one of the rockers and imagined the travelers who'd sat there and done the same; it seemed like a golden thread connected us through time.

Volcanoes National Park encompasses three of the island's volcanoes: Mauna Loa, Mauna Kea, and Kīlauea. The main park area is located at a four-thousand-foot elevation around the Kīlauea volcano, making a visit pleasantly cool most times of the year. The Visitor Center and Jaggar Museum are located on the stable rim of Kīlauea's caldera, along with the century-old Volcano House Hotel.

We walked along the Crater Rim Trail, a level hike of several miles that encircles most of Kīlauea's summit caldera. Huge *hāpu'u* tree ferns arched over the path, interspersed with thick stands of red-orange *Kahili* ginger, a showy invasive plant. The decorative ginger blooms filled the air with sweet fragrance, the perfect balance to the melodic, piercing songs of a healthy population of native birds. These brightly colored red and green jewels of the forest, nectar feeders called i'iwi, 'amakihi, and 'apapane, flitted from one *ohia* tree to the next, sipping from the red poufs of *lehua* blossoms.

In between stands of this serene, lush, multi-textured forest, glimpses off the edge of the caldera stole my breath. The Halema'uma'u Crater well was close to three hundred feet deep and more than half a mile across, a giant awe-inspiring, steaming open pit. Natural vents along the trail emitted veils of steam beside us, suggesting with their undulating wisps that *Pelehonuamea* (Pele, volcano goddess of the sacred land) still resided here.

After traversing the crater rim, we drove a short distance to explore the Thurston Lava Tube. This ancient tunnel, formed by lava flowing underground, is approached down a long walkway in some of the most spectacular fern forests of the park. A walk through the large, dimly lit tube, damp with seepage through the porous rock, is another memorable experience of a natural phenomenon seldom seen. There was a sense, as I walked that well-worn cement path, that at any moment a dinosaur could poke its head out from among the massive fern trees.

After an excellent dinner at the Volcano House's fine dining restaurant, full dark had fallen. Rumor had it that this was the optimal time to view the lava lake bubbling at the bottom of the crater. We returned to our rental car and drove out to where the Jaggar Museum, with its excellent fine art, culture, and history exhibits, clung to the cliffside farther down the Chain of Craters Road.

From Jaggar's popular lookout areas, lava, bubbling in the center of the caldera, was clearly visible at night, an otherworldly red glow like a glimpse into Mordor from *The Lord of the Rings*. To add to the drama, light drizzling rain blew past a full moon riding high over the deep black plain, creating a three-hundred-and-sixty-degree moonbow.

Mike dug out his tripod and set up for several photos of this hypnotic sight, as down in the caldera the bubbling lava lake glowed red, steam rising in a yellow haze above it like a glimpse into hell. The whole scene was so theatrical and dramatic that it hardly seemed real. I experienced such sensory overload that it would not have surprised me a bit if Pegasus had flown across that brilliant sky, too. I sat there on the stone parapet around the rim, soaking it in, until the drizzle thickened to a downpour.

We finally had to call it a night and go back to our beds at the hotel.

As of this writing, the Halema'uma'u vent and the stable situation at the caldera has changed. The steady eruption of Kīlauea that began in 1984 is over as of September 2018, after an enormous explosive and ongoing event that damaged the park and closed the Jaggar Museum and much of the Chain of Craters Road up until the date of this writing in 2020. Please research the park for updates online before making any travel plans.

CHAPTER FIVE
KALAPANA LAVA FLOW

I said goodbye to Volcano House reluctantly the next morning, and we continued on toward Hilo. We planned to hike across the open lava plain near a former village called Kalapana to witness the outflow of the Pu'u ō'ō vent, a slow-moving stream of liquid rock that was pouring into the sea some distance past the abandoned settlement that had been wiped out by eruption years before. Still a little stunned by what we'd seen the prior night, we were eager to witness the well-publicized spectacle of the lava dripping into the ocean.

Everything along the highway from Volcanoes Park to Hilo is supersized: gigantic ferns, towering Albezia trees, wild orchids, and enormous swathes of dangling vines, thick and strong enough for Tarzan to swing on, border the road. It's worth taking your time along the smooth entry into town to really soak up the unique sights along the way.

The turnoff to the lava viewing location was just outside of Hilo, so we took a little extra time to check into our hotel on Hilo Bay, knowing we planned to be back late at night. We wanted to stay at the viewing area until after sunset—in daylight, the heat of the liquid stone hitting the ocean creates so much steam that seeing its activity is difficult. The lava area could only be reached on foot, and the hike was reputed to be several miles, so we knew it would be a long day.

Mike was in the hyperfocused frenzy that happens when he wants to get the shot. After dropping off our luggage at the room, we headed back to the Kalapana area. The area outside of the former village, had become an informal staging spot for lava trekkers.

"Is this a park or something?" I wondered as we came upon lines of cars parked along the former street, up to where it dead-ended at a six-foot-high black stone flow that had permanently closed the road.

"The state owns all new land formed by the lava where it meets the ocean, but the people who had houses in Kalapana still own their original sites," Mike replied. "I think the Park Service monitors everything for safety, but it's kind of hard to tell what's going on."

Indeed it was. Milling tourists meandered along the abandoned route. Food and shave ice trucks did a brisk business, as did the porta-potties and racks of bikes for rent promoted by huckstering teenagers.

"Let's get some bikes!" I assessed the hot expanse of black lava and my heavy water and picnic-laden backpack with a jaundiced eye. Mike's pack, filled with expensive camera gear, was even heavier.

I was still anointing myself with sunscreen and making sure I had everything I could imagine needing for an extended time out in the lava wilderness (it was only 1:30 p.m., and we planned to be there past dark) when Mike returned from checking out the bike situation. "Those highway robbers are charging ten dollars an hour per bike! I found us a guy who'll give us a ride out to the viewing area, one-way, in his vehicle. We'll have to hike back, but it'll be cooler at night—and at least it's only twenty bucks."

I had some doubts about this, but a little mental math told me that the bikes really would cost a fortune, given the hours we planned to be out at the viewing site. We locked up the car, donned our packs, and set off.

"Stretch," our driver for this adventure, was an enormously tall man with feet the size of swim fins. He wore Birkenstocks, a tie-dyed bandanna around his forehead to hold back Fabio-esque curls that tumbled over leathery shoulders, and a beard that touched his belt buckle. "Hey, there, little lady," he greeted me, with an appreciative eyebrow bounce.

"Hey there, yourself, sir. Interesting setup you've got," I said, as Stretch ushered us to a battered minivan with no doors, whose rust was held together by a bright collection of eclectic bumper stickers.

"Here's a little extra for your trouble," Mike said, handing Stretch a tip. "We appreciate getting a ride."

"Well, for that, I'll give you the grand tour," Stretch said. "Little lady, you come on up with me in front."

I turned to glance at Mike, and he shrugged. Stretch seemed benign enough, but my crime writer mind went into overdrive —*maybe this giant was going to take us out onto the lava plains, rip us off, and leave us stranded!*

I unobtrusively slid my phone out of my pocket.

No service. Well, damn.

Mike got into the open back area with the packs, and I sat in the passenger seat up front as our erstwhile guide fired up the engine. "Better for the tourists to see the sights without the doors," Stretch told us. "I'll take you through our neighborhood. You can see what the lava did to Kalapana back in the early nineties."

We drove through a rickety gate marked *Private—Residents Only* and bumped down a potholed track etched over the raw lava toward the distant ocean.

"All of this used to be beautiful." Stretch gestured at the black plain with a ropy arm. "Then the lava came and buried it. Those of us who owned property still owned it, so some of us built on top of our old houses."

"You must have really loved it out here."

He shrugged. "It's home."

The ramshackle collection of dwellings we were driving toward resembled something out of a Mad Max movie. We got a house-by-house description of Kalapana's bizarre and colorful collection of off-the-grid, unpermitted lava wasteland shacks, their perimeters marked with white coral boundaries and fences made of loosely piled rocks. Stretch indicated his own hut, built of recycled glass windows, shipping pallets, and plywood. "I get by, giving folks rides, renting a few bikes, and growing some prime grass." He raised a brow in my direction. "You folks need any *pakalolo*?"

"No, thanks. Not our thing," I demurred politely.

We bumped around a looping road through the remains of the town and ended up at an interior residents' access road that reentered the route being taken by troops of tourists. Only a few hundred yards later, we hit another gate. Stretch turned the van around and stopped.

"I thought you were taking us to the lava flow," Mike said.

"This is the end," Stretch replied, with an unrepentant shrug. "Hope you enjoyed the tour."

There was nothing to do but get out, put on our packs, and start walking with the rest of the pilgrims who'd set out to pay homage to the fire goddess Pele's entrance to the sea.

"How much do you think we carved off the hike by taking Stretch's cab ride?" I asked, putting one boot in front of the other, conscious of the hot sun on the top of my head and the heat shimmer on the black rock around us.

"Maybe a mile? The security guy said it's four miles each way," Mike said. "I'm sorry. We probably should have rented the bikes."

"Oh, well. It was worth thirty bucks to get that grand tour," I said, glancing at my husband with a grin.

He nodded. "Priceless."

We eventually reached the area we'd come to see, a long bluff with waves crashing into it and gouts of steam blowing up into the air, marked by caution tape wrapped around a few boulders. We made our way around knots of tourists into the viewing area.

The lava was scarcely visible at all where it met the ocean—all we could see was steam. "We have to wait for the sun to go down." Mike surveyed the scene with his hands on his hips, clearly disappointed by the lack of visibility.

"Then why did we come out here this early?" I asked. "We could have stayed at Volcano House longer. Or our hotel."

But I already knew the answer. We came this early because Mike was so gung ho; and I'd gone along with it because resisting him when he's in that determined mode isn't something I'm good at.

Mike tried to jolly me out of my grumpiness. "You're a trooper, but you need to get out of the sun." My redhead complexion was no joke now that I did every-three-month skin cancer checks after a bout with melanoma. Mike created a little nest in a spot overlooking the lava outfall. He padded the rough stone with his sweatshirt and erected a huge red and white golf umbrella he'd lugged along, tied to his backpack. "Here you go. Don't want you to get sunburned."

"You're just setting me up here so you can ditch me and tramp all over the place to get the shot." I was wise to his moves. I lowered myself stiffly into the shady nest, and sighed with relief as a cool breeze blew up from the sea and the umbrella threw blessed shade over me. "I'll be fine. Just go, do your thing."

Off Mike went, springing away with the excitement of the hunt. Before he took up photography, he'd gone after surf with that same single-mindedness, and I'd been along for many a wave quest then, too.

I settled in for hours of waiting for the sun to go down.

After a snack and some water, I revived enough to arrange my phone camera to take a time-lapse of the glowing, oozing blood of the earth dripping off the cliff and hitting the ocean. The lava exploded when it hit the water, erupting with bursts of steam and crackling crazily with the sound hot glass makes when bursting apart. Fine black stone threads with drops on their ends, generated by the explosive contact with the water, flew to land on the rocks. People called these "Pele's tears," and I found some of the threadlike filaments in the crack beside me, and holding them in my hand, the shiny, jet black color reminded me of Hawaiian girls' hair.

In the funny way of things, I remembered a girl I'd worked with at my counselor job, a fifth-grade foster kid moved to my school due to a recent placement. She had been sent to me because she was having what her teacher called "adjustment issues."

I HAD A LOVELY CLASSROOM AT THE MAUI ELEMENTARY SCHOOL WHERE I worked as a "behavioral health" counselor three days a week. Various stations were set up for play therapy activities, but I especially liked to prepare art materials and see what a student was attracted by when they arrived at my counseling office for the first time.

I greeted the new girl. "Hello. I'm Ms. Toby."

She nodded shyly but didn't speak. She sat down at the little table beside me, picked up the paintbrush I'd laid out, and dipped it in water.

I was curious what color she'd choose.

Black.

She carefully printed letters with the paintbrush, but her name was too long to fit on the paper. She lifted sad chocolate-brown eyes to me. "I made a mistake."

"That's okay," I said. "It can be whatever it is."

"No. I can't make a mistake." She set the brush down with finality.

This child had a face made for laughing, with beautiful Hawaiian features: round satiny cheeks, a wide shapely nose, and a full curling mouth that made her look as if she were smiling.

Only she wasn't smiling.

Her thick black hair was bobbed crudely at her ears, as if the cut had been done with kitchen shears. The mass of curls sat on her head like a heavy wool hat, coarse and hot.

This was not how her hair was meant to be—it should have been swishing around her waist or hanging down her back in a great braided rope. Someone who meant to hurt her had slashed her hair off this ugly way. I felt an angry burn near my sternum.

"Well, at least tell me your name," I teased her, ripping off another sheet of paper and putting it in front of her. "I bet you have a good one." Names that make a statement and have family or spiritual value are important in Hawaiian culture.

"Kaikamahine Lani Moana Kai Kuuipo," she said softly. Her voice rippled over the syllables like water over stones.

"Kaika-? But how come they call you Lani?" I stumbled over her name a little, exaggerating my *haole*-ness, my white outsider status —asking her to be the teacher.

A dimple appeared for a second in her cheek, but she shook her head. She began her name again on the fresh sheet of paper, each letter painstakingly perfect.

That angry burn in my stomach was worse this time. *Who made this beautiful child so cautious and perfectionistic?* This was *watercolor*— have a little fun with it!

But she'd probably never been able to simply be a kid and make mistakes.

"What does your name mean?" I asked.

"I think it means Daughter of Heaven and Ocean, Beloved Sweetheart," she said softly. She knew exactly, of course, but even so, had softened her statement with "I think."

"That's gorgeous."

"My mother gave me my name," Lani said. She'd begun to surround KAIKAMAHINE with magenta hearts. *A good sign.*

"Seems like she wanted to tell the world how special you were," I said. "I wish I had a name that was a message, too." My mom had named me after a red-haired boy named Toby Tyler, in a movie she'd seen at the hospital.

"Not special enough for her to stop using drugs," Lani said matter-of-factly.

"Maybe she can't help it," I said. "Sometimes people are sick with an addiction, and they can't stop."

Lani didn't look up. She was not buying that line of propaganda. I decided on another tack—since this was our first session, I wanted to establish rapport, and something we could build on. "I have an idea. Since your name is so beautiful, how about we make a book out of it? Each page could be one word of your name. You can decorate it and translate it. You have the first page done already."

Her dimple lasted longer this time. "Okay. Can you help me fill this page with more hearts?"

"You sure you want me to help?" I dipped my brush into purple. "I like different colors than you. I might mess it up."

"It's okay," she said—the beginning of trust, of flexibility.

We filled the page entirely with purple, pink and red hearts—a brave and crazy declaration of love around her name.

I set the painting carefully aside, and we played a board game. By the end, she'd smiled at my exaggerated woe over losing.

I felt her name page—it was dry.

"Putting this up for the world to see how special you are," I said, and clothes-pinned the art to a clear fishing line strung high across the ceiling. The paper flapped a little in the wind from the door, and Lani jumped up and touched it. I chuckled because that hop was the kind of thing a happy kid would do.

The bell rang. Lani turned to wave to me from the doorway, though she didn't smile.

"See you next week," I said.

Lani nodded and left. Her butchered hair bounced as she trotted toward the bus. It looked better from behind, and after all, hair grew back.

If only I was as resilient as Lani; but she, and all of the beautiful, wounded children I'd seen and known over twelve years working in the public schools had taken a toll on my heart.

I remembered them all.

I'd cared too much.

The chance to escape into a life of writing stories for a living was too much of a dream come true for me to resist.

I set the delicate black threads into a crack beside me where I'd be safe from them. Pele's tears could be as sharp as glass and had been known to stab right through skin and break off.

I'D NEVER PLANNED TO LEAVE MY JOB WITH HAWAII DEPARTMENT OF Education working with at-risk kids. Twelve years of college and training to reach my Master's in Social Work degree, plus licensure, had been a huge investment of time, money, and love. I'd even been rumored to be one of the best on Maui; they'd called me "the kid whisperer."

I'd loved it. But it had left me bruised.

Therapy with kids is not scientific, not a matter of stimulus-response-reward. It's a little bit magic, a little bit creative, and a lot of fun, observation, intuition and play. Really effective child therapy is not speedy, and it's not easy to do well in a box of measured goals and calibrated minutes. Looking for a better setting, I had expanded into the private sector, and worked at a wonderful and discriminating child therapy clinic, as well as my school job.

I had always wanted to be a writer, but I wanted to be 'normal' more. I'd put my writing dream aside to get an education, to have a real career; I wanted to make a decent living and raise my children with all of the comforts and stability I'd never had.

Not only that, I wanted to write "the great American novel." My first book would be literary and highbrow, revealing some great new truth but in an opaque way; no clear heroes, no happy endings.

I'd tried to write that book for years; my drawers were filled with the dusty skeletons of abandoned stories that I'd lost interest in finishing—frankly, writing "literature" bored me, but I couldn't admit it. Embarrassed by myself and but still compelled, I began writing a blog under a fake name. My kids were almost grown, I was forty years old, and if it was ever going to happen, I had to start somewhere.

So, I entered online writing contests, wrote short stories, and sometimes I wrote about what happened at work. Writing about the therapy I did helped me process; I always felt better afterward, and people seemed to enjoy the glimpses I shared of that secret world.

The day that was to change everything didn't begin like the others.

My phone rang at 5:00 a.m. with an emergency phone tree call that there had been deaths at the high school; I was to report to the teacher's lounge by 6:00 a.m., to be part of a grief response team supporting the students.

The staff lounge of the high school smelled dusty, with a slight sour tang of mold. I stood with several other staff members, leaning against the cold metal counter that ran along one wall, my fingers curled around the edge for support; bracing myself to hear about the tragedy that had stolen the lives of two of our students, young girls aged fourteen.

I was dressed but uncaffeinated, my hair a damp snarl down my back, and my heart thundered in my ears with dread as two burly Hawaiian police officers in uniform, one sharp-faced woman in plainclothes with a detective shield on her belt, and the police department's chaplain, a small man with a cross dangling at his neck, entered the room.

The chaplain faced us, backed by the somber-faced officers. "Preliminary investigation indicates the girls' deaths were a homicide, sexual in nature. They were drowned in the sugar cane irrigation ditch. Their bodies were found bruised and missing clothing."

The room filled with gasps of shock.

We'd known the girls were dead—that's why we were there—but

we'd expected a car accident or suicide, much more common. This was Maui; we had one of the lowest crime rates in the nation. Terrible sexual murders didn't happen here under our sunny skies and waving palm trees.

Why hadn't I chosen some other career—any career—other than that of a therapist? How could I do anything for anyone else, when my own emotions swamped me like storm waves, roiling my stomach and stealing my breath?

The chaplain described the discovery of the bodies by some kids fishing in one of the irrigation ditches. "If the students ask what happened, tell them we're working hard to find answers; don't say anything more. There are rumors flying all over the community and we need to help contain them," he directs, and moves right into how we should begin the grief response with a school-wide announcement that the two students have "passed away," and that staff counselors are offering support in the school library.

The female detective steps forward. "And if you hear of anyone knowing anything about who these girls hung out with, or more about what happened to them, call me over. I want to interview them."

We weren't just consoling. We were helping with the investigation. My attention sharpened as I went on point like a bird dog spotting game.

I could help find answers. I could do more than pass tissues and process grief, an emotion that always threatened to overwhelm me, covered as I was in unhealed places.

We went to our table stations in the library and our principal made the announcement over the intercom. The officers opened the doors.

Soon knots of girls and a few boys, clinging to each other and sobbing, entered the library.

I asked gentle, open ended questions and helped them tell their memories. I pushed a box of tissues here, there, and everywhere.

Never had I hated my job so much, even as I tried to find out if these distraught teenagers knew anything useful.

They didn't. Some of them are just there to fish for gossip or escape a disliked class. They cried crocodile tears while darting glances around the room to see who else was there.

My gaze often found the detective with her watchful eyes, working in the room with the gentle chaplain beside her.

I went home at the end of the day, completely wrung out, a husk; my emotions battered me from within while the emotions of others had battered me from without, and all the while I'd maintained a calm and loving smile.

Mike looked up as I came in, took one look at my face and said, "rough day?"

I just nodded.

I went straight to my computer in the corner of our bedroom and sat down; opened a text window on my blog and begin a story of what had happened that day, seen through the eyes of a woman detective.

I projected into this character all the questions that I'd struggled with; the anguish, the challenges, the emotional exhaustion, the urgency to find answers.

I re-wrote the entire day from fictional Leilani Texeira's perspective in an active role, not the passive one that I had been assigned, passing Kleenex and offering pats on the shoulder.

Lei even saw me in the scene and described me: "The red-haired counselor had the kind of soft face that invited confidences, but misery hid in her eyes."

When Lei went home and stripped out of her sweaty clothes, getting under the shower, she became even more real to me, an alter ego through whom I could vicariously solve this crime. She looked at the scars of self-inflicted cuts on her arms, hidden from the world beneath long-sleeved shirts—and showed me that she'd been sexually molested as a child and was living with secret crippling shame, something too many of my clients struggled with.

Tears poured down my cheeks as I inhabited the body of a woman who was violated at a young age with no consent, forced to pretend and lie for so many years that her own memory refused to reveal the truth; and yet she was driven from within, from that dark and wounded place, to find justice for others.

I stumbled to the bathroom and took my own shower, releasing my emotions in tears that washed me clean. I slept soundly that night.

I checked the responses to the story on the blog the next morning before work. The comments were more engaged and passionate than I had ever experienced. "This is gut-wrenching!" "What happens next?"

Still raw from the experience, unable to talk about it or process with anyone because of the confidential nature of everything, I pounded out another chapter...and in it, Lei found a clue, and carried the investigation forward. I felt rejuvenated when I got up from the keyboard.

I had not become a counselor without doing my own therapy, so I made an appointment to talk about all of this with my therapist. In her office, I poured out the situation that happened at the high school, the real-life investigation that seemed to be leading nowhere, my frustratingly passive role as a counselor, and the way it had all come together in the form of this new character who had emerged on the page.

"It's not literature," I told the therapist. "It's a murder mystery." My lip curled as I said it. *Genre fiction!* Not real art.

"Who cares what it is? This is clearly a way that you're processing the events happening in your life; maybe it's a way you will find healing," she said. "Keep going."

I kept going.

The real-world investigation into the girls' drownings ended when it was declared a tragic accident; but I kept going.

As Lei revealed herself and her world on the page, I discovered the energy, the power, the compulsion, to keep writing a story that compelled me. No more abandoned drafts of arty prose that led nowhere; I was on a mission.

I continued to add chapters every day to the mystery, completely departing from the facts that had inspired it, moving the setting to the Big Island of Hawaii so that people wouldn't associate it with the terrible thing that had happened in my community. Other characters appeared, like Lei's dog Keiki, modeled after my own Nalu, a little tiny chihuahua terrier with the heart of a Rottweiler, and Michael Stevens, Lei's love interest, who looked suspiciously like my husband.

Lei felt real to me, and she resonated with my readers, too, who clamored for more and more.

One day, I realized I had written enough to finish a whole novel; somehow, I'd outwitted my inner critic enough to get that far.

At that point, we were dropping my daughter off at college.

On the way back from that rite of passage, Mike, Caleb and I meandered down the California coast on vacation for a few days. We stopped in Mendocino, a picturesque village on the edge of the ocean, lined with flowers, swaying grasses, and tiny fisherman's cottages. The boys went fishing off the rocks while I sat in our hotel, feeling the story of Lei pounding on the inside of my heart, saying *finish this, finish this, finish this. Do something crazy for once in your life. Let this story completely come out.*

I grabbed a directory and looked for a cabin nearby. I booked a cottage in the redwoods for two weeks; then informed my husband and son when they returned that I was not going to be going back to Maui with them; I was going to stay in Mendocino and finish my book.

Alone.

For the first time in my life.

They dropped me off at my cabin in the woods the next day, and it was just as cute as I'd imagined. I was excited about my big step forward, claiming my future as a writer. I was saying, *yes! I will finish this book. I do believe in myself. I am more than a mom and a school counselor!*

But as soon as the car drove out of sight, I was cut off from the security of the known. I had a massive anxiety attack and could do nothing but pace in circles, holding my phone in the air, trying to get a signal to call the whole thing off.

I had married my husband early and young, and I'd always had him, or my children, nearby.

This was my dark night of the soul, and I had chosen to enter it on my own.

The first two days were terrible; I had insomnia and heart palpitations. I was unmoored, adrift. I didn't know who I was without my familiar roles: wife, mother, sister, people helper. I diagnosed myself with separation anxiety; I could have written my own evaluation of classic symptoms.

But Mendocino felt safe, and so did my cabin. The elderly couple who owned the place loved the idea of a writer on retreat and looked in on me daily and brought firewood and cups of tea.

I took walks. Sometimes I rocked in the chair on the porch and stared at the trees, doodling in my notebook. I would write, but reluctantly—because I'd put myself in a position where there was nothing else to do.

By day three, the words began to come.

I set my laptop on the table in the over-decorated country cabin with its chintz fabrics, china bulldogs and silly fire irons in the shape of animals... and I wrote.

I woke up at night and it was cold; I'd never made a fire in a woodburning stove before, but I chopped kindling in the dark and figured it out, and I wrote until dawn overtook the sky.

I wrote and wrote and wrote, at all hours of the day and night. I had no one to please, no one to care for, and nothing to do but release this story—and in the two weeks I'd set aside for the task, I finished the book.

Only I, and now you, know that the character of Lei arose out of tragedy. Through fifteen novels, Lei has shown the course of a woman's healing from child sexual abuse through a loving relationship, therapy, and the detective work of one who brings justice to those who need it most.

One book led to the next, and the next, and the next. Meanwhile, my DOE job became more and more challenging. *Staff attrition. Budget cuts. No Child Left Behind.* I was asked to do more and more with less and less, while litigious parents hovered, and Individual Education Plan standards pressured.

At night, on the weekends, during holidays, whenever I could—I wrote my Hawaii-based crime novels, escaping into an alter ego who fought back against injustice. Solving crime through my main character Lei healed something in me.

By 2013, things had exploded with my books. My income from royalties overtook the salary of the DOE and the children's clinic combined. Stretched too thin, physically and emotionally exhausted, I made the tough choice to leave one career for another.

By then I was the wrecked woman on her back in the doctor's office, longing for the freedom to fly like a bird over the hoodoos of Bryce Canyon.

AT FIRST, THE FLOWING LAVA REMINDED ME OF REFRIGERATED HONEY when poured: slow, bulgy, and somewhat translucent. But I watched it long enough to notice a chunkiness—it was more like cream of wheat: thick, gooey, with congealed bits. As the afternoon wore on, the light shifted, and the brightness of the lava increased. By nightfall, the little nest where Mike had set me up had become a prime viewing spot of multiple glowing streams cascading in slow motion into the crashing, restless sea, broken by occasional large blobs exploding with a *crack!* like a rifle shot, accompanied by a huge burst of steam.

The whole thing was entirely hypnotizing. I lost all track of time.

Mike eventually returned, and we drank our remaining water and ate our picnic, our eyes never leaving the spectacle. I apologized for being grumpy, and he apologized for the fiasco with Stretch and reaching the observation area too early.

"It's fine. I could watch the lava flow all day, in sunshine or at night, and not be bored," I told him.

We were finally satiated by nine p.m. and ready to begin the four-mile trek back to the car. My pack was lighter by then, since we'd eaten our food and drunk our water, but Mike still had a very heavy load with his camera equipment.

We set out in a kind of reverent silence; our souls deeply satisfied by the sights we'd seen. We didn't have flashlights, but the huge yellow moon that had worn a rainbow the night before rose over the waves and lit the path, a narrow ribbon of crushed gray stone across the black plain. The air cooled, and the few tourists returning with us also spoke quietly if at all. The Milky Way, a garland of diamond fragments directly overhead, shone over red rivers of lava glowing on the volcano's sides, visible from miles away.

There was no sound but the metronome of our footsteps, the shushing of the waves, and far off in the green belt, the shrill *"Ko-kee! Ko-kee!"* of the tiny, invasive coqui frogs from South America, their high-decibel shrieks rendered picturesque by distance.

Even the hike back was a long, slow slice of magic.

CHAPTER SIX
WRITING DAY

Hilo is a utilitarian city grown up organically around its harbor, with a quaint oldtown area, and urban sprawl outskirts trimmed in big box stores. Mike successfully did the business of wood buying, I did my book marketing, and we met some friends for dinner at a favorite restaurant on Hilo Bay, The Seaside. As warm, velvety darkness fell, filled with the call of the frogs, we headed out of town to look for our lodgings.

Within an hour, after only a few wrong turns, we located the small, family-owned "ohana" rental we'd booked in the lush, sprawling grassland that's part of the Hāmākua Coast on the west side of Hilo. We spent a peaceful night in the cottage, broken only by the grunting and snorting of a large band of feral pigs as they tore up the grass verge on the road outside the property.

Mike was already long gone when I woke next morning savoring a pleasant feeling of anticipation. Today was to be my writing day. I was blissfully alone in this peaceful setting to work on my latest book. Mike was hiking with his photography friend and guide Sean King, navigating the lava to photograph it from a new angle, and wouldn't be home until evening.

I fixed coffee in the kitchenette, realizing as I did so that we'd forgotten to buy any food for my day alone out here in the country.

Oh well, my hips could stand a day of fasting.

However true that might have been on a logical level, I'd grown up with real food scarcity and various health food elimination diets imposed on me, an instability that had left me with lasting scars. These had taken the form of a love-hate relationship with food since my teens; I'd spent my twenties and thirties caught in a secret binge and exercise purge cycle. While I didn't do that anymore, I constantly dieted, and barely managed to keep my weight under control.

So, while it was true that my thighs wouldn't suffer from a day without food, not having any food, or any way to obtain any, unsettled me more than it should have.

I paced nervously around the little cottage, checking every cabinet and the freezer for something to eat, though I wasn't yet hungry after the previous night's rich dinner.

Nope—nothing to be found but a bottle of Aloha Shoyu and a few sugar packets. I could eat those if I had to; I'd done that before.

I put the packets in my pocket, just in case, berating myself for the insanity. Shame filled me at this evidence that I still wasn't "normal" despite all my efforts to heal myself.

I would drink more coffee.

I would be fine.

Nothing bad was going to happen besides a few hunger pangs. I had to make the most of this wonderful quiet to write.

I settled in front of my laptop with my mug, staring out the window as I considered my latest mystery. Eventually out of reasons to procrastinate, I put my fingers to the keys, and disappeared.

∼

A KNOCK CAME AT THE DOOR, STARTLING ME OUT OF THAT HYPNOTIC trance writers enter to create their imaginary worlds.

The cottage was so far out in the countryside that there were no neighbors anywhere nearby. Whoever was at the door had to be someone from the nearby main dwelling.

"Maybe it's the lady of the house, bringing me some banana bread," I muttered hopefully. I answered the door, grateful I'd shed my pajamas for my writing outfit of T-shirt and yoga pants.

No lady of the house bearing banana bread stood in my doorway.

Instead, a twenty-something young man with the distinct facial structure of the developmentally delayed fidgeted on the welcome mat.

"Hello," I said.

The young man blinked through heavy glasses and addressed my right shoulder as he wrung his hands. "You like play video games?"

"I'm sorry. I can't. I'm working." I glanced behind him, looking for parents or a caregiver. *No one in sight.* "Thanks for stopping by and have a nice day." I smiled and shut the door gently but firmly.

I hadn't yet reached my chair when another knock came.

I returned and opened the door again. Young Man continued to wring his hands and address my right shoulder. "We can play cards?"

"No, thank you. Where are your mom and dad?"

"Went go swap meet. You no like video games?"

"No, thank you. I'm working."

"But you get laptop." He pointed at my computer on the little table. "Can play games on dat."

"I work on my computer."

He grinned hugely. "Me too! I go get mine and show you." He darted off.

I couldn't bring myself to be harsh enough to scare him away; the kid was isolated and had seen a chance for interaction. His parents probably rode herd on him most of the time, but he likely got overstimulated at the swap meet (or wherever they'd gone) and had to be left at home. I'd worked with clients like this in my practice, and their obsessive persistence for high dopamine activities like video games was legendary.

I shut the door, wistfully hopeful that Young Man would get the hint, but had barely sat down again when the knock came again. There the kid stood, a battered laptop under his arm. "I like play with you."

I blew out a sigh. "You can come sit on the couch to play your game, but I have to work."

"I be good." He brushed past me and took up residence on the couch with aplomb, plugging his computer into a socket behind him with the ease of frequent practice. Clearly, he was right at home in the space.

"What's your name?"

"I play Zelda. My character's a warrior. His name's Ikaika. That means "Strong" in Hawaiian." He was already zeroed in on his game.

I clapped my hands lightly to get his attention. "What's *your* name?"

He looked up, a fleeting glance at my shoulder. "Ikaika."

"My name's Toby."

He didn't respond. Maybe he didn't understand, or didn't want to, or his name really was Ikaika, like his Zelda character. It didn't really matter—*he wasn't my client*. I didn't need to work on his social skills with him.

Truth was, though, part of me still missed being a school counselor and therapist. I'd been a part of teams identifying children in need of services, like Ikaika. One of those times flashed to memory.

I walked toward the kindergarten area, clipboard under my arm, to do a behavioral observation of a student showing developmental delays. I'd always loved walking through this particular elementary campus, with its dramatic view of the ocean and the huge plumeria trees dropping pinwheel flowers on the cement walks.

Bright shapes, labeled "Octagon," "Triangle," "Square," and so on, dangled over the low round tables in the classroom. A colored rug littered with blocks took up one corner, a book nook another, and a large plastic house filled a third. Clusters of children were playing at each of the stations. The teacher sat at one of the tables with several kindergarteners, doing stamp art with cut potatoes.

"Hey, thanks for coming!" Kumu (teacher) Lokahi greeted me. She was a fit Hawaiian woman with bands of tribal tattoos winding around her neck and up her arms. She indicated the child I was to be observing with a tilt of her head.

"I'll be doing data collection," I said. "I'm just going to be looking at what he's doing every thirty seconds and recording it. Is there somewhere you'd like me to sit?"

"Anywhere's fine. We're doing Center Time, so the kids get to pick what they're doing and switch activities when they want."

I grabbed one of the tiny, knee-high plastic chairs and wedged myself into the book corner, where I had a good view of my target student, Mano. He was lying on the rug in the block area, rolling a toy car back and forth and humming softly.

I reviewed the notes on my clipboard from the referral: *young for kindergarten, never been to preschool, odd behaviors during kindergarten screening, difficulty with directions and learning routine, poor social skills.*

I began the data sheet with a physical description: *slight build, curly brown hair, brown eyes.* I set my phone app to beep every thirty seconds and ticked the boxes on the assessment form for *Repetitive Motor Movements* and *Vocal Self Soothing.*

Per the protocol, I looked away for thirty seconds at the rest of the class. A little girl in pigtails caught my eye and walked over to me, carrying a doll.

"Can you feed her, Aunty?" Kids in Hawaii often call adults 'aunty' or 'uncle' as a sign of respect. The girl offered me a bottle of magically disappearing milk and the grubby plastic baby.

"Sure." I took the doll and set her on my lap, applying the bottle to her mouth. *Time to check Mano.*

Mano was still rolling the car—only now another boy, freckled and smiling, came over to play. He held out a block, entering Mano's visual proximity. Mano used the toy car to bat away the boy's outstretched hand, and it must have hurt. The wannabe friend dropped the block and wailed.

Three seconds were up, so I looked away, watching the teacher, who flew across the room to sit Mano on the Time-Out chair.

"No hitting," Kumu said firmly.

The pigtailed little girl came back with another doll. "Feed this one too, Aunty." She piled another baby on my lap.

Time to observe Mano again. I looked back at the boy.

He'd slithered off the Time-Out chair and was lying on his back, masturbating while gazing at the ceiling. I marked the boxes for *Sexualized Behavior* and *Repetitive Motor Movements.* I made a note: *touching penis inside of shorts.*

Kumu returned and removed his hand from his pants. "We don't touch our privates in school," she said, and bustled away after catching my eye—she'd wanted me to see that.

Something prodded me—a kid was poking me with the corner of a book. He held it up. "Can you read to me, Aunty?"

"Just a sec." I looked over at Mano. He was still on his back, only now he was spinning the wheels of the car. I ticked the *Repetitive Motor Movements* box again, then turned back to my newest acquaintance. "What's it about?"

The boy looked at the cover. "Papayas?" he asked hopefully. I couldn't resist giving his sleek black hair an affectionate pat. Papayas were indeed featured prominently. I opened the book. "*Tutu Makes Papaya Jam,*" I read. My new friend sidled into my lap, dumping the babies on the floor.

Time to observe again.

I glanced over at Mano. He was rolling the car over the play-house, humming to himself once more. Kumu called him: once, twice, three times. Finally, she got up and touched him on the shoulder. I checked *Repetitive Motor Movements* and *Vocal Self Soothing* and made a note: *"Requires physical cue to follow directions."*

My seatmate wiggled. "Read, Aunty!" he commanded.

"One day Tutu (grandma) decided to make papaya jam before the mynah birds ate all her papayas." Another boy joined us, hanging over my knee. *"Tutu took her long bamboo pole with the basket on the end and reached way, way up into the tree."*

I looked up. Kumu Lokahi was trying to get Mano to sit and paint at the art station. "Dip your brush in the water," she coaxed.

Mano held the brush oddly, with the tips of his fingers. I asked my lapmate to hold the book for me, and I checked *Working 1:1 With Teacher* and made a note: *"Adaptive brush grasp."*

Mano made a swirl or two on the paper with the paint, then hopped down, arrowing back to his car. Kumu glanced at me, lifting her hands in a confused gesture. Normally one-on-one attention from the teacher was highly sought after by kids this age.

"Did the mynah birds eat all the papayas?" my lapmate asked. He'd been very patient.

"Tutu picked all the papayas that were yellow and orange on the sides," I read. *"Only one of them had a mynah bird hole."* I showed him the illustration. *"She was just in time."*

The little girl returned. She picked up the baby dolls, and hung over my shoulder to see the story, too.

I looked over at Mano. He'd grabbed a little girl passing by, and, in the first sign of trying to make contact with another human that I'd seen, planted a big wet kiss on her cheek.

"No, Mano!" the girl shrieked.

He tried to kiss her again. She wriggled away. "No!"

Kumu swooped in, caught him by the hand, and took him to the

Time-Out chair. "No means no, Mano," she said. "We ask before we kiss."

Words to live by. I reached around my new friends to check the "Sexualized Behavior" box again and made another note: *kissed peer without consent.*

I finished out the half hour and set the clipboard aside. Tutu ended up making some very good jam in the story, and Mano continued to exhibit behaviors indicative of an autism spectrum disorder.

I went down to the playground during recess to continue my observation, stationing myself under a jacaranda tree, the blue-purple blossoms fluttering in the light breeze. The bell rang, and kids poured down the steps onto the field.

Mano emerged, his slight body a blur of motion as he ran, knees high, back straight, hands flapping. He beelined across the field without slowing and bounced into a kid, then spun off in another direction, zooming across the field to body-slam yet another child. His teeth were bared in a slightly crazed grin as he made another turn and kept going. The school counselor who'd worked with the teacher on the referral walked up to me.

"He runs this pattern every day," he said. "I think he picks someone out, heads for them, then tries to 'make contact' by running into them. We intervene as soon as he strikes someone, which he usually does."

As he spoke, Mano wound up like a World Series pitcher and smacked his latest target, a large older boy. That kid grabbed Mano by his skinny arms and prepared to teach him a lesson.

"Hey!" Fortunately, the counselor and the playground aide reached them in time. The counselor towed Mano over to a nearby bench.

Mano's feral grin was still in place, only now he banged his head on the counselor's hand and writhed, trying to escape.

"Help," the counselor said. I sat beside Mano on the bench, my side touching him to give him a cue, and I put my arm over him to anchor him there. Kids with Autism Spectrum Disorder often prefer a firm pressure touch. The counselor let go as Mano calmed. I put my finger under his chin, tilting the boy's head up. His eyes met mine briefly—then skittered away.

"Mano," I said softly. His eyes swiveled back. "It's okay. We're fine right here."

He stopped struggling and sagged on the bench, leaning against my side. We sat quietly until recess ended, then I walked him off the field and back to class by holding his hand. He settled down with his toy car on the carpet.

We had an emergency team meeting that afternoon to discuss further testing based on my observations. Mano's impossibly young mother had the same slight build, large brown eyes, and curly brown hair as her son. We sat on tiny chairs under the "Octagon" sign.

"I think we need a full battery of evaluations," I said, as kindly as I could.

Tears welled instantly in her eyes. She'd been terrified of this.

"Your son has some concerning behaviors that look like they could be Autism Spectrum Disorder. I'm working on a support plan right now to give him close adult supervision during transitions and free time, because he seems to have difficulty interacting with others, and makes contact with peers inappropriately."

She nodded—and her tears spilled.

"I just knew something was wrong." Her voice was a whisper. "His dad can't handle him. He goes in his room to get away because Mano won't leave him alone. We need help. We don't know what to do."

"It's okay," I said. "That's what we're here for." The teacher pushed a box of Kleenex over after taking one herself. "This is the first step in getting him help. It's going to take all of us to keep him supervised, safe, and help him learn."

"We'll do whatever it takes, if it's forever and a day," the young mom said.

Forever and a day was a long time. Hopefully, it wouldn't be that long. But for some kids, that's how long it would be.

~

I ADDRESSED TWENTY-SOMETHING IKAIKA AS HE SAT WITH HIS LAPTOP on the couch. "I'm going to work over here, and you can stay if you play quietly. Okay?"

He didn't reply.

I looked at my work in progress. I was just at the part where my heroine had realized that the case she was working was much bigger than it had initially appeared. She texted her trusty partner, Pono, that she was going into the valley without him . . .

"Come see! I fight da big boss!"

"Ikaika. I'm working. No talking."

"I like show you now!" Ikaika yelled, full volume. "You come!"

It occurred to me, belatedly perhaps, that I'd allowed a young man who was bigger, stronger, and heavier than I was, to come into my personal space while we were alone. Now he was trying to order me around, and I didn't know anything about how volatile he was or how physical he could get.

But I wasn't about to let him bully me.

"Ikaika—indoor voice." I spoke low and firm. "Ask me nicely."

"I sorry. You come sit with me. I show you da big boss," Ikaika whisper-shouted. "Please come. You my friend." He looked at me this time. His eyes were the color of melted chocolate behind those thick glasses.

Oh, man. This guy really needed company. "That's a good indoor voice, Ikaika. I'll come for a minute. But then I have to work."

Needless to say, Ikaika was still in the living room and I was still sitting next to him when his parents finally returned well after noon. His mother apologized and dragged him off, but by then my focus was fractured by hunger and having watched "the big boss" in the Zelda game.

Mike returned to the cottage shortly afterward, much sooner than expected. I could tell by his tight jaw and the way he slammed the car door that something was wrong. "We have to go."

"I'm ready." I'd already packed while Ikaika was showing me each level of his game. "What happened?"

"I lost my gear." He grabbed our bags and threw them into the trunk.

"Oh, no!"

My husband's face was haggard, his eyes devastated. "I hiked in with Sean, and we reached the lava flow from the opposite side than where we were yesterday. While I was down near the water trying to get a photo of the lava dripping off a ledge, a rogue wave came up and washed my Pelican case, lenses, tripod, and two extra cameras into the ocean."

I clapped my hand over my mouth in horror. Mike's equipment had taken years to accumulate, and every piece of it was well used. A bargain shopper, Mike slowly saved and bought each thing he needed over time, and then made everything pay for itself by selling photos taken with it.

"I jumped into the water and grabbed what I could find. I was able to get one of the lenses, the case, and one of the camera bodies —but I don't have insurance on any of it. Thousands of dollars of equipment, gone. Ruined." Mike held up his foot for my inspection. "Not only that—I stepped in a hot spot on the lava and melted my new boots."

"That's terrible!" The soles of the new boots he'd bought after our Haleakalā hike looked like a big black piece of bubblegum with little pebbles sunk into the tread.

"Did you have a nice time writing?" His question was perfunctory.

"No." The fact that I was seriously hungry and frazzled from the morning with Ikaika didn't compare to his disaster enough to describe. "Let's just get out of here."

We sniped at each other, venting frustration, as we left the cottage.

We were headed for Saddle Road, a "shortcut" from Hilo to Kona. This narrow two-lane road wound over the volcano plain between Kīlauea, Mauna Loa, and Mauna Kea volcanoes, a much shorter route than around South Point had been.

Before we got too far out into Saddle Road's famous isolation, we stopped at a gas station, where Mike fueled up and I looked for food in the store's mini mart. I bought a Spam musubi, that deliciously *badforyou* Hawaii snack made of fried Spam and compacted rice wrapped in nori seaweed. This delicious treat had been invented by Japanese workers as a handy lunchtime "sandwich" to eat while working in the sugarcane fields.

I'd been looking forward to my first drive on Saddle Road prior to this morning, but now I just stared out the window thinking about the disaster of the camera loss and how hungry I still was, even after eating the musubi.

Mike was stonily silent as he drove. The pall of our mutual bad mood felt like a cloud as thick as the vog—Hawaii's volcanic emissions—surrounding us.

I sneaked a glance at Mike's hiking boots. The thick rubber was beginning to puddle at the sides—*the lava had seriously melted the tread!*

Camera equipment and footwear could be replaced, but my husband's life could not.

I put my hand on his arm. "I'm sorry you lost your stuff, but I'm glad you're okay."

Mike glanced over and patted my hand. His eyes crinkled at the corners in an almost-smile. As he ages, my husband looks more and more like the actor Sam Elliott, but with crystal-blue eyes. "I'm sorry you were stuck there with nothing to eat and didn't get to write. Let's find somewhere to hike and clear our heads."

I was glad, in that moment, that none of the many challenges we'd faced in thirty years of marriage had pulled us apart—though as Mike said, "We're all just one decision away from stupid."

Mike's parents divorced when they were in their seventies (for the second time); mine, when they were in their mid-sixties. There were no guarantees of anything in life. But we knew two things: going out in nature made us both feel better, no matter what else we faced, and sharing our burdens made them easier to bear.

CHAPTER SEVEN
SADDLE ROAD KIPUKA

South winds had blown even more vog than usual in over Saddle Road, and visibility was spookily poor. The sky was rendered dim by the phenomenon, the sun a mere red dot. Crusty black *a'a* lava, forming lacy ledges, collided in a frozen black tableau with older flows of smooth *pahoehoe* lava alongside the two-lane scenic old highway. Gazing off to the right, we couldn't see massive Mauna Kea through the gloom at all, and it was usually a highlight view on the route.

Taking an opportunity to clear our heads as Mike had suggested, we took a break from driving and left the rental car at a roadside park with a path leading through the lava plain wilderness to a *kipuka*.

Kipuka are raised areas of old-growth forest surrounded by recent lava flows that have found their way around the pocket of elevation. *Kipuka* support many of the oldest and largest trees left in Hawaii and a host of wildlife in their microclimates—but the Big Island is so large that efforts to fence out the pigs, goats, and spotted deer that ravage the native forests have not been systematically implemented as they have on Maui.

As we hiked the crushed-stone path through strange coruscations and bizarre lava formations, I hoped that the *kipuka* we were headed for hadn't been mown down by the kind of feral pig incursion we'd just experienced at the vacation rental. I was a little afraid of the pigs; they were big and had tusks—but from what I'd heard, they were scared of people and not aggressive, except for sows who might defend their young.

The *kipuka* rose from the dark sea of lava, a verdant island wreathed in misty vog. Native birdsong wove a sweet spell around us as we ducked under the branches of old-growth koa and flowering *ohia* trees, weaving our way through stands of *hapu`u* and other ferns as we went deeper into the native jungle.

I turned off the trail and waved goodbye to Mike. "I just want to sit here a while and listen to the birds."

"And I'll try to get some pictures of them." Mike strode off with his one remaining camera, the one he'd been holding when the ocean disaster happened.

Once my husband was out of sight, I tipped my head back to gaze up into the giant koa tree I was standing beneath. Above me, in the umbrellalike canopy, a plethora of local birds tweeted and sang. I'd never seen koa trees this big before; most of the mature trees on Maui and Kauai had been harvested for lumber.

I wanted to be closer to both the tree and to the birds. The native birds, often invisible to visitors due to their habitat, are endangered because they fall prey to avian malaria carried by mosquitoes. They're only safe from this scourge at elevations too high and cold for mosquitoes to survive.

Impulsively, I hopped up to grab the lowest branch of the tree. I used to climb trees all the time as a kid, but I hadn't been up in one since our children were little, a quarter century ago.

My body felt stiff and awkward, but I scrambled and hauled myself up onto the branch and climbed even higher into the canopy. Eventually finding a good spot on a wide limb, I pressed my face against the rough, silvery bark of this most special of endemic trees. I closed my eyes and listened to the sweet voices of the honeycreepers as they hopped and sang among the sickle-shaped leaves.

Being in the tree took me back to growing up on Kauai. I used to love being up high in trees; I built forts in them and played or read in them for hours. Reverent shivers ran up and down my spine as I rested in the arms of this koa, with high, pure birdsong heard nowhere else in the world swirling around me. I was my truest self in that moment; I hadn't aged a day from the nature-loving, athletic girl I'd been.

The *kipuka* was at about six thousand feet of elevation, and with the vog blocking the sun, the temperature began to drop. Goose bumps rose on my arms and legs; my thin T-shirt and yoga pants were no longer enough coverage.

I climbed back down to the lowest limb. Sitting there, I discovered I could not get out of the tree without dropping more than six feet to the ground. *Crap!*

Over the years, I'd developed tricky knees along with a hip and ankles weakened by old running mishaps; jumping down that far was a serious risk of injury.

Mike had hiked off somewhere, my phone had no signal, and he didn't respond to my hails—so I was stuck there. I contemplated my situation as I wriggled around on the rough branch, trying to get comfortable.

"I guess I'm too old for this." Admitting it physically hurt.

But nature was a balm to me. Even chilled and uncomfortable, I still felt restored by being in the tree.

I thought about my mental health clients and their suffering. If only everyone could be alone in the forest, surely, they'd be healed.

Sometimes, though, a wound was always a weak spot—the way my ankles, knees, and hip had become after all those years of exercise purging as I tried to outrun my past.

Balanced on the branch, I composed a poem on my phone's note feature about the bittersweet sorrow I felt about leaving my profession, even for one as fulfilling as being a full-time novelist.

Datebook:

My life goes by, a book of little boxes
Penciled names and times containing
No hint of the stories
The sorrows, compulsions, memories, grief,
The rage, depression, drugs, and abuse.
Just little boxes filled with names and times.
I wish those names
Left no mark on me but
They do.

I witness their stories
I hold the box of their secrets
I hear their songs:
street rap full of fuck you
ukulele ballads spun out of loss
Some songs are just broken poetry cut into arms
or the tattooed names of stillborn children.

I take those stories and songs
I weave them into new tapestries
I make them fiction and put them somewhere new
My alter ego heroine kills rapists and imprisons pedophiles
She patrols the streets of my imagination making them safer
A big Rottweiler by her side and a gun in her hand.

In real life, I pass a box of tissues.
It's never enough, but I guess
It's better than no one ever knowing the stories
At all.

∾

FINALLY, I'D RUN OUT OF WAYS TO STAY DISTRACTED. I WAS COLD AND stiff, and my butt was numb. "Mike!" I hollered, hands around my mouth. "Mike, I need help!"

"On my way!" This time he hollered back from off in the distance, and he broke into a grin at the sight of me clinging to my perch. "Stuck?"

"Yeah. I didn't want to jump down and break something."

He got underneath my branch, reached up and caught me under the armpits, and eased me down onto the ground. "What made you get up there?"

"I wanted to get closer to the birds."

"That's my girl." He kissed me on the nose. We walked back to the car holding hands and drove the rest of the way to Kona Airport in much better spirits.

I'd added onto the trip at the last minute, so we'd booked separately. Mike had a flight on a different airline, and he left ahead of me through the main terminal area, while I walked over to the departure shed to wait for the little puddle-jumper I'd reserved on.

Maui and the Big Island of Hawaii are so close together that they're visible to each other on a clear day. If all goes well, a flight from Kona on Hawaii to Kahului Airport on Maui, takes less than half an hour.

My ride was a tiny turboprop run by a company that shall remain nameless and is no longer in business. The company had no ground staff, no office, and no apparent budget. The breezeway between two metal trailers, our "lounge area," was filled with twenty-two members of a Micronesian family. A six-foot-high mountain of boxes and bungee-corded coolers marked their possessions, which I eyed dubiously as the pilots, two young men with Russian accents, weighed the stuff and argued with the Micronesians, trying to convey that it wouldn't all fit on the plane.

The two pilots were delayed a further half hour by sorting out exactly which passengers, none of whom spoke English, were flying with us. To my gratitude, the pilots refused to carry the chickens and baby pig, which went back into the pickup with departing folks who'd apparently been hanging out to offer moral support.

Finally, seven of us got on board, filling all of the seats in the tiny craft. My knees tight to the seat in front of me and my apprehensive gaze on the Russians just ahead of me in the cockpit, I prepared for the bumpy journey to Maui by praying.

The engine, firing up, sounded exactly like the 1976 Volkswagen Karmann Ghia Mike had bought me when we were first married. That car was adorable, but it had a bad day pretty often, and I'd gotten good at doing a running push-start and parking so that the car was always pointed downhill.

The props started whirling. The Russians checked various switches and dials, chattering unintelligibly. All looked good. I shut my eyes and kept praying.

And then, the thing sputtered, died, and refused to start again.

We all filed back off, climbing down the rickety ladder and walking back to the open breezeway. The situation was kind of third-world funny at that point, and I texted Mike to let him know that I'd been delayed, again, by mechanical failure this time. The hardy passengers and I sat on benches in the lounge area and waited for the airline's mechanic to come check out the plane.

Darkness fell as the sun was snuffed out by the heavy vog. Wind whistled between the metal trailers. Mosquitoes swarmed. The Micronesians lay down on the benches and went to sleep.

I wasn't able to nod off that easily. By then, I was cold, tired, and hungry. Wearing my Volcanoes National Park hoodie, listening to music to calm myself, I scrolled through alternatives on my phone. Nothing was available that didn't involve a lengthy, expensive cab ride into Kona, a hotel room (if I could find one), and another attempt the following day to get back home. Assistance in the form of shuttles or help rescheduling was not offered by the pilots, and I had to *work* the next day.

I decided to gut it out and keep waiting for the plane to get fixed. Sitting on the bench, my knees tucked up inside my roomy sweatshirt, I desperately wished myself somewhere else—somewhere with dinner, a warm bed, and *no adventures.*

The mechanic flew himself in three hours later on a three-seater Cessna, arriving at 12:30 p.m. Clad in board shorts, rubber slippers, and a T-shirt, he approached the parked plane with toolbox in hand. He fetched a stepstool, climbed up, popped the hood of the little plane, and poked around, asking one of the pilots to hold a flashlight for him.

We heard banging, "Move the flashlight up a little, willya?" and other reassuring comments. Finally, the engine started and kept going long enough for him to slam the lid and pronounce it fixed.

I ascended into the little coffin with the other stubborn survivors of our airport hell. The Russians fired up the sewing machine of an engine, and soon we were hurtling through pitch-black skies over heaving seas, packed tightly in the lurching metal tube and hanging on for dear life. The only illumination was from the flashing tips of the wings and the green dials of the control panel between the pilots. Twenty minutes later, the crappy little thing bounced down onto the runway on Maui.

When you say yes to adventure, you say yes to the whole enchilada—not just the fun parts.

But there was no doubt that I felt keenly alive, and at two-thirty a.m. when I finally kissed my pillow, my bed at home had never felt so good.

CHAPTER EIGHT
TRAVEL DAY

Departure day had finally come. We were doing it at last! From a dream in a doctor's office to reality in less than six months—what a way to celebrate turning fifty!

Our plan was to fly into California and rent an SUV. From there we'd begin our trek in Yosemite National Park; swing through Arizona; hit Colorado, New Mexico, Utah, and Nevada; and then loop back to California—a route of around four thousand miles. We planned to stay in park lodges, but we'd also packed camping gear for days we couldn't find accommodations.

We did last-minute errands, zipped up duffels and backpacks, watered the plants, and tried to reassure the anxious dogs. My mom was coming to take care of our place, so we knew they'd be fine. We patted their heads, closed the front door, said goodbye to our house on the side of Haleakalā, and set off for a month of adventure.

Adventure, by definition, involves risk. Sometimes that risk starts out as innocent fun and devolves into something much less pleasant. The very spice that makes any experience exciting can turn things sour, as I'd had occasion to realize already. Even so, champagne bubbles of happiness filled me as I settled into my window seat on the plane to San Francisco.

Window seats have always helped me overcome plane anxiety, because I figure I'll be able to see whatever disaster might be coming. I inflated a brand-new, fuzzy-coated plastic neck pillow I'd bought at Longs, inserted my ear plugs, put on my eye mask, and fell asleep as soon as we were airborne.

Suddenly I woke.

The pillow's air had expanded or something, and the support felt tight around my neck, as if it were strangling me. I ripped the pillow off, but I was overheated and unable to catch my breath. Spots filled my vision, telescoping to black. "Help! I can't see! I can't breathe!"

Panicky, I gasped and flailed, trying to get to the aisle. All I could think of was reaching the open space and lying down on the floor, but I was wedged against the window by Mike and another passenger.

"What's the matter?" Mike caught me as I lunged across him.

"I don't know! Something's wrong! I can't see! I can't breathe!" I wheezed.

The flight attendants were amazingly fast to respond as Mike and the other passenger moved out of the seats in my row. They helped me lie down across the seats, encouraging me to stay calm and focus on breathing.

Someone called over the intercom, "Is there a doctor on board? Medical emergency!"

I was too terrified to be embarrassed as one of the attendants covered my mouth and nose with a plastic mask and turned on a cylinder of oxygen. "Just breathe. Count slowly and breathe." I shut my eyes and focused, feeling a trickle of oxygen moving through my constricted airway.

A doctor and two nurses answered the call and came to examine me, getting ready to hit me with the plane's emergency EpiPen, as I was clearly in respiratory distress.

I remembered my son's asthma inhaler, which I still carried around in my purse even though he was almost thirty and lived six thousand miles away. Mike dug the inhaler out and I sucked in the mist.

Gradually, I felt it working; the tight alveoli opening.

They put the oxygen back on me, and eventually I was able to take a full breath. The black spots receded as I lay prone across the seats. I refused to be parted with the green metal oxygen canister for the remainder of the flight, cradling it in my arms like a baby.

The doctor speculated that I'd had an allergic reaction to some chemical associated with the inflatable pillow, which was brand-new and smelled strange. Washing that kind of thing before use might be a good idea in the future.

By the time we landed, I felt fine. I looked all over the baggage area to thank my rescuers, but they had vanished. I was left with deep gratitude for their time, expertise, and generosity. Thank goodness I'd had the inhaler! I greatly hoped I wouldn't need it again as we took off for a month in the wilderness.

As we settled onto low-quality sheets at the optimistically named Good Nite Inn in Fremont, California, I made a resolution: this trip, for me, would be about allowing what was happening to just happen . . . without getting stressed-out, worried, or controlling.

On this trip, I resolved to assume that everything would work out, that people would be positive and helpful, and that we'd be safe and comfortable as we traveled. Falling back on my therapy training, I'd even prepared a self-hypnosis recording on my phone of my favorite affirmations, in case I needed a reminder, such as "The world is a friendly and loving place that responds to the energy I put out."

My throat still hurt that night, but I hadn't had a panic attack. Something had been physically wrong with me, and that was real. There might still be other things amiss; the itchy hives on the back of my hands were worrisome. But I wasn't going to let anything get in the way. I would be "Zen" and enjoy this adventure, no matter what bumps in the road we encountered.

And in case you ever wondered, airline personnel really do go on the intercom and call, "Is anyone on board a doctor?" And God bless them, those folks answer.

~

WE CHECKED OUT OF THE GOOD NITE INN THE NEXT MORNING AND had breakfast with our daughter, who had driven out to join us, coming all the way from San Francisco to the forgettable stretch of urban sprawl that is Fremont. Many hugs later, we went shopping for camping and food supplies and got lost, shopped, and got lost again.

The five-hour drive to Yosemite finally began, much later than anticipated, and we drove toward roiling and ominous clouds; a thunderstorm blanketed the freeway with pellets of water as we left the Bay Area.

"Hope this isn't a sign of things to come," Mike muttered, peering through the whipping wipers at the barely visible road. "Check that Lady Google has us on the right track, will you? She hasn't said anything in a while."

Turns out, our affectionately named GPS had gone offline some time ago. Our phones only had one bar of signal, not enough to run the app.

"Guess we're really out in the country," I said as we meandered through acres and acres of blooming almond orchards—spectacular, but not necessarily where we'd meant to go. "Do you know where we're going without Lady Google?"

"I used to, but it's been a long time." Clearly, we had taken a wrong exit somewhere. Mike eventually found a gas station and a paper map, and we got back on track "old school," heading up through hills already gone buff and brown with California summer.

I clung to my resolution to stay Zen no matter what, even when a state patrol officer burst out from behind a bush to pull us over on a stretch of deserted country road. Mike navigated to the shoulder.

"Did you see what the speed limit was?" he asked. "Because I sure didn't."

"Nope. Guess we missed the sign."

"I didn't think I was going all that fast, but I bet that's the problem." Mike reached across me to dig around in the glove box for the SUV's rental information.

Turns out it was—we'd been doing 45 in a 35-mph zone. Watching buzzards circle in the bleached blue sky as the officer wrote us up, I did my relaxation breathing: *in through the nose to the count of five, out through the mouth to the count of five.* "Nothing bad is happening right now. Everything's fine," I muttered aloud.

"Yeah, until we get home and have to write a hefty check for this ticket," Mike said.

"It's a one-time thing. First and only ticket of the trip," I stated. "Now it's out of the way."

Mike shook his head, setting the cruise control at thirty-five. "I'm not taking any chances."

After a few more wrong turns and lost miles due to poor map-reading skills, we pulled into Yosemite at dusk—and every mile, hassle, and penny it took to get there was made worthwhile.

CHAPTER NINE
YOSEMITE NATIONAL PARK

I first visited Yosemite thirty years ago, soon after Mike and I got engaged. We hiked in Tuolumne Meadows up above the Valley and ended up camping in the bushes beside the trail, when the light ran out long before we reached our destination.

The only picture we own from that trip shows us smiling in front of a wooded vista. My golden-coin hair is a-frizz from the mist of Bridalveil Fall, and Mike's muscular arm is draped over me in casual possession. His physical presence dwarfed me, and it was intoxicating to be tucked against his side—truthfully, all I remember about visiting Yosemite back then was how intensely in love we were.

People who read *Freckled,* my first memoir, have asked how we went from that first meeting at the end of the book to falling in love, and I promised that in *this* memoir, I'd tell that story.

Like all good love stories, ours almost didn't happen.

I met Mike in 1983, on a brief visit to my parents on Kauai before I left for college.

At eighteen, I was on my way to Boston University on the East Coast, escaping a childhood spent growing up in the jungle on Kauai. My parents had moved to Hawaii in 1967, and we'd spent a good portion of the next fifteen years living in a van, tents, and various rentals as they scratched out a living in paradise while pursuing a surfing lifestyle.

I wanted something different for myself: I wanted to be "normal." I'd relinquished the yogis, gurus and "love feasts" I grew up with for a Christianity that promised a whole new life and a handbook of rules to live by in the form of the Bible.

Highly romantic and idealistic, a kind of surfer-girl Anne of Green Gables complete with red hair, I wanted to have a Great Big Passionate Love. I saw myself with a clean-cut fellow college student, a guy who wore polo shirts with an emblem on the chest, boat shoes with no socks, and perhaps had a Jr. or III after his name —the kind of man I could build a solid financial future and guaranteed normalcy with.

Mike did not fit this template at all.

He filled a room with his presence. He wasn't just tall—he radiated a crackling energy that magnetized not only me but everyone around him. His crystal-blue eyes seemed to see infinity and befriend it. Tousled brown surfer hair told of many hours in the ocean. He was too rugged to be traditionally handsome, but I couldn't look away; I was riveted by his physical grace and the competency he showed in everything he did, from cooking lobsters he'd caught on the reef to fixing someone's car.

I'd first met Mike when he came to my parents' house for dinner, but during five days at a Christian youth camp where we were both volunteers, I had two encounters with him that made a big impression.

In the first encounter, Mike came into our staff prayer meeting stripped down to board shorts and carrying a big bowl of soapy water with a washcloth floating in it and a towel draped over his shoulder. He declared that he was going to wash all of our feet "like Jesus served the disciples" during the prayer meeting, and then he got on his knees and started working his way around the room.

I prayed from my sticky plastic chair, too, fervently entreating

God for Mike to pass me by, but He didn't answer that particular prayer.

Mike removed my foot from where I'd tucked it under the chair and placed it in the warm, bubbly water, cleaning the dirt away from my peeling toenail polish with precision and tenderness. He then did the other foot, ignoring my stiffness, my embarrassed resistance. When both feet were clean to his satisfaction, he took my feet out of the bowl and patted them dry with the towel. I stared at his broad tanned shoulders and the sun-streaked top of his head, my cheeks on fire with embarrassment and vulnerability.

This guy was spiritual, and he didn't care how it looked to others.

The second encounter occurred during an all-camp tug-of-war. We were stationed beside each other, sandwiched between other teammates on the rope. Together we hauled and strained, crashing into each other, grunting and heaving with effort, getting dirty and chafed by the heavy rope—and we hauled our team to victory!

Dropping the thick, rough rope, shouting in triumph, we hugged —and as his body pressed against mine, sweaty and heart-pounding, I had a flash of what it would be like to *be* with him.

Epic. Earthshaking. Everything this romantic virgin had been waiting and hoping for.

Mike was not someone I'd ever be able to boss around. This was a man who would challenge me—a *man*, not a boy. I was hugely attracted—but also terrified.

A week later, on of the eve of my departure to Boston University, twenty-nine-year-old Michael Ray Neal gave eighteen-year-old Toby Wilson his address on a scrap of paper. "Write me," he said, "if you want to be pen pals."

"Pen pals." So old-fashioned and innocent.

He'd given me his address in a big brother kind of way. Our age difference and lifestyle choices were huge barriers. I was fairly sure I hadn't made the kind of impression on him that he'd made on me, but for some reason I wanted to—*and writing was my thing.*

I wrote him from the plane as I flew, alone, all the way from Kauai to Boston, a city I'd never seen before.

I wrote him from the sunny windowsill of my dorm looking down on Commonwealth Avenue. I wrote him from the Boston Library, at a table shrouded with green lampshades and overlooked by walls of books gleaming with the patina of time. I wrote him from my little twin bed in a suite with three freshman girls determined to have fun, and me—a recent convert, clinging to brand-new Christianity like a fig leaf to cover my nakedness.

I wrote him of the changing autumn leaves and what it was like to run along the Charles River with the Harvard rowing team sculling faster than I could jog. I wrote him on a field trip to Maine of the first time I saw an apple growing on a tree. I wrote him of what the stars looked like through the university's giant telescope and of the first falling snowflake this Hawaii girl had ever seen and of how it tasted, melting on my tongue.

I wrote him of the contrast between Boston's glittering high-rises and the ancient graveyards right beside them, where the powdered bones of our nation's forefathers lay beneath rough slate tombstones marked with names that time and wind had worn away.

I wrote him of my homesickness for Hawaii, as winter deepened and my thrift-store wool coat no longer kept out the cold. I wrote him of my struggle to keep my faith alive in the face of my roommates' constant partying, and I wrote him about the guy I'd begun to date, who liked me more than I did him.

Mike wrote me back, thick missives on lined paper, filled with a misspelled black block print scrawl that slanted backward in his hurry to nail down the words. Vibrant and bold, riddled with pictographs, doodles in the margins and Scripture verses, his letters arrived weekly, filling me with anticipation as I ran to check my mailbox.

I didn't tell anyone about our correspondence—its spiritual focus, its soul-searching, radical connection. *"Who are you, Mike Neal?"* I asked, deep in our ongoing dialogue. *"Tell me who you are."*

His reply was searing in its intensity: *"No one has ever asked me that before. No one has cared enough to want to know."* And he did his best to tell me who he was.

Something had shifted, and we both knew it.

I dropped out of Boston University to transfer to a West Coast college, the city life and harsh winter too big of an adjustment for me. We met for a visit at the end of that first year; I stayed with friends of his in the Bay Area, and he showed me San Francisco.

We weren't dating; just spending time together as Christian pen pals. Our age difference, between his thirty years and my nineteen, loomed large.

But as we went skimboarding in Half Moon Bay, fishing for cod off the rocks, riding the carousel on Pier 49, wandering through the zoo eating cotton candy—I knew I felt something for him.

Something big.

Something different than I'd ever felt before.

And, every now and again, I'd get a glimmer that he might feel the same.

After church one day, Mike led me over to his old white station wagon, a car he'd nicknamed La Bomba. "I've got a surprise planned." He blindfolded me with a bandanna and ushered me onto La Bomba's big bench seat.

We drove out of the church parking lot. He played classic rock on the radio, and we got on the freeway—or at least, the feeling, the smoothness, the wind whistling through the windows and stroking over my skin told me it was the freeway.

"It's as if I'm flying through space, like I'm on the Starship Enterprise," I said. "Strange how different everything is when you just take away one of the senses."

"I'm a Trekkie too." He tugged my hand. "Come over here and snuggle. We've got a ways to go."

He'd held my hand before, but only briefly, to help me over a boulder on the trail or across a slippery spot. Once, we'd lain on our backs on a sand dune at night, watching the stars, and he'd put his arm around me. We'd hugged, too, but not for long. This was the first time he'd invited me to come closer in a way that could be interpreted as romantic.

I slid over on the bench seat and cautiously settled, lowering my head to rest on his leg. I shut my eyes, relaxing at last behind the blindfold, submitting to this adventure, letting go.

The springs of the old horsehair-filled bench seat creaked as we bounced over a pothole; the wind blew across us, hot as summer in California can be, smelling of diesel and dust; Fleetwood Mac sang of a landslide.

I felt his thigh beneath my cheek, flexing as he drove, one hand on the steering wheel and the other playing with my hair, resting on my shoulder, stroking my arm. Deep bliss welled up in me, making my eyes prickle. It was utterly perfect just to lie here, a blindfold over my eyes, trusting this man I'd come to know deeply through letters.

Wherever he was going, even if I couldn't see the way, I wanted to be along for the ride.

But the enchanted drive eventually ended. A deeply rutted road bounced me around so hard that I had to sit up and brace myself by clinging to the door handle.

We stopped.

"Shoot," Mike muttered. "This is not what I planned at all."

I smelled an overwhelming stench of rotting fish guts and garbage. I took the blindfold off.

Buzzing flies swept in through La Bomba's open windows. We'd pulled up in front of a loaded dumpster in a dirt parking lot at a lake. A small bait shop, mobbed with people, crowned a rickety dock. A huge banner hung over the area trumpeting, "FISHING TOURNAMENT TODAY!"

Mike turned to me; his mouth pinched with embarrassment. "I thought I'd bring you to my favorite little lake for a picnic." He gestured to the back seat, where a wicker hamper rested, along with a Mexican blanket and a pair of fishing poles. "I didn't know it would be so crowded."

"That's okay. I'm sure we can find somewhere to fish." I avoided inhaling because of the dumpster smell. "Let's just go find a spot."

"That's my girl," he said. "Sorry the surprise was not so great."

My heart broke open. *He called me 'his girl!'*

We got out and, holding hands and carrying fishing poles and the picnic hamper, walked around the edge of the lake, looking for an open space.

The lake was completely packed. Every square inch of decent shoreline was already occupied with noisy families or serious fishermen. We trudged a long way, until finally Mike pointed down a steep tumble of rocks and dirt to a tiny ledge above the water, deep in the trees. "I think we can have a little privacy down there." He slanted a glance at me to see how I'd react.

"No problem." I scrambled and slid down the embankment to the water. I'd grown up a tomboy on Kauai; getting muddy didn't faze me.

The ledge was just wide enough for our butts to fit on if we sat close together with our feet in the water. He was so much bigger that my head barely topped his shoulder. We put our bait out and held our poles, but sitting there, actually touching him, knowing he'd wanted to be with me and show me a favorite place of his ... that was all that mattered.

Mike had packed a picnic. And he called me 'his girl.'

My whole being vibrated with happiness.

We talked, but I don't remember what about. We ate roast beef sandwiches and drank root beer he'd packed in the picnic basket. My feet were getting pruney; I wiggled my toes when little fish nibbled on them. The light was greenish from the leaves above, and sunspots danced over us. I wished I could hold his hand, but I was too shy to reach for it.

"I think I have feelings for you," he said, eyes front, trained on the tip of his pole.

I'd had "feelings" for him for a while now, but some inner voice had chanted, *"Don't show it, don't show it,"* and I'd heeded that.

"Oh, yeah?" I kept my eyes forward too.

"Yeah. Strong feelings."

"What kind of feelings?" I didn't mean to sound breathless.

"I think I love you." Mike's voice was low. "I've never felt like this before."

I turned and met his eyes, deep-set under dark brows—a blue as bright and clear as the noon sky. "I've never felt like this before, either."

"I can't stop thinking about you. I want to be with you all the time." He paused a long moment. "In every way."

"Me too." I knew what that meant, and I heartily agreed. I leaned into him, rubbing my cheek along the bulge of his shoulder muscle, all but purring. "I love you."

"We should get married," he said.

A whoosh of heat exploded in my belly, roared up my neck, and lit my face bright red. I didn't need a mirror to see what that blush looked like; it had plagued me forever.

Was he proposing? Was that what just happened?

I probably should have thought more about how strange it was that we'd admitted we loved each other, and the next step was marriage. We'd never even kissed.

But I didn't think it was strange. I wanted to be with him, too. All the time. In every way. I was a chaste Christian; so was he. Therefore, we were getting married.

"Okay," I whispered.

"So. We're engaged?"

"I guess we are."

"We're engaged!" Mike stood, and grabbed me up in his arms. "We're getting married!" We jumped up and down in the water, hugging and laughing.

Such extreme happiness swamped me that it was agonizing, as if at any moment the top of my head was going to blow off. We whooped and shouted and splashed each other and hugged repeatedly.

We packed up the poles and the basket and scrambled back up the hill. We ran and skipped, holding hands, all the way back to La Bomba, stopping periodically to yell to the people fishing along the lake, "We're getting married!"

And, sometime between that day when we got engaged and when we eventually married at the green Wai'oli Hui'ia Church in Hanalei in 1986, we'd gone hiking and camping together in Yosemite—but I was too in love back then to notice anything but the man beside me.

∾

As it turned out, dusk, in May, was a splendid time to enter Yosemite National Park.

We emerged from a short tunnel and pulled over to gasp at a view of the sunset striking the magnificent cliffs of Yosemite Valley, and gleaming off the swollen Merced River. Mist from gushing waterfalls created tender scarves of drifting vapor that enhanced the vast, sheer lines of the mountains, and the dark lushness of the forest. We took picture after picture of the waterfalls jetting and thundering off the granite sides, filling the flooded ribbon of river snaking through the valley floor.

Yosemite National Park was established in 1864 and is one of the brightest jewels in the National Park System (NPS.) Yosemite is famous for its many stunning waterfalls, but the park also includes nearly twelve hundred square miles of mountain vistas that include high cliffs, deep valleys, ancient giant sequoias, and a large wilderness plateau area (Tuolumne Meadows).

The last rays of daylight filtered down on us through a haze of foliage as we found our way to the "Housekeeping" camping area on the Merced River, directly across from Yosemite Falls, where we'd be staying for the next few days. Dogwoods bloomed everywhere, their white flowers floating like stars in the green gloaming of new leaves.

Housekeeping Camp was mostly deserted this early in the season, and even as we set up in the dark, we were delighted with our shelter. Consisting of three cement sides, two spring-loaded cots, and a canvas roof with a front flap that tied shut, our shelter was a quasi-tent that came with a steel anti-bear locker in which to store our foodstuffs.

We pushed our beds side by side to snuggle close, glad to zip together our sleeping bags, so recently purchased that they crackled, as the temperature plunged during the night to well below freezing.

Waking the next morning to the roar of the falls and the presence of my beloved beside me, still together more than thirty years after first visiting this place as a couple, felt so fulfilling that I teared up as I snuggled close to Mike.

We'd almost separated several times over the course of our thirty-plus-year marriage.

We loved each other intensely, passionately, and to the exclusion of anyone else. Love was never the problem—but we were two strong-willed firstborns with different ideas about how our lives should go, what we should do, where we should live, and how we should spend our money. When people asked what the secret to staying married so long was, we'd always answer, "Stubbornness."

We are both *very* stubborn. Neither of us was willing to be the one who left, even when we were miserable together. So, we stayed: through thick, thin, unemployment, illnesses, family drama, deaths, multiple moves and career changes, and the stresses and strains of birthing, raising, educating, and releasing two amazing young adults out into the world.

And now here we were, reaping the benefits of having survived those tough times. We were still together, still in love, and on an adventure at the place where we'd begun. *Full circle.*

Mike got up first, pulling on clothes in the freezing dawn and departing for the kitchen area. Shortly after, he came back to get his cameras, and bent to kiss me. "G'morning, Sleeping Beauty. I'm off to get a picture of the sunrise on Yosemite Falls."

"Excellent. I can smell the coffee perking." I was in no hurry to get up.

"Of course. See you later." Mike grabbed his Pelican case, restocked with equipment he'd rented for the trip, and vanished.

I got up at my own speed, poured myself a cup of warm brew, and walked outside the shelter area to the gasp-worthy sight of the great horsetail of Yosemite Falls plummeting thousands of feet directly in front of our campsite from gigantic cliffs a mile away.

I opened one of our camp chairs, sat down, and sighed with happiness as I feasted on a breakfast of natural beauty. More than thirty years after my first visit, Yosemite hadn't aged a day, and she made me feel young again too.

CHAPTER TEN
A STORM IN YOSEMITE

Mike eventually returned, and we spent a sunny morning in the park exploring the valley floor. Yosemite rises up steeply in spectacular cliffs and bluffs, but the central meadow is flat, nice for riding through with a bike or gentle walking. I needed pants, boots, and a parka as we trekked through the chilly springtime forest, spotting deer with fawns, squirrels, chipmunks, ravens, and the bright blue Steller's jays that love California. I kept a sharp eye out for bears, but mercifully never saw any.

After we returned to camp in the afternoon, Mike had a specific photo shoot he wanted to do and took off for that. I drove to the public restrooms near the campground, feeling sticky, ready to get clean after a couple of days since the Good Nite Inn's tepid showers.

Clouds had blown in over the valley, and I shivered getting out of the SUV. The park facilities consisted of a row of pay-per-minute stalls in a big central shower house. I paid for a small towel, chose a stall, and soaped up quickly, one eye on the timer.

Sudden thunder boomed directly overhead—so loud that I squealed in fright, joining three other ladies occupying the building in a chorus of shrieks. We burst into nervous giggles and exclamations, which were abruptly drowned out by the machine-gun rattle of hailstones on the clear fiberglass roof.

I couldn't remember the last time I'd seen a hailstone—perhaps when we'd lived in Michigan twenty years ago. Hailstones are not to be sneezed at. They inflict millions of dollars in damage every year and come in sizes ranging from the diameter of a frozen pea to the biggest ever recorded, roughly the size of a volleyball.

The stones pelting the shower house were pea-sized, but when combined with an ongoing blitzkrieg of thunder and lightning, being naked and wet felt incredibly vulnerable. I hurried through my shower and threw on my clothing, running through the storm to the SUV and moving to park it under the trees so the rental's paint wouldn't be damaged.

Mike met me back at our shelter. Storms excite him. He was in a great mood, running around adjusting the shelter's tarps to deflect the now-streaming rain and intermittent hailstones. He set up a camera on a tripod and aimed it, covered with a plastic trash bag, at the top of Yosemite Falls, chanting, "C'mon, storm, just one good lightning bolt over the Falls is all I need!"

Mike is one of those people who hears a storm warning and heads *toward* it rather than away. Floods we've dealt with have been an occasion to go out and see if people need help. Tsunami warnings in Hawaii meant Mike sneaking past barriers to take up a vantage point to observe the event, and hurricanes were some of his favorite times to go surfing. After my adventurous childhood on Kauai, I had a healthy respect for natural phenomena, though I shared Mike's aesthetic appreciation.

The hail segued into buckets of freezing rain. We dug a trench, using our hands and firewood sticks, to redirect water collecting on the tent's roof from pouring onto our bed. When the soaked canvas structure overhead was as secure as we could make it, I heated some water on the stove for hot chocolate, and we sat on plastic garbage bags in our wet folding chairs to watch the show.

Lightning lit the churning purple-gray sky. Thunder shook the pines until cones pelted down. Across from our camp, Yosemite Falls pumped water so hard that the plume of the waterfall disappeared entirely in spray, emitting a roar like enormous waves on a big day at the Jaws surf break on Maui.

The skies cleared suddenly in another freaky weather shift, and a sunset of vivid red and gold, as dramatic as the storm had been, lit the famous Half Dome cliff formation. Mike and I grabbed cameras, hopped in the SUV, and drove and ran from vista to vista, filling our eyes and lenses with transcendent, iconic beauty. The sunset was so over the top it seemed like a green screen projection with majestic nature views playing from every direction. Every picture I took looked fake—but each was the truth of just one of Yosemite's many moods.

We got our fire going for the night by drying wood on the propane stove, a process that involved holding the wood with tongs as it hissed and steamed like a hot dog, making me giggle. We cooked steaks and made s'mores once we got the wet wood going, praying the rain hadn't turned to snow and closed Tioga Pass, the mountain exit out of the park we were planning to take. If Tioga wasn't open on Saturday, we would have a very long drive around the wild end of California to our next destination.

A young English couple arrived after dark and took the campsite space that backed up to us, which we'd enjoyed having empty. They didn't have proper gear and ended up needing help with their fire, opening cans of food and their bottle of wine. They appeared to have arrived in the USA, thrown a few bags of groceries into their rental car, and set off for Yosemite with no real idea of how to camp —but they were polite and had cute accents, so we didn't mind.

Later, the couple definitively answered whether the bedsprings on the cots squeaked. (Yes, and loudly.) Mike and I looked over at each other and grinned. We'd had the previous two nights all to ourselves and hadn't had to worry about that.

CHAPTER ELEVEN
GAS AND FISHING

We set out the next morning to get fishing licenses and go up to Tuolumne Meadows above Yosemite Valley for stream casting, an activity we'd done back on our engagement trip thirty years before.

"We need gas before we drive to the top of the mountain," Mike said. But we drove all around the lodges and shops of the park's village and didn't see any stations. Buying the licenses and tackle at a sports shop, Mike asked where the nearest gas was.

"There's none in the park," the attendant told us. "Nearest station is seventeen miles outside the park, in El Capitan."

This significant fact was not in the literature about the park.

Or on the blogs we read about Yosemite.

Or on any of the signs we had seen so far.

There is pretty much nothing I dislike more than running out of gas—a close second to getting locked out of the car. During our many years of marriage, I'm pretty sure both of those have happened to us much more than the national average.

We started our married life flirting with the raggedy edge of broke, driving "restoration project" cars that Mike was always working on. Every other week or so, we seemed to lose the keys, run out of gas, get stranded on the side of the road with a break-down, or lock ourselves out—and often with two little kids in tow.

Those hard times were behind us. I now drove a new car with a spare key hidden somewhere on it, and always filled up with a quarter tank still on the gauge.

But Mike had rented the vehicle we were currently using and was handling everything to do with it on this trip, so clearly this issue with the gas was his fault.

I lost the Zen I'd been trying so hard to practice.

I stomped around the store, glaring at Mike as he bought a map and asked the clerk to mark the shortest route to a gas station.

"It's all downhill—just coast," the guy said, highlighting the route with his pen. "Good luck!"

We got in the SUV in tense silence. I took only one look at the gas gauge, already set at E. "We'd better not run out of gas," I growled.

"You were with me when we drove in. Did *you* see any signs, or have any idea that there was no gas in the park?" Mike challenged.

"No." I knew it was illogical to be so angry.

"We'll make it," he said. "We'll just hitchhike if we run out before we get there."

I folded my arms and scowled. "We're too old for hitchhiking to get gas."

"It's not like you're going to have to do it," he said. "That'll be me."

Hell, yeah. This was all his fault!

Following the map, we exited the park on a back route. We coasted as much as we could, all the way out of the valley, for seventeen white-knuckled miles down an unknown road.

Fortunately, it was mostly a downhill slope, as the clerk had promised. I did relaxation breathing and kept from snarling by biting my lips.

Mike tried to jolly me out of it. "We've been through worse than this. Remember that time we went steelhead fishing with the kids?"

"How could I forget?" We'd set out for a river rumored to have a run of steelhead. Caleb was an avid fisherman at five, and Tawny was already a rugged Neal ready for anything at only three. I was the only one of us who expressed concern about the lateness of the day, the sketchy verbal directions from a crusty fisherman describing where the river was, and the fact that it was Sunday and we had only a half tank of fuel.

The river was much farther than we'd been led to believe. I'll never forget watching the gauge as we went over yet another mountain, and—of course—coasted to the shoulder as we ran out of gas. I hated the sinking sensation of gliding to the side of the road with wilderness all around us and young children in the back seat.

I stayed with the kids in the hot car while Mike jogged off with the empty can he kept in the back. He managed to hitchhike to the nearest hamlet, where the gas station was closed due to it being Sunday. Getting creative, Mike begged a gallon of gas from the proprietor of a general store that was open and hitchhiked back to us . . . but it wasn't enough to get us all the way home. We were stranded in the hamlet until the gas station opened on Monday.

We ended up staying in a motel overnight, and then discovered the river with the steelhead right nearby.

Everyone but Tawny caught fish, and on the way back over the mountains, Mike bought me a lovely miniature china tea set I had admired in the window of the village gift shop as a make-up present. I still have that set, and it has been used in innumerable tea parties with the kids and their friends over the years. The sight of its delicate, miniature cups decorated with pink roses reminded me of a fiasco that eventually had a happy ending.

The real problem was that I'd grown up poor, and I'd sworn off living like that—and then I'd married a man who made his living with his hands and had an adventurous streak a mile wide. I regretted nothing, but it was important to understand and overcome how triggered I was. After all, I'd become a mental health therapist in part to heal my own past.

So, what was the worst that would happen today, if we ran out of gas? *I'd sit on the side of the road in the hot sun while Mike hitchhiked to get gas, and an axe murderer would come along and kidnap me (or him).*

My imagination was not always a friend.

We glided silently around another bend in the road, down another gentle slope.

"Eureka!" I yelled, pointing. A large placard declaring *'No Gas in Yosemite!'* marked the sandy lot of a decrepit gas station with an attached convenience store. We coasted on fumes up to the pumps. "Thank you, Jesus!"

Mike filled up the vehicle and went inside the store. He came back and handed me a round, chocolate-covered ice cream sandwich, and flourished his own. "When I was a kid, we used to buy these *It's It* sandwiches from a concession stand at Playland-by-the-Sea at Ocean Beach in San Francisco," he told me. "I can't believe they have them out here."

"Thanks," I said. "It looks yummy." And it was: crispy oatmeal cookies encased top-quality vanilla ice cream, and the whole thing was enrobed in chocolate.

The silence as we headed back up the incline we'd coasted down was broken only by lip smacking as we ate; an ice cream treat had never tasted that good, seasoned as it was by a potent cocktail of hunger and bone-deep relief that we weren't walking along that narrow, steep road in the hot sun.

We stopped on the Merced River as we reentered Yosemite, separating to go fishing by mutual nonverbal agreement: I tromped off in one direction, while he went the opposite.

Finding a likely spot, I tossed my lure into a deep, swirling, jade-green pool, soon tangling the gold and yellow Panther Martin spinner in the new-fledged leaves of cottonwoods along the edge. I clambered and splashed across the river to retrieve it, only to start over again.

There's something meditative about stream fishing with a good lure. It induces a "flow state," as psychologist Mihaly Csikszentmihalyi defines it: an activity that's completely absorbing because it falls into that perfect window between too difficult and too easy— that place where time seems to stop.

I could have worked my way along the boulder-rimmed river all day, choosing difficult spots to cast into, working my lure just so: into the shadowy notch between two rocks, to the left of the waterfall; that undercut mossy bank where the muskrat lived, roots dangling into the water making the cast extra difficult; the crystalline bowl of bubbles where a cascade purled, pebbles mingling their colors at the bottom.

Casting is almost enough to make fishing fun all by itself, but when a fish is on your hook, there's a deep excitement. Keeping the rod's tip up and the tension exactly right to maximize the fight, guiding the line to keep it from snagging, and gently bringing the tired fish to shore all require the total focus that's a part of "flow." I'm always respectful of fish, keeping them in the water to get the hook out if I'm releasing them, and killing them right away if not.

I set free the sweet little spotted browns I caught after admiring their perfect, colorful camouflage spots, sleek bodies, and the deep pink of their gills. Eventually I returned to the car, right at the same time as Mike did. We often found ourselves perfectly in sync that way.

"Look!" I pointed, and we both froze, staring.

A doe stood in the underbrush nearby, a pair of fawns at her side. They seemed to blend with the forest when they stood still, as if conjured from shadows and the colors of the trees and earth surrounding them.

"Dang it, I don't have my camera handy," Mike muttered.

I blinked, and they were gone. "Guess it's time to go back to camp."

We'd seen a lot of wildlife in the park so far. While commonplace for California, as Hawaii residents who seldom saw anything but birds, we'd both enjoyed glimpses of deer, sleek patterned garter snakes, huge shiny black crows, curious blue jays, gray and red squirrels, and bold chipmunks (one actually hopped into the car to grab a peanut off the floor when the door was open.) So far, we hadn't seen any bears, though we were surrounded by signs reminding us not to leave anything smelly out to attract them.

Mike wanted to get more sunset photos as evening drew near, but I was tired of all the to-ing and fro-ing. I opted for an evening alone, hanging out at camp and doing domestic chores. Little homely routines seemed to anchor me, to provide a calm I was craving.

I straightened up our tent and trekked up to the communal laundry room with a pillowcase full of grimy clothes.

At the little sliding window near the entrance, a young man with giant gauges in his ears and an "I'm too cool for this Laundromat attendant job" attitude explained to an upset German guy that the reason his clothes weren't dry yet was that he'd run them through a washer, not a dryer. I stifled a smile. Figuring out the English instructions was obviously no picnic.

A clutch of Mennonite ladies stood inside, guarding their washers and cliquishly gossiping in some almost recognizable dialect. They were lovely, in their long pastel gowns and gauzy caps, and never left their laundry alone for a minute. *Do they think we'll run off with their long skirts and headgear?*

After starting our load with a fistful of quarters, I left to take another shower in the steamy shower house. Just as I realized that I was there at approximately the same time as the day before, a thunderclap rattled the fiberglass roof overhead.

This time I just laughed, reveling in the experience and not to be shortchanged of one expensive, delicious minute of hot water. Thankfully, no hail added to the cacophony overhead.

I spent the remainder of the afternoon pleasantly: trying to get the campfire going with damp wood while watching the lustrous plume of Yosemite Falls from my folding chair, then fishing along the turn of the golden-pebbled river, casting into a nice, deep pool where the water carved under the roots of a leaning sequoia. Eventually, I watched the setting sun slide down the great slab of Half Dome like a candle burning low.

Then I filled a pot on the little stove to make a cup of hot chocolate and watched the water boil. I felt my heart rate slow, along with my breathing and my busy brain. I was totally present to watch the formation of pearly microbubbles in the pan, to see them coalesce and partner, to notice them swell, and to witness them lift off the bottom of the pot in the beginning of a concert of a chemical reaction so commonplace I'd forgotten the complexity of its dance.

I remembered a child who'd showed me how delight in a moment could heal.

I WAS SUPERVISING AN INTERN FOR HER MASTER'S IN COUNSELING AT the time. This helped me, because the one day a week that I could give to that school, out of all of my other job duties spread over several schools, was not nearly enough to meet their needs—and it helped my intern, Kealia, because a good practicum site is hard to find. My mission was to expose her to a variety of training opportunities that captured the basics of therapy in a school setting.

Our first client that day was a kindergartener whose mother had called the principal asking for counseling after he'd witnessed what she called "a traumatic event." His teacher had also turned in a referral form: "He won't pay attention, he cries, and he won't talk."

I looked at the two forms that had appeared in my mail slot and explained to my intern, "We need more information from the child's mother to find out what we're dealing with, and at least a verbal consent directly from her. I'm going to call the parent and model a phone interview for you."

My intern nodded, making a note in the little square notebook she carried everywhere. Kealia was a quiet young woman who might be too shy to be effective in this setting, but she'd already shown me that she was smart and empathetic with good listening skills, essentials for an effective therapist.

I phoned the mother, introduced my intern, and put Mrs. Ching on speaker. "I'm going to meet with your son, but I need a little more information to help me work with him. What are your concerns, specifically?"

Mrs. Ching had many concerns, all stemming from her husband's recent suicide attempt. Her three children, with her in tow, had returned from an outing to find their father in the act of hanging himself in the living room. The mother and the older two children cut him down and were able to revive him with CPR—but now, the couple were getting divorced.

The youngest child, who had witnessed everything, had been showing regressive behaviors ever since: anxiety in separating from his mother; disliking visiting his father on weekends, per the custody agreement; bedwetting. Most worrisome of all, he hadn't spoken a word since that day.

After assuring Mrs. Ching we'd do the best we could, I hung up. My intern's eyes were wide with worry over the severity of the situation. "How are we going to help such a serious case here in school?"

"We'll create a safe place where Jordan can process the trauma using art or play. Just watch for now." Kealia nodded and went behind the desk to observe; we'd decided on a client-centered play therapy approach.

I called down to the classroom and had an aide bring Jordan up to our counseling room. The boy's serious, reserved demeanor and haunted eyes reminded me of Haley Joel Osment in *The Sixth Sense.*

I gestured to the therapy area, where my toys were spread: a playhouse with a box of action figures and dolls, a plastic pirate ship, a pile of puppets with a small puppet theater, and a variety of art materials invitingly displayed on a child-sized table.

"I'm Ms. Toby, and I'm so glad you could come to my room. This is your time to do whatever you want," I said. "What would you like to try first?"

Jordan surveyed the toys, his hands loose at his sides, his face expressionless. Then he looked at me and shrugged, an exaggerated movement that brought his shoulders up by his ears. He was waiting for me to tell him what to do.

I imitated his gesture, smiled, and waited.

After a long moment, he realized he was really going to have to choose. The adults in his life probably never stopped filling his silence with their anxious directions.

Jordan walked over to the playhouse.

I followed and sat nearby on the carpet, cross-legged.

Jordan took out all the action figures and set them around the house: plastic soldiers, a Spider-Man, a G.I. Joe, Tarzan, Buzz Lightyear. He ignored the traditional family figures. When the house was bristling with defenders, he rolled an action figure on a motorbike around and around the house. I observed aloud what he did as it occurred. The metaphor seemed clear—he felt unsafe and was defending himself.

Little boys usually make lots of sound effects, and a motorbike is one of the most fun to do. Jordan made no sound. He put the figures back in the box and looked at me.

"What do you want to do next?" I asked.

He shrugged.

I shrugged.

I waited quietly until he walked over to the table, then I sat beside him on the other tiny chair, as he chose a crayon and drew on the paper. With surprisingly good fine motor skills, he drew a yellow fish, its mouth curved up.

"That looks like a happy fish," I observed.

He nodded, decorating the fish's body with big black dots. I took out some more art materials in case he wanted something different, and a decorative glass egg rolled out of the box.

Jordan caught the egg, positioned it underneath the fish, and traced around it. He set the egg aside and colored the water around his egg shape dark blue.

"Is the water warm or cold?" I asked, not really expecting him to answer.

"Cold," he whispered.

I carefully didn't react to this breakthrough—he'd spoken! "It looks like the fish is guarding the egg."

"Yes." His voice was barely a wisp of air.

"Maybe the happy fish is taking care of his egg in the cold sea." I put it all together.

Jordan looked up at me with his serious, sad little face, and pushed the drawing over to me.

"Do I get to keep this?" I picked it up.

He nodded, slid off the chair, and walked over to stand by the door.

"Are you ready to go back to class?"

He nodded.

"Do you want to come back next week?"

He nodded, vigorously this time.

"Okay. Miss Kealia is going to walk you back to class." I gestured to my intern. "I really enjoyed playing with you today, Jordan."

They walked away—no smile, not a backward glance.

I sat down to write my case note. I'd asked my intern to write one too, for us to compare as a teaching tool. I started:

Client exhibits constricted affect and selective mutism. Engaged in play using action figures with a guarding, vigilant motif. Chose to do artwork and continued theme . . ."

I sat for a moment, staring at the drawing. There was something very hopeful about it—the bright, spotted yellow fish smiling and hovering over the oval egg, with blue ocean all around. I stuck the artwork on the bulletin board behind my desk with a thumbtack, and I noticed my own feelings; the tension of the morning, the stress of demonstrating good skills to my intern, anxiety engendered by the daunting phone call to the mother—had all drained away.

I was relaxed, confident, hopeful. This little boy wanted to heal himself, and he was going to.

Kealia came back and threw herself onto the couch in the corner. "What's going to happen to him? He's so shut down, it's like nobody's home." She blinked rapidly—she was holding back tears.

I remembered being that scared.

"Jordan's going to be fine. He was telling us what he's feeling through his play and artwork. He'll keep practicing these metaphors until he resolves them. We just have to trust the process."

She shook her head. "I don't know."

"You don't have to know. *He* knows. He's the one in charge of his healing, and it'll happen when he's ready."

"Okay." She was still skeptical. "It'll be interesting to see."

Kealia fetched Jordan for our session the following week. No smile, no greeting, but he walked over to the play therapy area without a prompt. The toys were invitingly displayed, as were crayons, pens, watercolors, clay, and a stack of paper.

Kealia sat down on the couch where she could observe, a clipboard on her lap.

Jordan walked over to the art table, opened a brand-new Crayola watercolor set, and stuck the dry brush into the paint.

"You might want to add some water so it's not so dry," I said, my only suggestion so far, and the last one I planned to give.

He dipped the brush in the plastic cup of water.

And, as I observed out loud, Jordan progressed from painting colored circles on the paper to pouring the cup of rinse water over the watercolor set. He then poured the water off the set onto the paper, spreading the puddle around with the brush.

"It's so interesting that all the colors together make green," I commented, observing the vivid swamp shade he'd created.

No response. Throughout this whole experimentation, he had

not once looked at or acknowledged me. I sneaked a glance at my intern. She shook her head in bafflement.

Pouring the rinse water off the colored paint disks had washed them. They glowed, bright and fresh as Easter eggs.

"The paint is all clean again," I observed, as Jordan examined the tray of colors.

He picked up a pair of scissors and used the tip to pry the pans of watercolor out. He set the color discs in the puddle of green water and rubbed them around with his hands.

"That looks like it feels nice," I said.

Jordan held his hands up to show me that they were now green too, and made eye contact for the first time. "I need more paper," he said distinctly.

My intern gave a muffled gasp—*he'd spoken a whole sentence, unprompted!*

I pointed to a box of old-fashioned computer paper in the corner of the room. "Help yourself."

Jordan hopped off the chair, marched over to the box, and pulled off a five-foot swath. He returned to the table and laid the paper over the colored puddle, smacking it hard. Watercolor flew out from the sides.

"Looks fun," I said.

Jordan looked up at me with a sparkle in his eye; I couldn't yet call it a smile. He peeled the paper up and showed it to me.

I clapped my hands in delight. "Amazing!"

The watercolor puddle had somehow made a butterfly shape, and the tablets of pure color had created a beautiful design as they stuck to the paper. He picked the tablets off and handed me the paper. "Thank you, Jordan."

He put the color tablets into the empty cup. He looked expectantly at me, waiting, stirring the tablets around in the empty cup with the brush. He'd used up all the water in his pouring and experimentation, but I was not going to solve the problem for him.

I shrugged and smiled.

"I need more water," he stated. *Another whole sentence!*

"What should we do?" I asked.

Jordan shrugged, then spotted a water bottle on my desk.

He hopped off the chair and fetched my water bottle. He poured a little of it carefully into the cup and stirred all the watercolor tablets together.

He then spread out about three feet of fresh computer paper, and with a flourish, poured out the cupful of colors. He took two paintbrushes and stirred the color around. Finding that unsatisfying, he set the brushes aside and put both hands in the paint and slid it around, swirling and mixing it. My hands tingled, watching him.

His hands now thoroughly covered, Jordan found an empty corner of the paper and smacked handprints down repeatedly. Splats of paint dotted his cheeks, shirt, and hair till he looked like a tiny, slightly crazed Jackson Pollock.

I peeked at my intern. Her eyes were wide at his vigor.

"Jordan, it's time for us to finish. We have to get you cleaned up, and we'll do some more art next week," I said.

Immediately, he hopped down from the chair, holding his hands up for me to see. They were purple this time. "I have to go wash."

"I know. Let's go!" I led Jordan down to the boys' bathroom.

We soaped up his arms, and he let me dab the paint off his face with a damp paper towel. As I did so, he looked away and seemed to disappear. His serious mask fell back into place. Once clean, he wiped his hands on a paper towel and took off for the classroom.

I followed him. He entered the room and rejoined the group sitting on the floor without a backward glance.

Someday he'd speak, and smile, and wave goodbye to me.

I returned to the counseling room.

Paint covered the low Formica table. Yards of computer paper littered the room, decorated with evidence of Jordan's fearless exploration of the limits of a Crayola watercolor set.

Kealia stood gazing at the mess with one small paper napkin in her hand, clearly overwhelmed. She looked at me, and we burst out laughing.

"I can't believe you just let him keep going! I could hardly handle the mess," she said. "I've never seen anything like what he did! He was so confident! What was going on with that whole thing?"

I opened the broom closet and fetched a roll of paper towels and a squirt bottle of cleaner. "I think he was both exploring what he could do with a watercolor set and testing us. Are we safe? Are we going to accept him no matter what he does?" I shrugged—I was starting to like shrugging. "Play therapy's a little bit magic, a little bit mystery; but it's working."

"He talked!" Kealia clasped her hands together in a prayer gesture. "I feel privileged to witness it."

"Me too," I said. "Our job is to hold the container for the client to do the work." I quoted an excellent child psychologist I'd learned from, delighted to be passing that wisdom on to someone else who "got it."

Jordan eventually recovered from his traumatic event, and even gave me a hug and said goodbye at his last session. Kealia went on to become an exemplary play therapist.

THIS SIMPLE CHORE—WATCHING WATER BOIL—WAS SO LUXURIOUS, SO beautiful unto itself. I made my cocoa and then a grilled cheese sandwich for dinner, and sat beside the fire, utterly content.

Mike returned, energized by the conquest of his desired image of the meadow with a lit Half Dome in the background. He'd been planning to take me to dinner but was happily surprised that I'd fixed him a sandwich, too, and kept it hot on the stove.

"I think I like you domestic," he said, biting into the sandwich.

"Don't get used to it." I leaned over and gave him a kiss.

He smiled. "Of course not."

CHAPTER TWELVE
JUMPERS, CLIMBERS AND MOUNT WHITNEY

During our last hours in Yosemite the next morning, I walked alongside the road, getting some exercise. I'd been walking every day since our Haleakalā hike. I might not have been able to run anymore, with my tricky hip and sore knees, but I could still get out and move and enjoy nature now that I had time for regular exercise. I was getting my heart rate going when Mike drove up next to me, his cheekbones flushed with excitement. "You won't believe what I saw this morning!"

He'd left our camp before daylight to set up a 'sunrise at the rim of the world' shot from the park's highest lookout, Glacier Point. As he was positioning his tripod and checking his light meter, two BASE jumpers came up beside him on the edge of the massive cliff, and, wordless and matter of fact, jumped off into space beside him.

"It was unreal. The drop was astronomical, and these two guys hardly took any time at all to consider it or work up to it. They just fluffed up their squirrel suits a couple of times and jumped!" He and one other photographer at the edge had yelled at each other. "Did you see that?"

They'd peered over the ledge of the lookout, almost hysterical with adrenaline, looking for the chutes, the bodies, anything—but the jumpers had vanished.

Mike said it made him dizzy to even look down at where they'd gone—seven thousand, two hundred and some-odd feet into the darkness of predawn Yosemite. Worst of all, the BASE jumpers had moved too fast for him to get any pictures of them.

"Is jumping there legal?" My eyebrows went up.

"Of course not." Mike's eyes flashed. "How do you train for something like that? There's no room for error. It makes surfing Jaws on Maui look like kid stuff!"

"Would you have wanted to try that in your younger days?"

"Oh, yeah! What a blast!"

BASE jumping was invented in 1978 by Carl Boenish, a man who went on to die performing the sport in 1984. The acronym "BASE" stands for four categories of fixed objects from which one can jump: building, antenna, span, and earth (cliff). El Capitan in Yosemite was one of the early famous recorded sites where the sport was born. Serious jumpers try to record a jump off of each of the four categories.

Mike showed me, from below, where the "guys in squirrel suits" had jumped off from. A tremendous granite ledge protruded out of the cliff face right above Yosemite's Curry Village, and apparently the sleek suits with arm-to-leg wings the jumpers wore enabled them to glide out far enough to miss that ledge.

I was glad he hadn't ever witnessed that adrenaline-junkie sport up close until now. Our age difference has never been a factor physically—he'd always been athletic and competent at anything he tried. But he was way too much of a risk-taker for my comfort. For instance, we both liked surfing, but I liked bodyboarding mellow waves—while he enjoyed extreme surf with dangerous reefs and huge barrels.

We both liked diving, too. I liked cruising around in less than twenty feet of water, looking at coral and fish and searching for shells—and he dove deep into caves and spearfished, or pulled out lobsters by hand. He dove for abalone in Northern California, unfazed by the possibility of Great White sharks, while I stayed on the shore and prayed he didn't get eaten.

Mike never did anything by half measures. Only now that he was over sixty were we able to do more activities together because he'd "slowed down."

We packed up and said goodbye to our wonderful spot in Housekeeping Camp, and on our way out of the park, pulled over to ogle the sheer, dazzling form of El Capitan, the tallest of the valley's rock walls. Mica on the cliff face sparkled in the sun like fool's gold, and we spotted some climbers close to the top, tiny as mites against the sheer, vast stone. It scared me just to look at them.

But it was Saturday by then, and the park was filling up fast.

There seemed to be four kinds of people visiting Yosemite: foreign tourists of every tongue and shade; oblivious families with milling, dangerous children whizzing around on wheeled gadgets of various types; elderly, paunchy folks with black knee socks and binoculars; and hard-core fitness/hiking/climbing buffs in zip-leg Columbia pants. I'm not sure what category Mike and I fit into, as middle-aged, semi-fit artist/nature lovers!

Here are a few notes of advice to anyone traveling near and around Yosemite National Park: Bring a big state map! Don't rely on your GPS; chances are it will be useless. Also, if you can, go to Yosemite in early spring, midweek, with a LOT of gas, and music downloaded on your player or phone. And lastly, bring extra patience if you have the misfortune to be driving through Yosemite Valley floor on the weekend.

After leaving the main park area, we drove up to explore Tuolumne Meadows, a large plateau traversed by winding streams. Tioga Pass, our route out of the park which led down the other side of the mountains to Highway 395, had very recently opened for the season. The high-elevation fields of the mesa were still patchy with snowmelt, revealing the picked-over bones of deer and smaller animals, harsh reminders of winter.

We fished our way out of the park and descended out of the Sierras, eating Jelly Bellies from a Ziploc bag as we wound down Tioga Pass through arid slopes striped in shades of dun and tan, peppered with cactus and tumbleweeds—and ended up directly facing Mono Lake.

I'd had no idea that this landlocked, highly alkaline lake existed, a shiny metallic-looking shield of water surrounded by what looked like snow.

"That's salt or something," Mike said. He pointed. "Check out those formations." Strange shapes that looked like the hoodoos I'd seen photos of at Bryce Canyon poked up through the surface of the lake, and not a living plant was visible anywhere near it.

Delighted to have some phone reception again, I did a quick Google search on Mono Lake. "The formations are made out of limestone," I read off my phone. "They're called *tufa towers*. Brine shrimp live in the lake and support millions of migratory birds every year. It's alkaline, with a pH of ten, and it's almost three times as salty as the ocean."

"I heard if you swim in it, it's hard to sink."

"I would imagine." Where we'd parked at an overlook was close to a hundred degrees, but the mercury-like surface of the lake still didn't look appealing to me. "It's supposed to be okay to swim in. We could go if you want to."

"No. I'd like to reach Mount Whitney by tonight. I hear there are spectacular views and hiking trails there."

"What's special about Mount Whitney?" I asked as we got back in the car.

"It's the tallest mountain in the United States, and it's on the eastern side of Sequoia National Park. People like to climb it and hike around there. It's the next closest thing to us that's worth seeing before Joshua Tree National Park, near Palm Springs."

That sounded great to me. I'd left the planning up to Mike, and he'd only made a few reservations for the trip as we wanted freedom to be able to take our time and discover new things. We turned south on Highway 395 and drove on past Mono Lake. "Mount Whitney or bust!" I said.

Smooth jazz accompanied us as we rolled down a wide, silky stretch of empty highway, bordered by the snow-covered Sierra Nevada all along one side of the stretch of high desert we were traversing. *This was the road trip I'd craved and dreamed of!* I enjoyed the views, and the road unspooling before us, lovely and uncrowded, for hours.

But by the time we pulled up at a bend in the highway called Lone Pine, near the base of Mount Whitney, we were tired. The motel we spent the night in featured delaminating Formica furniture and dangling fly strips, but after the long travel day, we were too beat to care.

Mike rousted me from bed before dawn. "You have to see the sunrise from Mount Whitney. C'mon. You'll be glad you did."

"I like to have time to rest and restore," I complained. After arriving so late and going directly to bed, I wasn't ready to get on the road again.

"The sunrise will restore you more than a few more hours in this crappy room," Mike said. I hoped that was true as I blearily packed and we checked out and got in the car.

We held tepid Styrofoam cups of coffee made in the room's pot as we drove a narrow, winding route, higher and higher, up the stark granite crag that stood out from the wall of ridges around it: Mount Whitney had the magnificent feel of the Lonely Mountain in the *Lord of the Rings*.

The road switched back and forth as we worked our way up until it ended at an unexpectedly spacious and forested park. An extensive network of trails led in various directions, but we weren't there to hike this time. We backtracked down to the best vantage point we could find, trying to beat the slow welling of golden light from the east as we pulled off to the side of the road.

A breeze was up, and the air was bitingly cold. I hadn't dressed properly and huddled beside a boulder as Mike, seemingly oblivious to the temperature, set up his tripod to capture the sunrise. Once his camera was in place, he joined me and drew me close to share his warmth.

The sunrise hit the desert floor as dramatically as it had on Haleakalā, filling the air with gold, bringing featureless cliffs to life as it illuminated hidden layers of rust, umber, mustard, and violet.

I breathed deeply, inhaling the smell of wild pennyroyal, dust, and stone. I leaned into my husband's comforting wind shadow and folded my hands in a gesture of prayer and awe, as morning broke across the desert below.

"Thanks, God." I was so glad that I'd left the fleabag motel to watch the birth of a new day. More and more as time went by, reverent feelings I'd experienced in church as a younger woman occurred outside, inspired by nature. My soul was restored. "And thank you, honey," I whispered.

"You're welcome." Mike kissed my forehead. "Time to go, before the desert heats up."

CHAPTER THIRTEEN
PALM SPRINGS TO ARIZONA

Our next stop after Mount Whitney was at the Palm Springs art gallery that represented Mike's photography and wood sculpture work.

I hadn't expected the wave of emotion that arriving in Palm Springs would cause; but as I got out of the SUV, the smell of dusty date palms, oleander, and desert sage filling my nostrils, I flew back in time to one of the "landscapes that live inside us," as my novelist friend Holly Robinson puts it.

That particular landscape of my history lies in a deep canyon that cradles the northern end of Palm Springs and flows up into the Agua Caliente Indian Reservation in Andreas Canyon: a walled compound with its own restaurant, golf course, Olympic-size swimming pool, professional tennis courts, bocce ball lawn, croquet court, movie hall, and riding stables.

My grandparents owned a colony home there, in that exclusive resort settlement called Smoke Tree Ranch. They wintered at "the Ranch" from November through May, when La Jolla was cool and foggy on the California coast. I had visited that enclave nearly every year for the first thirty-five years of my life.

The Ranch wasn't a glitzy or fancy community, but it was definitely a hideout for the wealthy. Founded in 1936, its colonists were people who bought or built resort homes within the Ranch's four-hundred-acre boundaries and aspired to a "certain way of life," according to the Ranch's charter. These colonists included an American vice president, bankers, CEOs, and even Walt Disney. The emphasis was on families gathering and enjoying traditions with other people of "the right set"—all very *Mad Men*.

I stood next to the SUV on asphalt already softened from the heat and looked to the southwest, toward arid dun-and-gray mountains that seemed to spread open ridged arms. The Ranch was nestled to the back of that side valley.

Mike walked to the gallery door and reached for the handle. "You coming?"

"Just a minute," I said.

He nodded and went inside.

I walked over and stood in the sliver of shade provided by the building's roof overhang. *Will I ever see that place again?* A bittersweet nostalgia rose up in me. That whole era had died with my grandparents, and I hadn't even known I grieved it until this moment.

The aesthetic of the Ranch was not ostentatious; although most of the colonists were millionaires many times over, even the grandest houses kept a low profile and were decorated in the subtle tones of the desert. Everything at the Ranch was kept natural looking; even the street signs were engraved rocks.

Grandma Gigi and Grandpa Jim lived on Rock 10. Their house was a long, low sprawl, with a flat graveled roof and large, multi-roomed wings that embraced a kidney-shaped pool beside a big shady tree to the back. The property was tucked into a frilly apron of orange, tangerine, lemon, and grapefruit trees that draped around a gracious turnaround drive.

My first memory of the Ranch was of swimming in my grandparents' pool. The chlorine smell, the taste of it, and how the water dried my mouth out were so different from the ocean where I swam in Hawaii. I loved how aqua-blue the water was when I dove down and kicked, and how it stung my eyes when I opened them—because of course I opened them, to see the way the light made lacy, netted patterns over the smooth white surface of the bottom.

I liked to swim underwater as far as I could and shoot back up to surprise Gigi, who'd be standing waist deep in the pool in one of her flowered bathing suits with the skirt on the front, wearing a rubber swim cap covered with fake plastic flowers.

Gigi was always a little shocked by how vigorous I was—how I wanted to jump in from the side, how I clambered over the large, decorative inflatable white swan that always floated majestically in the pool. No matter how many times that swan tried to buck me off, I'd ride it like a bronco.

The pool had a hot tub attached to the side, lined with pretty tiles for sitting on and bubblers for the grownups' backs. My parents, grandparents, uncles, and their wives would lounge there in the late afternoon, talking with martinis in hand as I swam, pretending to be a dolphin or a cowboy, and played with my sister Bonny when she got old enough—and eventually, my cousin Jennifer and two younger sisters Anita and Wendy.

I had a personal thing I'd do when I first arrived at the house that no one knew about: I'd throw my bag down on whichever of the twin beds I'd been assigned on that particular visit. (There was the "junky" guestroom in the left wing, which had a bathroom with a shower that hardly had any water pressure, but on the plus side, its own adjoining TV room. Or there was the "good" guestroom in the right wing, with gold-accented headboards, antique coverlets, a collection of vintage perfume bottles on the desk, and a private patio and bathroom with crystal and gold fixtures. Gigi oversaw the room assignments, and they depended on how many people were at the house.) After dropping my belongings, I'd go out and greet the citrus trees.

Hawaii didn't have trees like the ones that surrounded the Ranch house.

These freaks of nature grew right out of the sand, watered on a drip system. Bright green and healthy, groomed into lollipop shapes, they were always heavy with fruit as fake-looking and glossy as Christmas balls. When we visited, usually around Easter, I liked to work my way inside them, burrowing in under their tight, well-groomed branches and shutting my eyes to breathe in their heady citrus scents. I couldn't climb them because they were equipped with razor-tipped thorns, but I would have if it had been possible. I liked to pick a few of the waxy, intensely sweet white flowers and tuck them behind my ears, delighted with the naughtiness of having picked future oranges, grapefruits, or lemons before they could mature.

Mom and Pop, our surfer-hippie parents, hated the annual visits to the Ranch. "It's plastic fantastic," Mom said—but the yearly pilgrimage was part of our family's traditions.

Easter at Smoke Tree was pure magic for us kids, with its own egg hunt, treat baskets filled with candy, and first-run movies shown for "free" in the Walt Disney Hall donated by its most famous resident.

Bonny and I would get up early in the mornings and sneak outside, when the air was cool and the dawn light lambent silver, and look for baby bunnies, ground squirrels, and the famous and elusive roadrunners that lived in the area, which were, to our astonishment, completely unlike the cartoon one.

We spent mornings swimming in the various pools (our hair went green and straw-like from the chlorine every time) and hot afternoons hiding in the air-conditioning and glutting ourselves on TV and sugary snacks, which we didn't have on Kauai.

Bonny and I could go all over the Ranch by ourselves, since it was walled in and "safe." We loved riding bikes Gigi rented for us through the smooth, quiet avenues of the Ranch's enclosed streets as we searched for lizards and snakes. We were ruthless hunters of both, grabbing them behind their heads and putting them in our pockets and the rolled-up fronts of our T-shirts to play with for an hour or two. Thankfully, in all the years we did that, we never saw a rattler.

At least once every visit, we'd take a guided horseback trail ride up into the Reservation's canyon that ended with a giant breakfast for the Smoke Tree families and their guests, served on tables made of sawhorses and logs. Most of all, we loved the mad dash the horses made all the way back to the Ranch, as they galloped to the stables for their grain, water, and well-earned rest in the shade.

I stopped going to the Ranch after Mike and I married—he was not of the "right set" and they never let him forget it—but I resumed visiting again when our children were old enough to travel. I loved being able to share the things I'd once enjoyed with them. The Ranch had done a great job of marketing itself to the next generations of colonists' offspring, and every time we went, it seemed as if time had been closed outside that iron gate with its guardhouse, and those high, stucco walls.

On what was to be my last visit to the Ranch, Caleb was ten and Tawny eight. Grandpa Jim had begun a gentle slide into senility that blunted his hard-driving businessman edges; he was now content to sit on one of the lounge chairs under the wide roof extension that provided shade, staring out over the natural pinkish slate tiles at the turquoise pool.

A bright fuchsia bougainvillea grew up the side wall overlooking the water, and Gigi had her gardener train it to grow under the roof on the inside as well as the outside. Every year, turtledoves nested in that sheltered corner. I led Caleb and Tawny over to try to peek at the babies just as my sisters and I had, when we were young.

Gigi brought out my great-grandmother Nanee's hats to show my children on that visit, an especially fun one we were taking with my mom, traveling the state of California on the train, a trip we were calling the Grand Granny Tour.

I'd never seen the incredible collection of cloches, pillboxes, boaters, sunbonnets, tam-o'-shanters, buckets, and berets, all of them encrusted with rhinestones, pins, or glass gems (Nanee loved sparkly things) along with bits of veil and clusters of feathers. Tawny, her cheeks burnt pink by hours in the pool, posed for pictures Mom took, wearing a cream-colored cloche with a little veil. She stood beside elegant Gigi (pale as bleached muslin in her late eighties) while Caleb, grinning widely, wore Grandpa's huge ten-gallon cowboy hat on the other side.

Gigi closed up the Ranch house after that visit, and the house wouldn't be opened again until after she'd passed, when my father and uncles emptied it, spruced it up, and sold it.

I didn't know that would be my last visit. Didn't know that I'd miss my grandfather's memorial because Gigi "didn't want to make a fuss" and I wasn't invited. Didn't know they'd both donated their bodies to science so there was no gravesite to visit. The thought of medical students dissecting their bodies makes me nauseous; and I wonder if they are still around in some lab, floating in a formaldehyde bath forever.

I never knew what happened to those hats; I never said goodbye to the citrus trees or turtledoves or the pool with the lacy patterns on its white bottom. Weirdly, I was now near the same age as Gigi had been when I had first come to the Ranch as a child. If all went well with our kids' relationships, I'd soon be a grandparent myself.

How would I create a connection, a sense of tradition, with our grown children, their spouses, and future offspring? I had no idea—but now I knew that I wanted some thread that drew us all together, year after year. I appreciated the Ranch and what it had been in a whole new way, as I stood there on the hot asphalt and stared into the heat shimmer on the mountains.

If only I could have said a better goodbye. Maybe this was that moment.

When the temperature at Joshua Tree National Park was discouraging and Mike's art rep suggested we try to get somewhere cooler to camp, such as the hills of Arizona, I agreed with alacrity.

Nothing but the past was left for me in Palm Springs.

Highway 10 out of Palm Springs was scary to this little Hawaii bumpkin: two lanes of heavy traffic packed with speeding semitrucks and worn, pitted asphalt that made our teeth clatter together. I jumped nervously when we came up on big rigs, grabbing for a nonexistent sissy handle and gasping aloud as they passed us. This tried Mike's patience for several hours, until we turned off onto Highway 60, heading into the backcountry for Prescott, Arizona.

Mike was tired by then from all that heavy concentration, and for the first time on the trip, I took the wheel.

With wide-open desert, saguaros raising their prickly arms, and foothills beginning to add a little interest to the monotonous desertscape, we both began to relax, listening to classic rock oldies: ZZ Top, Eagles, Rolling Stones, Eric Clapton. With a mellow scenic road and those tunes, I could drive forever.

There's beauty in the spare, supple forms of the desert, in the open bowl of space overhead, in a landscape filled with nothing but occasional birdsong and the rustle of a ground squirrel. Blooming cactus flowers were lovely for their lush, delicate brevity, bursting like bright ruffled party decorations from their thorny parents. There is no waste, anywhere, in the desert. No excess but that of the luxuriant and endless blue sky. Nature finds a way to survive and thrive even in the harsh heat, and I admire that.

We'd started the day with a fierce sunrise seen from Mount Whitney in Lone Pine, California, and we ended it in the foothills outside of Prescott, Arizona, after covering a total of five hundred and seven miles, a great deal of it desert.

Yes, there's beauty in that landscape, but I was glad we were headed for the red rock splendors of Sedona and the legendary panorama of the Grand Canyon beyond.

CHAPTER FOURTEEN
SEDONA AND CALL OF THE CANYON

Perhaps we overdid it on the long drive day, or maybe the Red Lobster Ultimate Platter I ate late the evening upon reaching Prescott didn't agree with me, but I woke up not feeling well: my stomach was upset, and the mysterious, prickly red rash I'd gone to the doctor for just before we left Maui had returned in full force, spreading from my hands to my arms, neck, and face. The rash, mostly on one hand, had completely cleared up in Yosemite, and I'd thought it was gone.

I still had some leftover hippie attitudes from my youth; western medicine was so focused on treating the symptoms, not the cause, and that was a pet peeve. But a major road trip was not the time to be messing around with wishful thinking. I resolved to press in to find real answers about this increasingly chronic problem when we got home.

In the motel bathroom, I slathered skin oil and eczema lotion over my entire body, hoping that would take care of things, and as I did so, I ruminated.

I don't like being hot. The realization that most of our remaining route through the Southwestern National Parks was going to be well past my heat tolerance limit of 85 degrees made me grumpy as well as itchy.

"Your wife is a delicate flower that can't bloom in this harsh climate," I told Mike when he returned from his early morning shoot of the outlying areas of Prescott (pronounced "press-kit"). I showed him my rash. "Maybe I should have kept taking that steroid pill they put me on."

"Of course, you should have kept taking it," Mike scolded. "Let's get on the road and keep you in the air-conditioning."

We headed out, and I perked up as we explored the interesting historic mining town of Jerome. The sight of Sedona's red rock formations, glowing under the noon sky in the distance, lifted our spirits so much that I put ZZ Top and Santana back on and drove us across the valley toward Sedona while Mike took pictures out the window.

We pulled in at the Sedona Motel, which we found through geography (central location) and Tripadvisor (4.5 stars). Its main amenity was a wonderful host named Bill, who smelled of sage and marijuana, and directed us to the best places to take photos when I told him Mike was a photographer.

We retired to siesta through the heat of the day, as humans in hot climates have been doing since the dawn of time, collapsing for a travel-weary nap in our cool, air-conditioned cave of a room.

We went separate ways in the afternoon—me to brave the temperature and walk to a little reproduction Mexican arts village called Tlaqueplaque, and Mike to do his evening sunset shoot.

As I walked the mere two blocks to the village area, sweating profusely but unable to feel it due to instant evaporation in the arid heat, I knew I had to adjust my expectations.

Forget tent camping in these temperatures.

I had to be cool while sleeping—perimenopausal hot flashes were bad enough without overheating in earnest. And, for sure I'd want to wash off the BO at least daily, which meant showers. It would also be okay if we didn't do any more major hiking. My tricky hip and persnickety skin were making such things a memory, sad as it was to admit.

Having come to these conclusions, my spirits lifted, and I was able to really enjoy browsing the lovely art galleries of Tlaque-plaque. Every terra-cotta courtyard was enriched by fountains that cooled the air. The tiny bright creatures landing on the potted flowers that I'd thought were butterflies were actually humming-birds, a delightful surprise.

The town of Sedona is surrounded by layered rock, for all the world like towering, red stone wedding cakes decorated with melted mineral frosting. Full of art, culture, and New Age arcana, Sedona vibrated with signs advertising psychic readings, aura photos, tarot, crystal healing, singing bowls, and every kind of therapy.

When I asked a young Native American woman in a bead shop where a coffee could be found, she took the time to discuss the various options with me, asking me what kind of coffee I was in the mood for (something strong, sweet, and cold) and not just brusquely directing me to the nearest Starbucks (a prohibitively hot several blocks away). In return, I browsed the shop and bought a vivid strand of heishi turquoise that I might have missed otherwise. We parted with smiles—it felt like truly connecting with someone.

So far, the people we'd met on the trip had been wonderful. If I acted positive and kind, even in a frustrating or difficult situation, that's what I got back from others. The world really *was* a friendly and loving place if I behaved as if it were, and my decision to believe and practice that was paying off.

Meandering and shopping completed, I returned to our room and poured myself a glass of the nice Merlot the art dealer had given us in Palm Springs. I wrote in my journal by the motel's window, enjoying the way the sunset moved down the incredible rock formations like hours on a candle.

Mike returned when that light had vanished and took me out to dinner in the warm, cinnamon-scented dusk. We promised ourselves to come again, when it was cooler, and stay longer in the magic of Sedona.

WE PROBABLY WOULDN'T HAVE TAKEN THE EXTRA TIME TO HIKE ON the way out of Sedona if Bill, the aforementioned motel manager, hadn't underlined one trail heavily on the map. "If there's only one hike you do in Arizona, it should be the West Fork Trail, or 'Call of the Canyon,' off Highway 89. You don't want to miss it!"

Bill had steered Mike to some other great sights around Sedona to photograph, so we planned our drive day around going to this spot. "Anything with a name as fancy as 'Call of the Canyon' must be worth seeing," I said, lacing up my trusty hiking boots once we found the turnoff and sandy parking lot. The rash I'd been struggling with, which seemed to be aggravated by heat, was better now that I was taking the medication, and my hip was feeling good after a couple of days of relative rest. I was ready for action.

Call of the Canyon turned out to be everything I love in a hike: a flat trail alongside a stream, with crossings every half-mile or so, lined with budding deciduous forest, stunning sculpted red bluffs, fields of unfamiliar wildflowers and ferns, constant birdsong, and cool shade under sheltering trees. My hip didn't start acting up until the last of the seven miles we walked, and we could have gone farther if we hadn't run out of time, water, and snacks.

After that lovely interlude, we got on the road again, determined to reach the south rim of Grand Canyon National Park by evening. From the beginning of that day, a high thin cloud cover had lessened the intense heat, a relief as we progressed through Arizona toward the Grand Canyon. We made it, and arrived at the South Rim at 4:00 p.m.

We were beat after seven miles of hiking and many hours of

driving, but we parked in a gigantic parking lot and joined a herd of lemminglike tourists headed for the rim. I was immediately stunned by the sheer magnitude of the Grand Canyon when I reached the edge and looked over.

Bands of color played with shadows, enhanced by the glitter of the faraway Colorado River below, a mile down at some points. We wandered a well-traveled cement path along the edge and took some inadequate pictures.

I held my notebook and pen like talismans, struggling to find words, light-headed every time I looked over the guardrail. I wanted to sit and soak in the view in reverent silence, but instead, I was engulfed by noisy herds of fellow humans also there to gawk at this natural wonder. The cacophony of voices and different languages swirled around me like leaves in wind.

"I need a rest," I told Mike. Eager as I was to explore, I was also tired from the long day, and completely oversaturated by the grandeur of the Canyon and its crowds. Mike, in contrast, was energized. He roared around at top speed, and miraculously found us a room in one of the lodges near where we'd parked.

After stowing our gear in our room, we had a brief but intense argument.

"I need an hour to recharge," I told him. "I want to watch the sunset with you at the rim, but I'm too tired right now."

"Well, there's a shuttle bus to a more secluded lookout spot, but it leaves in ten minutes. I want to go."

"I told you I'm too tired." I felt tears well up. "I don't like being yanked around without time to absorb what's happening."

"Then you stay here and do what you need to do. I'll go catch the sunset. You can't have it both ways this time." Mike picked up his camera case, grabbed a jacket, and left.

I took a shower, and under the flow of water, I cried. I was disappointed with myself. Why wasn't I tougher, hardier, better able to just keep going? At least after all these years, I knew when I'd reached capacity. I was as fragile now as a balloon blown too full, and in danger of bursting.

After the shower and a brief nap, I went outside and sat on the patio outside our room, looking at the clouds and the nearby pine trees, trying to assimilate the day. The Canyon beckoned, only a few hundred yards away, deep, and wide and glorious—but I just couldn't handle any more glory.

I hated missing out on what Mike was seeing right now. I'd wanted him to stay with me, for us to rest and rejuvenate, then go watch the sunset together. That wasn't fair, because he was energized by the Canyon's magnitude, not overwhelmed by it as I was. We were different people that way.

This was our first real argument of the trip; and I wallowed in self-pity for a while.

The Canyon was nearby; I could walk there easily from the lodge. But that too-full, brittle, fragile feeling persisted. I couldn't process any more of its vastness without the buffer of Mike's presence.

I GROUNDED MYSELF INSTEAD WITH NOTICING SMALL THINGS: washing my hands with a freshly unwrapped sliver of soap in the bathroom, drinking from a plastic cup of water, the way a pine cone rolled on the ground at my feet.

I eventually wrote a poem in my notebook.

The Grand Canyon
Veins of water carved the earth
Deep through granite tissues, coursing hundreds of miles
A great rent in the skin of the planet
revealing
A rainbow of stone bones and
Glitter of the water blade below.
Trees sculpted by wind.
A hawk cries and soars.
A daisy clings to the cliff.
Awe strikes. Words fail.
Meanwhile . . .
A mass of humanity
A river of ants
Insignificant and transitory
Pour around the edge of the abyss
Looking and wondering as they always have
Busy eyes, hands, feet and cameras documenting
In a cacophony of tongues and images
Their tiny moment in eternity
While the heart of the land
Beats on, unchanging
Far below and way above.

I closed my notebook. I shut my eyes. I listened to the wind in the nearby pines.

The wind whispered, "It's okay that you need space and quiet and a measured pace. Your words are a lens for other people to experience the world; your writing conjures it for them, and you need certain conditions for that. Mike shares the world through his images, and he is perfectly calibrated for capturing them. Together, you are each bigger than yourselves alone."

"Thank you," I said to the wind, and went inside and lay down to rest. I'd visit the Canyon tomorrow, when I was ready for new adventures again.

CHAPTER FIFTEEN
SOUTH RIM OF THE GRAND CANYON, LIPAN POINT

We were unable to get another night in the lodge, so we were tent camping for the first time on the trip at the South Rim of the Grand Canyon. After checking out of the lodge the next morning, we found a spot at the Desert View campsite area, a featureless acreage dotted with cactus and tumbleweeds.

We'd kissed and made up over dinner in the lodge the night before, chalking the fight up to tiredness and our different needs—a considerable improvement in turnaround time. We'd fought a lot in our younger years, each of us wanting the other to be different. Thirty years into the marriage, we were both reasonably sure that kind of change wasn't going to happen, and that happiness lay in mutual acceptance.

This was our first time putting up the new tent, inflating the air mattress, and rolling out the brand-new sleeping bags that hadn't been used since Yosemite. After my 'Breathing Incident' on the plane, we both wanted to be sure everything was thoroughly aired out before bed, so we took the time to assemble everything at our site.

Mike put up the tent, fiddling with its mysterious interlocking supports, while I tried to save time by inflating the queen size air mattress with the foot pump. That didn't end up helping, though, because the darn thing wouldn't fit through the doorway once the tent was up. I let some air out, dragged it in like a limp sponge, and refilled it inside.

"Your wife may be spatially challenged," I said, once the bed was inflated and positioned correctly. "However, she is not blonde."

"Maybe a little bit blonde. But you said it, not me!" Mike chuckled.

"Let's keep it that way," I replied.

Another old joke. We hadn't used them all up yet.

The Desert View area of the South Rim park was near the amazing Watchtower; we spotted the six-stories-high building and decided to walk over and explore it once the camp was set up.

Here's my Grand Canyon travel tip: if you only have time for one monument visit at South Rim, *go see this.* The tower's exterior, a golden buff made of local stone, seemed almost to have grown out of the landscape, and its shape echoed ancient Anasazi construction. I walked in slow wonder up a spiral staircase through five pie-shaped layers inside the tower, a pinnacle of Native American art and carefully framed views.

The ceilings and walls glowed with murals that vibrated with the captured history of the Hopi people, whose world this really is. The Eagle's Nest overlook at the top of the Watchtower was roofed with light-drenched Native American paintings and featured three-hundred-and-sixty-degree windows mounted with telescopes from which to view the Park and the Grand Canyon below.

Enamored with the experiential nature of the building, I searched to find a plaque about it and was surprised to discover that the tower had been built in 1932. Its aesthetic and respect for native culture seemed contemporary, and the whole tower itself was almost organically well-designed and ahead of its time.

The building's designer was Mary Colter (1869–1958), an American architect and interior creator whose distinctive nature-inspired style was steeped in the look and feel of the Southwest, though she'd earned her art degree in California. She spent her career from 1902–1948 as the primary architect for a well-known railroad company. In that role, she designed hotels, shops, and rest areas along one of the Southwest's major train routes. Colter's most famous projects, though, were the four that she created in South Rim Grand Canyon National Park: the Hopi House, Hermit's Rest, Lookout Studio, and Desert View Watchtower.

Our souls inspired by human-made artistry, Mike and I were ready for more undiluted natural splendor. We trekked back to the campground, packed up Mike's photo gear and my journal, and hopped in the SUV. We stopped at a small variety store where we bought a couple of sandwiches and cans of root beer. Thus fueled, we set out for the afternoon/evening sunset vista view in the Lipan Point area, which we'd picked out to explore the night before.

Walking along the cement rim trail with its embedded metal railing, we were frustratingly distant from any dramatic views of the Canyon.

"Let's check out this side trail around the guardrail. See if it gets us to that outcrop the map shows." Mike gave his brown leather hat a tug and squinted into the lowering sun. He looked like a tall, silver-bearded Indiana Jones in his boots, jeans, and camera backpack.

"Fine." I set my jaw in determination—*I'm not going to wimp out and be left behind again.*

We embarked on a perilous trek down the trail to find an optimal spot with no other people around. Climbing the rocks didn't scare me—it was the stretches of slippery pebbles and sand, where it would be easy to slide into infinity.

"This looks good," my intrepid husband announced when we reached a tongue of rock that protruded over the depths. He strode around with his usual physical confidence, oblivious to danger, looking for just the right spot to set up his cameras as I imagined what one misstep could do.

My once-conquered fear of heights reemerged. After my tree-climbing youth, I'd gradually developed vertigo over the years. However, I'd used daily climbs up onto our Maui home's rooftop crow's nest to get over it and hadn't had an episode in years.

Now, I was barely able to move, crippled by dizziness whenever I even glanced at the edge. Anxiety too weighty to express extended to Mike as much as myself, but I resolved not to complain or tell him about it. Watching Mike set up his camera for a time-lapse at the very edge of the tongue of rock was making my head spin, so I turned my back on him. I slowly lowered myself to my hands and knees and crawled to the edge on the opposite side of the promontory.

"Are you okay?" Mike asked, concerned.

"Just a little dizzy. I'm fine." I wasn't going to whine or wimp out. I was going to look over the cliff if it killed me.

I slid off my knapsack, carefully not looking at the rim. I'd brought a beach towel, which I spread out on the stone. Once that padding was established, I lay on the towel and eased forward until I could see over the rock lip. I lay there on my belly, gazing down into the vastness, as the Grand Canyon rendered me breathless, wordless, and overwhelmed.

Keening wind. Bits of dust hitting my eyes. The glimmer of water, far, far below. Bands and colors of stone and sky. A sense of flying while lying still.

I shut my eyes, turned my face to the side, and rested my cheek on the towel. The wind whistled, and a bird called: a unique sound, *tseeee tseee,* that was so high it might have been the voice of the stones. The sense of space pulled at me and I spun, even lying still.

I eventually withdrew into the shadow of a large boulder and sat there wrapped in the towel with my knees drawn up. The sensory overstimulation I was experiencing drove me to focus on little things: The shape of a nearby pebble. Tiny yellow daisies fluttering in the wind. A twisted cypress bonsai'd by extreme conditions, clinging to an edge with thousands of feet of space below it.

Mike joined me, and we watched the sun go through its evening dance on the vermilion, ochre, and indigo walls of the Canyon. A scrim of haze in the air enhanced the sunset's drama as it progressed. According to a ranger I'd asked earlier, the murk was pollution from Las Vegas and a nearby Navajo coal-burning electric plant—nothing to be excited about. But the particulate matter in the air added dimension, a sense of substance and weight, so that the light became textural. Rays played like lasers through the shadows of approaching dusk, bending around the Canyon's deep gouges and sensuous curves.

We ate our sandwiches and drank our root beer in reverent silence.

Finally, when the light show had dimmed, the sky gone purple, and the stars poked white holes in a black woolen sky, we made our way carefully back to the trail, the concrete path, the guardrail, and all that was steady and comfortable.

CHAPTER SIXTEEN
HEADING TO THE NORTH RIM

I slept like a hibernating bear in the double sleeping bag on the air mattress that night, thankfully having no breathing issues. Mike got up early, captured the sunrise, and pronounced it "Epic!" upon his return. I was okay with missing it, having conquered my terror of the depths the night before.

We made coffee on the one-burner stove, packed up, and were on the road by 7:00 a.m., heading for the North Rim of the Grand Canyon, the sister park on the opposite side.

Meanwhile, I'd become Camping Woman.

Camping Woman had wind-snarled hair filled with dust, ten broken, dirt-encrusted nails, and unshaven legs. She wore a pair of those awful Velcro strap sandals no person from Hawaii would be caught dead in. Camping Woman's beauty products were a travel bottle of shampoo, a tube of sunscreen, and rash lotion. She'd forgotten what day of the week it was, let alone the actual date.

She was married to Camping Man—bristly with beard, silver hair tufted in all directions, sunburn down his nose, and blue eyes alight with adventure. Yep, we had discovered our "real selves" on this trip, and maybe it was my hippie upbringing, but I couldn't help liking us rather a lot.

WE TOOK HIGHWAY 89A OUT OF THE SOUTH RIM PARK, A WIDE-OPEN ribbon of road, with unique natural features all around: the rift of the Canyon (or like adjunct of it), ravens against the sky, sagebrush and cornflowers, and the jutting spine of what became the Vermilion Cliffs, a geologic formation we'd never heard anything about. This wildly colored bluff in dramatic red and white stone ran alongside the highway for miles. We pulled off the road repeatedly, goggling at its multilayered grandeur.

Navajo Bridge was another spectacular surprise. This graceful, Art Deco style span was a visual treat. I enjoyed the contrast between the desert mesa and the calm, translucent green magic of the Little Colorado River far below its elegant struts.

We were hungry by then, so we pulled into nearby Marble Canyon Lodge, operated by a Navajo family. We were the only people in the rustic restaurant and enjoyed a great breakfast and friendly service. The Navajo version of eggs Benedict, called begay, was recommended by the pretty, black-haired teenage waitress, and we found it delicious. Their sauces, and even the bread, were homemade.

Feeling regretful that we were the only customers, I spent some time browsing in the attached gift shop, purchasing carved sandstone paperweights and woven leather bracelets for our relatives as future holiday gifts. Out in the parking lot, I used the restaurant's Wi-Fi to write a five-star review for the place; doing so seemed the least we could do to help when the family had provided us such a refreshing break. We'd found others' reviews very helpful as we traveled.

Onward we went, winding higher and higher into the coolness of pines that marked the ascent into the North Rim park, debating whether blues, jazz, or rock was better road trip music. Eric Clapton and Santana basically covered all rather well and couldn't be beat for consistency of mood.

North Rim Grand Canyon National Park was much smaller than the South Rim. I fell in love instantly with the combination of the park's funky, rustic log cabin-type charm at its lodge and its cooler temperatures at a higher, eight-thousand-foot elevation. But, after our initial excitement, we ran into our first major snag of the trip.

The only campground in the park was already full with a waiting list, and there were no rooms available for us at the historic Grand Canyon Lodge North Rim. Unlike South Rim, which contained multiple campgrounds and several inns, there was nowhere else for overflow visitors to stay until well outside the park.

"Guess we should have made reservations, for this park at least," Mike said, crestfallen.

We settled for lunch at the spectacular lodge, eating out on the flagstone deck overlooking the Canyon, while Mike called multiple places outside the park to find somewhere to sleep that night. He eventually was able to reserve a cabin for us an hour outside the park's boundaries. This situation precluded any further return to North Rim once we left, to our great disappointment.

We wanted to go on an hour-long drive along the park's overlook road to a famous point, Cape Royal, for the sunset, so we decided to make the most of our afternoon and evening there. Mike threw our sleeping bags out under a tree, and we crashed like hobos at a pullout for a nap before the evening light show on the Canyon's rim.

I fell asleep on a pine needle bed with the wind matting my hair and yellowjackets buzzing in to see if I was edible. Camping Woman had no problem with crawling into her sleeping bag and drooling onto her pillow on the side of the road, when tired enough. I really was getting back in touch with my childhood self as each new challenge popped up, and that made me smile.

After that spell of unconsciousness, we continued through the park to a spectacular, aptly named Valhalla Overlook. We hiked out to the very end of the very end, a bluff at the edge of Cape Royal Point, for our last sunset at the Grand Canyon. Our chosen spot, after hours and miles of driving, had brought us approximately opposite the location where we had been the day before at the South Rim side of the Canyon. Several other professional photographers, including a couple of Asian men dressed like ninjas in black ripstop hiking gear and matching black face masks, joined us on the point.

Mike tied a rock onto his tripod, anchoring it against gusts of chilly wind. He set the camera to record a time-lapse of the area of the canyon wall overlooked by the Watchtower; that worthy focal point was clearly visible in the distance, reduced from six stories to the size of an ant.

I had learned what my phone camera could and couldn't do, and I waited until most of the light had bled from the day into the gray haze emitted by Las Vegas to take my pictures. All of us photographers stayed after the sun descended over the horizon to see if the sunset would "kick," as Mike called it, his phrase for when a sky went up in flames—which sometimes happened well after the fiery orb appeared to have set.

We struck up a conversation with another photographer nearby, who introduced himself as Doug Taylor. "Waiting for the sunset to go off is like hoping my last girlfriend will be in the mood—hints of possibility and a certainty of cold," he said.

Doug was traveling around full-time as a nature photographer and was full of great stories and tips because he'd visited many of the places we were going to. Making a new friend on the Rim made our last night there sweeter. Connecting with other humans to share an experience of natural grandeur helped us savor it differently; I resolved to remember that.

The sunset never did kick. We eventually bumbled our way along another unlit path back to the parking lot and drove over an hour through the dark to locate the cabin Mike had booked.

"We'll be back someday," I promised the North Rim. "And really get to know you."

I like to think the Canyon blew us a kiss and agreed.

CHAPTER SEVENTEEN
ZION NATIONAL PARK

Arriving in Zion National Park feels like entering a cathedral: there is Outside, and then there is Within.

This experience is created by the way the road entering the park winds upward through ordinary enough hills and brings you through a standard ticketing kiosk. Then, around the very next corner, the incredible slickrock formations and stunning vistas begin.

The Zion-Mount Carmel Highway and Tunnel running through the park was designed to create an experience of the park, and to foster a travel "Grand Circle Tour" from Zion to Bryce Canyon and Grand Canyon National Parks. Begun in the twenties and completed in 1930, the one-mile tunnel through a stone mountain in Zion was the longest of its type in the world when completed.

I wondered how such an incredibly long passageway had been built back then. As we drove through it, we slowed to peer through deep bay windows carved in the stone. Turns out that blasting those gallery windows into the cliff face above Pine Creek Canyon was the beginning step of digging the tunnel! From these alcoves, the workmen were able to access the interior of the cliff and progressively bore their way through the rock, approaching from opposite sides. The gallery windows also served as ports through which rock debris from carving the channel could be pushed out and cleared from the work area, as well as supplying ventilation and lighting to crews working inside.

Mike and I so enjoyed the experience of the tunnel that we immediately turned around and drove back through it, trying to photograph the glimpses of the park that we could see through the deep rock archways.

The switchback road on the other side of the tunnel was stunning, too. The whole route through Zion had been mapped out to capitalize on the valley's natural features. We drove as slowly as we could down to the Virgin River, soaking in the extravagant, richly colored red and gold cliffs, rushing turquoise water, and lush cottonwood forest.

Zion elicited a sense of being somewhere holy and special that I've seldom experienced. I loved the grand, florid names that Mormon settlers had assigned to everything: Angels Landing, Temple of Sinawava, Court of the Patriarchs.

Mike had done some internet searches before we arrived, looking for "slot canyons," which he hoped to photograph.

"What are those?" I was unfamiliar with the term.

"Slot canyons are narrow valleys carved by water as it moves through soft rock, such as Utah's sedimentary deposits. I've seen pictures, so I know there are some here in Zion."

He handed me his phone. Pictures from Zion National Park had come up on his searches, but when we looked at the park's map and literature, we couldn't find any information about where these unique attractions might be.

Though it was well into afternoon by the time we arrived, we pulled into the attractive, historic Zion Lodge right in the middle of the park. We immediately asked for a room and got lucky enough this time to reserve two nights there.

At the lodge's restaurant for a late lunch, we asked our server about the mysterious gorges Mike had seen pictures of. "We're looking for an easy access slot canyon. Do you know where any might be?"

"I'm sorry, I don't. But my waiter friend is a canyoneer. I'll ask him," the waitress said.

"Oh, thanks so much!"

She bustled off after taking our orders.

"What's a canyoneer?" I whispered to Mike.

"Let's look it up." The Free Dictionary provided us this handy definition: *(kăn′yə-nîr′ĭng) The sport or recreational activity of hiking, biking, or boating through canyons, especially the sport of descending very narrow canyons by rock climbing, rappelling, and swimming. Also called canyoning.*

The server's canyoneering friend arrived, looking young, tanned, and fit in his white shirt and black pants. "You wanted to find a slot canyon?"

Mike took his phone out to get directions, but the way the young hipster described how to find it reminded me of how we give directions in Hawaii: "You know, outside the tunnel, you look for a parking lot on the left, past the bridge. Leave your car over there and go north, and you'll eventually find it. That's the easiest slot to hike in this park."

"Does it have a name?"

"Fat Man's Misery," he said. We all chuckled. "It's actually pretty challenging," he went on. "Bring rappelling gear to get the most out of it." He took off to attend to a table.

I looked at Mike. "Rappelling gear? Are you sure we're up for that?"

"You can stay at the lodge if it's too much." Mike slanted a glance at me. "But I wouldn't want you to miss out."

"I'm going." Yep, I was on a mission to rediscover the brave girl I'd been; canyoneering would have been right up that freckled tomboy's alley. I used to climb trees forty feet in the air. I'd never even seen rappelling gear—people in Hawaii climbed everything barefoot, even coconut trees. We settled in at the lodge and took a minor hike that evening just to limber up our legs for the more major expedition the next morning.

I was so nervously excited about the slot canyon expedition that I had a hard time winding down; Mike was sanguine as usual. We sat on the little deck outside our room with glasses of wine to take in the warm night, and I tried to relax.

A full moon rose above the serrated ridge of the valley, bats darted and zigzagged, and the song of cicadas filled the air as cottonwood fluff blew through the warm night like fairy dust; gradually I settled into the Adirondack chair, feeling the calm spell of Zion settle over me like a warm blanket.

Between the previous day and the next morning, the vague directions the waiter had given us to the slot canyon had become even more inscrutable in our minds.

"Which way is north?" I wondered. Once we left the lodge, our apps no longer worked, and we didn't have a compass or map for this.

"Did he mean before or after the big tunnel? Which side?" Mike said. "What bridge, exactly?"

We drove to the tunnel area, hoping we'd spot it once we were there, and pulled into a parking area that seemed like it could be the one the waiter had mentioned. There was no apparent trailhead, and nothing but a cliff of shale and boulders tumbling down into a deep canyon. Our dithering and wandering about was noticed by a park ranger. "Are you lost?"

We asked about the slot canyon, and he got snappy. "No roaming is allowed along the paved road or off the paths through open areas. Follow the signs to designated trails." He indicated a nearby trailhead. "You can hike there."

The way he was pointing led to the nice, well-groomed hike we'd already done the night before, called Canyon Overlook. "Thanks."

The ranger was looking at a sixty-year-old man and his pudgy wife and judging us as typical tourists. We probably looked like a rescue waiting to happen, from his point of view, and I didn't blame him for the skepticism. We walked in the direction he indicated, hoping he'd leave us alone and unsupervised. He soon drove off in his truck.

Mike has never been much for signs, and I've always thought of such directives as "best practice" suggestions rather than actual rules to be followed; rebellious attitude left over from growing up hippie, I suspect—but we both took "leave no footprint" and respect for nature very seriously. We had no intention of getting hurt or lost or damaging anything, but we were determined to find Fat Man's Misery. Canyoneering wasn't only for the young!

After the ranger drove off, we continued along the road, looking down into the ravine below. After one or two false starts bush-whacking through rocks and scrub, we spotted an open gulch that looked like it might narrow to a cavelike opening.

"This is it." Excitement made Mike's voice tight.

My palms prickled with nervous sweat as we picked our way down rocky scree toward the bottom of the arroyo. At any moment, I expected a ranger to blow a whistle and yell at us, but we managed to make it to the gorge's floor undetected.

I gasped at the sight before us. Hidden from above by a layer of vegetation and sheltering rocks, Fat Man's Misery slot canyon wound in multi-colored, magic secrecy for miles. Our feet were the first to touch the canyon's gleaming white sand floor that day—it had rained the night before and washed away any footprints. We felt like true explorers.

I took Mike's hand. "Stop for a minute. I want to savor this."

He was practically vibrating with impatience to enter, but he stood, letting me cling, and we gazed into the narrow, light-streaked, carved aisle of stone. "This looks like an Indiana Jones movie. Hard to believe it's real."

"It's real, all right."

There was no marked trail, and we didn't know where we were going nor how to get out once we started down into that enclosed route—but we were entranced as we stepped onto the gleaming sand of the slot canyon's narrow confines.

The play of light and shadow on the sinuous curves of the walls conveyed a frozen sense of motion, something ancient and mysterious—not to mention a little dangerous. We passed under logs caught overhead by floods, poised to fall any minute, boulders balanced on ledges, dead and rotting carcasses of animals that had fallen or been drowned by previous floods.

Sunlight pierced the cover above, landing in bright pools on the pale sand, reflecting off the brightly colored, banded stone walls to create a unique glow. Far from a strenuous hike, the canyon was an avenue of delights—and filled with warm, inviting corners for rattlesnakes to sun themselves in.

"I'm looking for the perfect stick," I told Mike. "I'm not being paranoid about rattlers. You know I like snakes. I'm just showing respect, because we're the intruders in their world. Plus I'm only wearing shorts and tennis shoes." For some reason, I'd left my hiking boots at the lodge, and my legs felt downright vulnerable.

We walked slowly, stopping to crane our necks and take pictures, because every twisted, striped turn of this maze was a new and breathtaking scene. The canyon could clearly be an oven in the summer, but today we had cloud cover and even a sprinkle of rain to cool it down.

I found the perfect snake-warding stick in a hollow of rock—the root from a hardwood tree, twisted and turned in a truly serpentlike form, silky from the water that had washed it into the canyon long ago. Light and strong, silvery gold in color, it felt like a magic wand in my grasp.

We kept going until we reached an impassable drop-off section. Peering over the edge, we could see pitons for rock climbing down to the next level. We'd gone as far as we could.

"Guess we have to go back," I said.

"Look up," Mike said. I tipped my head back and recognized the boulder-strewn shale cliff leading down from the parking lot where we'd left our car!

Of course there was no trail up, and now we knew why our canyoneer friend had suggested rappelling gear. I hooked the curved stick around my neck to begin the climb up the slippery-looking cliff.

"Leave the stick!" Mike said. "You're going to need both hands."

"No. I'm keeping it." I climbed with it around my neck, then threw the stick above me so that it caught on the rocks. I climbed up to it, refusing to look anywhere but at the next handhold, foothold, and my magic stick.

Mike toiled along beside me. Other people must have done this climb, but we saw no evidence of them. I never considered giving up, even once I'd concluded it would have been better to return through the canyon the way we came; this conclusion was solely based on knowing that getting down from the point I'd reached would be even more hazardous than continuing to the top, come what may.

I reached my stick, high on the cliff, at last.

I didn't want to lose it in the sheer area I was currently navigating, so I tucked it in my bra and clambered on, with the length of twisted wood protruding out of the neckline of my shirt. I made it all the way up a cliff that had looked impassable that way. Mike and I emerged at the parking lot, mere yards from our car, frowzled and triumphant as a pair of unlikely jack-in-the-boxes.

That evening, the stick rested in my suitcase among the many pairs of dirty socks, a testament to our incredible day, the perfect souvenir.

And, as always, the secret to climbing anything is: *Never look down.*

CHAPTER EIGHTEEN
AN ENCOUNTER AT EMERALD POOLS

I've always been a spiritually sensitive person. I saw an angel at eleven, chanted the Hare Krishna and ate off banana leaves at twelve, practiced meditation and yoga under a guru at thirteen, and became a Christian on a campout with Young Life at seventeen. Mike and I attended a Christian college and spent ten years in professional ministry before pursuing other careers.

None of those statements actually convey anything relevant about my ever-present thirst for the Divine. I was born with this longing—a persistent curiosity about a bigger meaning behind everything. That pursuit of purpose has continued throughout my life, a golden ribbon connecting me to something eternal.

As I matured, my faith took a quiet, personal form, an intuition-led dialogue with God supported by spiritual reading from many disciplines, but mostly the Bible. I came to prefer to let my life and actions be a testament to what I believe rather than to try to persuade others to "buy my brand."

Even so, I wasn't prepared the next morning, when I set out from the Zion Lodge at 6:00 a.m. with a cafeteria coffee in my hand, for anything more than a stroll along the Virgin River to the hyperbolically named Emerald Pools. Leaving the hotel via the trail to the

Pools, I was quickly engulfed in wilderness. The air vibrated with unfamiliar birdsong, so I tried a phone call to my bird-knowledgeable friend Holly, but couldn't get a signal.

Blooming flowers lined the well-groomed path: Indian paintbrush, cactus blossom, columbine, and gorgeous little pitcher-throated white blooms that reminded me of wild hollyhocks. A cascade of a waterfall fell from the bluff above, and the trail crossed behind it, utterly dry—I was enchanted to look through the waterfall at the valley below.

Mike had left our room at his typical 3:30 a.m. to shoot stars and the sunrise somewhere else in the park, and on my own, I was acutely aware of my solitude.

I was cougar-huntable, bear-bait, rattlesnake-prone alone, for the first time on this trip.

The hike turned out to be both longer and more strenuous than I'd anticipated, but sunrise was beginning to pierce the colorful peaks of sandstone around me with lances of gold, and whatever was at the top of the trail, I wanted to see. To test my resolve, the trail suddenly went vertical with boulder and stone stairs, arriving at a series of small green puddles.

I put my hands on my hips and surveyed them, unimpressed. "Some 'Emerald Pool,'" I muttered. "Those Mormons really liked dramatic names."

A little silvery-bronze squirrel greeted me with a chirp from a boulder in the trail.

Charmed, I took a picture of him. He hopped down, ran up the trail before me, then hopped on a rock to look back and see if I followed. It was still very steep, and I was puffing a bit by then, but I hurried after him, smiling at his persistent, adorable behavior.

Then, something began to happen with the light.

The trail headed toward a vast yellow slickrock wall on the left, with a red mountain on the right. The sunrise hit the peak of the ochre bluff and filled the air with an unearthly, almost powdered, glow.

I stopped, trying to absorb what I was seeing by taking a picture of it—but the phenomenon was impossible to capture. Belatedly I realized that something unusual and incredible was happening as the light seemed to dance and vibrate around me, the color of pure gold.

"Amazement" is too weak a word to describe the surge of feelings that rose in me: awe, wonder, anticipation, and a sense of being honored as if heaven had decided to throw me a surprise party, and all the angels had appeared, singing in the voices of stars.

The squirrel chirped and led me higher, hopping and stopping, flicking his tail to keep my attention. *He was my spirit guide!*

Never in my life had I seen a squirrel act like this. Every time I slowed down or tried to stop, he chittered and ran toward me, then back.

He led me all the way to the real Emerald Pool, a translucent green jewel of water directly below the looming golden sandstone cliff, now lit with the new day.

I felt the utter holiness of the place as the squirrel guided me to a boulder by the pool.

My worshipful impulse was one I'd never had before. I don't speak Hawaiian, but I've been around it all my life. From some deeper knowledge I didn't know I carried, a Hawaiian chant emerged from my throat, complete with inflections and vibrato and as confident as any *kumu hula* leading her dancers in worship. I would never presume such a thing in my whiteness in Hawaii, but here in Utah, in a land that belonged to another tribal people, it was the response that Spirit called up.

I headed toward the water as I called the chant.

My voice echoed between the still pool and massive walls, sounding to my own ears like someone else's, like something out of time, and beyond my own understanding, race, religion, or culture.

I walked, chanting, to a cottonwood tree by the pool, picked one leaf, climbed onto a rock, and dropped it into the shining green water.

The leaf floated on the water like a tiny boat, and I sang the chant again, the exact same words.

Pinkish-gold light filled the area and seemed to crackle with some contained lightning. Every hair on my body stood up with static as I was flooded and electrified with the Power that had decided to visit me and this place. I opened my hands and raised them instinctively, tipping back my head to take in the glory that surrounded me.

A few minutes later, the presence of the Divine gently faded.

I sank to my knees on the boulder. I couldn't help but sit and cry, kneeling beside the water in the deep notch between golden cliff and massive red rock.

When I could make my fingers work, I took a few pictures with trembling hands—pictures of the pool, the floating leaf, the cotton-wood tree, the rocks. Pictures I knew wouldn't show anything of what I'd just experienced nor give any clue to what it had meant.

Nothing changed outwardly, but just as suddenly as the event had begun, I felt my dismissal.

I bent my head and said, "Thank you. Goodbye."

The squirrel reappeared. I stood up and followed him. He hopped along ahead of me, leading me away from the pool. Eventually, he sat on a rock in the path and allowed me to come within a few feet of him, where he chirped, and we eyed each other.

I was still crying, tears trickling helplessly off my chin, and he seemed amused by this. With what looked like a wink, he disappeared into the brush with a flip of his tail.

On the way back, I thought of Moses, when he'd gone up to the mountain to meet with God and his face had to be covered from the splendor of that encounter.

A few bits of glory were still clinging around my shoulders, invisible to all but me.

CHAPTER NINETEEN
THE NARROWS

We begged four different times at the historic Zion Lodge for a room for another night, but even Mike batting his pretty blue eyes couldn't get a "yes." Still, we couldn't bear to leave this amazing park with so much as yet unseen. So, after Mike's morning photoshoot, he went to a campground already labeled FULL. While I was having my spiritual encounter, he had been driving in circles around the campground until he saw someone pull out. He drove in, threw down our cooler and folding chairs, and nabbed the spot.

We settled into a campground area with a lot of people around us and a few shade trees. We assembled our tent and mattress like old pros this time. Our nearest neighbor had one of those Winnebagos the size of a city block, with a generator running nonstop only twenty feet away, so we decided to escape and take the tram to the back of the valley for the sunset.

I loved walking with Mike beside the Virgin River under the Temple of Sinawava toward the famous Narrows hike at the back of the canyon. The two of us were both calmed and excited by everything about this park—the grandeur, the accessibility, the song of birds and rustle of new spring leaves, and the special light that happened at sunrise and sunset when the sun struck the mountains and reflected their colors.

The entry to the Narrows hike was clearly marked, and what was most interesting was that the path led directly into the water and up the stream for the duration. I stuck a hand in the stream. "This is cold!"

Mike had his hands on his hips, staring up into the steep, brightly striped canyon walls. "Let's do this hike."

"Yes!" I was fascinated by the brightly colored pebbles in the stream, the way the sunshine bounced around off of the sculptured cliffs and the water—and the possibility of attempting one of the most unique hikes in the world.

We read up on the hike at a nearby kiosk. The Narrows was rated "strenuous," and cold-water hiking shoes and poles were highly recommended because most of the trek was through the forty-degree, rushing Virgin River up into the steep canyon. Just glimpses of the beauty of it at sunset got our enthusiasm going for the next morning's adventure.

Dawn rolled around early. We didn't want to wait for the outfitting store to open at 9:00 a.m., so we decided to go without special water shoes and sacrifice our sneakers instead.

On the way to the Narrows, my hip injury flared up, sending shooting stabs of pain down my thigh and into my lower back; old injuries had come back to haunt me. It was frustrating to be hampered by chronic pain when I was so excited. If only I'd been given a whole new body when I had my spiritual encounter at the Emerald Pools! I hobbled, hunched and stiff, but determined to keep going with the help of a sturdy stick. Maybe my hip would limber up and feel better if I kept moving.

Mike stopped to take a photo, and I decided to walk on ahead so he wouldn't get irritated with my slow pace. We had a mile to go before we even got to the "hard part" where we would have to wade in the cold water, and I worried about how I would do.

I walked and walked, pausing to take pictures of the beautiful morning. Why didn't Mike catch up with me with his usual long-legged stride? I knew how eager he was to get going into the stream.

It was a little spooky on the trail alone, so early and dark, but that special Zion glow had begun at the tops of the cliffs hundreds of feet above as the sunrise caught the peaks, and I was entranced by the sunrise as I limped along.

I heard a sound far away. It sounded like someone calling for help, but it bounced off the canyon walls, so I couldn't tell where it was coming from or what the words were. We might need to help someone! I got my phone out to call Mike and let him know.

No Service.

The cries were getting louder, haunting and scary.

This was serious! Whoever was calling was in real distress, and I was in no shape to do much with my hip acting up. I needed to find Mike so that we could help whoever was in trouble. I turned back to look for him, limping as fast as I could at my shuffling pace.

Suddenly, coming around the curve of the trail, I recognized that the echoing shout was my name: *"Toby! Toby!"*

Mike must be hurt! My heart rate soared in panic. I ran back down the trail, as fast as I could go with my crabbed-up leg.

Around a curve, Mike came running toward me, red-faced and even more freaked out than I was. "Where the heck did you go? I've been looking and calling for you for a half hour!"

"You're not hurt?" Adrenaline overload at seven a.m. on a measly cup of coffee isn't fun.

"Don't run off like that ever again!" he exclaimed. "Couldn't you hear me calling you? I thought something bad had happened to you!"

"I thought something bad had happened to *you!*" I explained how I'd kept going along the path because my hip was acting up, and I was too slow for his usual speed. "Then I heard this scary noise and I came to look for you so we could help."

We couldn't laugh at our misunderstanding; we were too upset.

We walked on together for a while, not speaking, working off the adrenaline, and he stayed by my side in spite of my limp.

I took his hand as it swung between us. I love the shape of his hands; they're graceful and long-fingered and strong. I love the calluses on his palm and at the base of his fingers from building and creating and fixing and doing. How I love that hand, and the way it engulfs my square, sturdy little paw.

Mike finally squeezed my hand back. His frightened anger was passing; we were okay. We were together.

We turned to each other and said, "I'm sorry," at the same time.

"If we ever get separated, after five minutes we'll go back to where we saw each other last, and wait," Mike said.

"That sounds good." I kissed his knuckles. "Did you think a mountain lion got me?"

He shook his head. "I was trying not to imagine what it could have been."

We reached the spot where the Narrows access trail dead-ends into the clear, rushing, very cold Virgin River. *The way forward was in.*

We got excited again. "I'm going to go slower because of my hip," I told Mike. "You can go ahead."

"I won't leave you behind," he said, and I felt a giant gush of love that brought tears to my eyes. I blinked so as not to let on.

I had been leaning on a branch I'd found, but right at the start of the Narrows, other hikers had left a variety of stout sticks of every size and length. That row of sticks delighted me; though we were the first at the river that morning, I felt connected to everyone who'd done this hike before us and returned to share their sturdy support for the next traveler.

Mike had put most of his camera equipment in plastic bags and then into a lightweight backpack. We each chose a stick, and felt that "first explorer" feeling again, having beaten the crowds. We reveled in the new day blooming color over the Navajo sandstone walls all around us, captured and glittering in the clear water.

I went in first, and squealed. The river was bruisingly cold. My feet burned at first, then went numb. I hopped out of the water whenever I could, onto rocky little sandbars, and kicked my feet and wiggled my toes. I couldn't really tell if they were moving or not, and I worried about Mike, who said he "didn't feel anything" and stayed in the water much longer than I did. The cold was frightening; enough to distract me from the beauty surrounding us.

A brutally long stretch of walking in water to our knees ended in a glorious tumble of waterfall, where we were able to get out on a sandbar. Mike took pictures of it and I sat on a rock and enjoyed the sight.

The views couldn't possibly get any better further upstream; I was chilled, and my hip still hurt. I wanted to return.

Mike was focused with that intensity that he experiences when he's after something. "Go back to camp and rest your hip. Get comfy," he said. "I'll be back when I've seen what there is to see."

"Love you. Don't get frostbite!" I turned around and went back downstream, leaning on my sturdy stick and meeting a host of hikers coming up. I was able to say, "Wait till you see the sunrise on the waterfall!" as if I did it every day.

Hobbling back to the tram, my mind wandered back to my old job. Would anyone miss me at the Department of Education? I'd been at a junior high school for five years, at a high school for one, a supervisor for two, and then covering the counseling needs of three elementary schools for the last two years of my career—plus working at two private clinics after-hours with families. I'd loved my work, and it had taken years for me to get all the education and licensures I'd needed, not to mention special training in autism, play therapy, family therapy, couples work—*was I really walking away from all of that to write stories full time?*

I climbed carefully into the park's tram and sat on one of the seats, staring out the window. Becoming a full-time writer felt so frivolous, when I knew I'd made a difference in the field.

I tipped my head back, and the pure, puffy white clouds floating over the brilliant mountain peaks reminded me of a unique student and his art.

~

I WAS ASSIGNED TO A LITTLE ELEMENTARY SCHOOL OUT IN THE JUNGLE on the wet side of Maui when I worked with Ganesh. The area was home to holdouts from the hippie movement who were too stoned to get the memo that "Tune in, turn on, drop out" had been replaced by the Polo-Shirted Eighties, the Yuppie Nineties, and now the Crashed Economy 2000s. They lived in plastic tent villages, growing hydroponic pot and heliconias, forming naked drum circles, and bringing unkempt, unbathed kids covered with *ukus* (head lice) to school to be civilized.

I had been one of those kinds of kids, growing up near Taylor Camp on Kauai in the 1970's. Now I was on the other side of the fence, doing uku-checks and worrying about kids' hygiene and home life.

Ganesh was a child with serious learning issues, a broken front tooth, and long untamed brown curls that made him an object of scorn among the other fourth graders. Ganesh had never attended school at all until second grade, when his hyper behavior prompted his parents to enroll him in public school "to get a few hours of peace," according to his bead-bedecked mom.

Ganesh never walked if he could run, hopped if he could leap, or talked without shouting. But if I put a pencil in his hand, he calmed down and drew with Daliesque originality, and while doing that, could carry on a conversation. We were still assessing him, but the team's conclusion that year was that he was on the autism spectrum with ADHD characteristics. He had no social skills whatsoever.

After a recent fight with two girls (they'd teased him about his long hair, whereupon he banged their heads together and scratched their arms), I asked him to make a "comic book" on How to Get Along with Others. He retitled it, *Ganesh's Book of Nonviolence.*

The first five pages consisted of *What Not to Do.*

Stab someone. Light them on fire. Drop rocks on their heads. Call them names like "F-ING ASSHOLE."

Each picture was a battle as I tried to moderate the content, worrying what my principal would think if she saw it. Finally, I decided that the comic book would be a therapeutic exercise to get some of his feelings out and replace them with something prosocial. The gruesome thing would never leave my files nor see the light of day.

I let Ganesh rain destruction on his peers with his pencil, unfettered.

The second half of the book, consisting of *What to Do,* was harder for Ganesh to come up with.

He drew *Put a blanket on your dad when he's passed out and it's cold.* The eerily corpselike drawing of the father floated in the air with X's for eyes, and the blanket in the child's hands looked like a guillotine coming down.

I had an overactive imagination, too.

After that one drawing, Ganesh was out of prosocial ideas.

"What about school?" I asked. "What kinds of things could you do to make friends?"

He shrugged, long, tangled curls swinging forward over his tense little face. I smoothed them back gently..

"Ask someone to play?" Ganesh glanced at me for the first time, a side-eye out of seldom seen gray eyes. He drew a hopscotch board, the squares listing freeform into the sky. His self-figure was an attenuated balloon shape with the words *"Want to play?"* floating beside him.

"You draw the other person," he said, and pushed the paper over to me.

I was encouraged by this sign of engagement, itself prosocial, and quickly sketched a girl standing, looking thoughtfully at the hopscotch board. Ganesh waited patiently and quietly for me to finish, a first.

"What next?" I asked, handing him back the pencil.

"I don't think she wants to play with me," he said, his "self" immediately inserted into the drawing, his attention on the reserved little girl I'd drawn.

"She's wondering if it will be fun. She's not sure," I said.

"I think she doesn't like me," Ganesh stated loudly.

"No. She's just shy. Big voices scare her." I grabbed this chance to give him feedback at a safe remove.

"I'll be soft. Indoor voice." He lowered his bellow. "Maybe she'll play then."

"Yes, she definitely wants to."

He turned the page, with an air of getting down to business.

"Asking to help someone," he stated, beginning another drawing.

My girl figure ended up being the one in need of help, drowning in the ocean and grabbing onto his figure's surfboard. We ended the session, but I promised him we'd complete the comic book next time.

"I like my book, Ms. Toby." The gap of Ganesh's broken front tooth ruined what should have been a great smile. "Gandhi would have handled those girls better. I have to put him in the book, too."

"Gandhi would never have wanted you to scratch people," I agreed.

ON THE PARK SHUTTLE BACK TO THE LODGE, I LEANED MY FACE ON the window and said a prayer for Ganesh. Surely the Presence that had met me at the Emerald Pools would watch over that uniquely wonderful kid.

CHAPTER TWENTY
ZION TO BRYCE

The drive from Zion to Bryce Canyon National Park (the park with the hoodoos that had originally captivated me in the doctor's office) was only an hour and a half, so we decided to take a longer route up into the mountains to see a place called Cedar Breaks National Monument on the way. "Crowning a grand staircase of rock formations, Cedar Breaks sits at over ten thousand feet and looks down into a half-mile deep geologic amphitheater," I read off my phone as we drove. "Sounds like we need to see that."

"It'll be nice to cool off at a higher elevation," Mike agreed. We'd packed up our campsite and said a reluctant goodbye to Zion that morning, spurred on by a heat wave that had pushed temperatures up to over a hundred degrees.

We passed through fields of grain and alfalfa as we drove up into the mountains toward Cedar Breaks. Clouds engulfed us with the abruptness of an incoming storm. Light rain flecked the windshield, and Mike turned on the wipers. Both of us were still wearing lightweight clothing from the hot climate below; I was in shorts, slippers, and a tank top.

"Wow, this is a big weather change," I said.

"And now it's snowing," Mike said. Raindrops had abruptly transformed to whirling white flakes.

I hadn't seen snow falling since we'd left the Midwest almost twenty years ago, after completing our college degrees together—a story for another day. "Do you think . . . the road is getting slippery?"

Mike didn't answer. His white knuckles and intent gaze on the twisting route were my answer. The SUV was an all-wheel drive, so there was nothing further we could do to ensure we would be safe.

The snow fell harder, and he slowed down further.

Anxiety tightened my chest and shortened my breathing as I lost my Zen, assaulted by imaginings of us crashing off the deserted mountain road into a frozen chasm. Desperate to pull myself together, I turned to Mike. "Can we stop? I want to get some warmer clothes on."

We found a scenic overlook and parked. Snow blanketed the valley we'd driven up, obscuring it completely. I got out, shivering in the freezing wind, and dug around in the back for the duffle bag holding my clothes. I changed from my shorts and tank shirt into socks, jeans, tennis shoes, a long-sleeved tee, and a parka. The wind and blowing snow sliced over and around us as Mike took the opportunity to change as well.

Not one car passed us the whole time. "There's nobody else on this road, Mike," I said as we navigated carefully back onto the deserted highway. I put one hand on the sissy strap, and the other on the dash, bracing myself as we crept up the hill through the icy snow. "It's kind of spooky. Do you think they know something we don't?"

Mike frowned. "Why are you so freaked out?"

"I don't know." But I was, super freaked out in fact. Vivid mental movies of us sliding off the icy road and being lost forever attacked my brain like alien invaders. I shut my eyes and practiced relaxation breathing.

We finally reached the top of the mountain and discovered why there was no one else on the road: sawhorses, barely visible through the swirling flakes, supported a sign that announced, *CEDAR BREAKS MONUMENT CLOSED.*

Mike pulled over to navigate the shortest way from our location to Bryce Canyon, and I worked on calming my incipient anxiety attack, determined not to stress Mike out further when he already had his hands full. I put on headphones and thumbed to my affirmations recording. I shut my eyes to practice relaxation breathing for the drive back down the mountain.

Lady Google showed us an alternate route that led sideways along the ridge, and we drove slowly down to our destination, which was still at a much higher elevation than we'd been aware of. Mercifully, the snow lightened as we finally pulled into Bryce Canyon National Park, site of the magical, mystical hoodoos that had originally inspired the trip.

Bryce is much smaller than Zion and consists mainly of various lookout spots around the rim overlooking its famous valley, and trails down into it. The uniqueness of the rock formations that had first caught my attention were what had caused the area to be designated a national park. The hoodoos were formed when ice and rainwater wore away the soft, brittle limestone that makes up the underlying formations of this particular geologic zone.

The sun was going down as we entered Bryce, so we headed for the aptly named Sunset Point lookout. After a short trek in below-freezing temperatures, I found a spot near the edge, in the lee of a boulder, and drew my knees up under my roomy parka to watch.

By some stroke of kismet, I was sitting in the exact spot where the photo on the cheap calendar in the doctor's office had been taken.

I'd done it: I'd seen a photograph that compelled me, and now I was looking at that view with my own eyes.

And it was glorious.

Directly below the point where we were sitting and to the south, the group of hoodoos known as the Silent City rose from the canyon floor, a maze of humanlike fingers and fins packed in a tight formation of rows and clusters, like so many Chinese terra-cotta soldiers. Just below the overlook on the northern edge stood the famous formation known as Thor's Hammer, solitary and arresting. Colors welled and swirled, moving like water through the sandstone monoliths, receding into deep violet shadows as a spectacular sunset ebbed into night.

Tears filled my eyes. All the stresses and strains of travel felt worth it in that moment of fulfillment. Bryce Canyon National Park is stunning; the pictures of it tell the truth, but they can't capture the magnitude and power of the place. I gazed hungrily down into the great bowl of canyon, wishing I could somehow bottle this feeling of joy and wonder and dab it on when needed.

A memory sparked: when I was fifteen, I'd done just that—and in a wild, mystical way, *that* moment was tied to *this* one, thirty-five years later.

GOLDEN DUST MOTES ROSE AND SPIRALED IN A LANCE OF SUNLIGHT coming through the skylight as fifteen-year-old me dusted the upstairs master suite of the mansion whose grounds we lived on as caretakers. I wielded an ostrich-feather duster with more art than function—I liked to imagine it was a fancy fan and I a belle of the ball—but the suite was hot today, and I battled a feeling of hopelessness. *Would I always be stuck cleaning people's houses?*

Kauai was so beautiful, though, that it distracted me from my worries. I dusted a cobweb in the window and paused for a moment, staring out the great arc of glass overlooking a palm tree-rimmed pond, where a pair of imported trumpeter swans circled in the jade-green water.

I mentally embroidered a fantasy of waking up in the pure-white king bed with its fancy mosquito net and taking a bath in the giant tub that overlooked the pond.

I would write my story down later in my tiny room in our shack in the corner of the estate—*maybe someday, my stories would make a million dollars, and I could have a big king bed and a tub overlooking a pond.*

Mom, sweating and irritable, stuck her head into the suite. "Hurry up, we need to get the vacuuming done before the family gets home." She pointed to a large bottle of perfume perilously near the edge of the vanity. "Be careful of that. They say it's the world's most expensive perfume." She hurried on.

I walked over and picked the bottle up. "*Joy* de Jean Patou," I read aloud, pretty sure I wasn't pronouncing the French name correctly. I examined the heavy square-cut bottle with its plain embossed label. Darting a glance at the door, I pulled out the crystal stopper and took a sniff.

Like a genie rising, a voluptuous scent encircled me.

This wasn't the chemically enhanced bath spray I was used to. This was the blood of truckloads of real roses and bushels of delicate French jasmine blossoms, crushed to pulp and distilled into precious golden liquid.

With another glance at the door, I rubbed the crystal stopper on my wrists.

The scent enfolded me like the satin of an imaginary ball gown. How beautiful it was!

A heady feeling swept over me as I flew about my work: *I had stolen Joy!* Wearing the world's most expensive, delicious perfume, I'd become a suburban Cinderella, a princess disguised as a maid.

I volunteered to clean the master suite from then on. The level on the bottle of Joy got a little lower, but it wasn't noticed.

I'd stolen Joy! And someday, imagination would be my magic carpet to the good life.

It had taken a long time, but my stories *had* become my magic carpet. I could bottle this memory through my writing, share it with others, and savor it again and again.

ONCE THE SUN DISAPPEARED, BRYCE CANYON WENT FREEZING COLD.

Really cold . . . bits of snow blew past like a giant's dandruff as I sat on bare rock, my jeans totally inadequate. Dark enfolded us, and I had trouble getting up—my rear was as frozen as a side of beef, my tricky hip locked up and sore. Mike was moving slowly too as we made our way back to the vehicle, hoping like hell we could get a room at the only place to stay inside the park, Bryce Canyon Lodge.

THANKFULLY, THE LODGE HAD A ROOM AVAILABLE. WE SIGHED WITH relief, tossed our stuff onto the bed in our chamber, and hurried down to the dining room before they closed.

We hunched over our meal with an extra-large atlas and a hand-drawn grid I'd made of the days remaining of our month-long trip, along with our list of "must-sees" from friends, and we tried to plot the rest of our route.

Bryce Canyon National Park was small in terms of things to do, and we couldn't get a second night at the lodge. Camping outdoors in this degree of cold was out of the question, so we decided to ride horseback down into the Canyon the next morning, which was highly recommended, and then figure out where to go next.

Plotting routes is not as easy as it seems. Getting back to California looked like an unpleasantly long stretch of nothingness across Nevada, and some of the "must-see" sights were prohibitively far away.

"I've been noticing some amazing slot canyon pictures here," I told Mike, showing him a photo feed on my phone.

"Oh, that's Antelope Canyon, Arizona," Mike said. "It's not that far away. Looks like a cool place. But it's not a park—it's on the Navajo Reservation."

"Why don't we go? I want to see this." I showed him a photo: a beam of light leaned like a pillar between striped, coruscated red-and-gold walls like frozen waves of stone. "It's Fat Man's Misery in Zion, but on steroids."

"Sure! Let's do it."

We grinned at each other over the atlas. I loved the excitement in his eyes; I loved that we could just decide to go to Antelope Canyon. I loved that we were having this adventure—*together.*

The next morning, we rousted out of bed early to ride down into the canyon itself, to see the hoodoos up close. Just the smell of horses reminded me how much I loved riding—but I hadn't been on one since my thirties, and Mike had seldom ridden at all.

The stable gave Mike a large mule named Tin Man and adjusted the stirrups to maximum length to accommodate him. He still looked giant on the sturdy animal. I had more experience, so the guide gave me a soft-mouthed black gelding named Lucky Strike.

We moved out single file down a sandy path with hair-raisingly steep switchbacks that wound down into a conifer forest interspersed with limestone formations. Once out of the wind at the top of the Canyon, the temperatures warmed up. The sun beamed down on our heads, the smell of horse and pine surrounded us, the erosion-formed sandstones loomed close and the brightness of spring birdsong filled the air. "I'm officially in heaven," I said.

Mike didn't reply, so I turned in my saddle to see that he had dropped his reins. Tin Man carried Mike along unguided as he took pictures, both hands occupied by his camera. "This is much better than walking."

"Not for Tin Man," I teased.

We reached the Silent City area and moved in to observe the hoodoos. The formations looked like giant sandcastles layered in cream, buff, pink, and vermilion clay-like stone. They seemed less human, more like abstract sculptures when viewed up close.

The guide directed us to a lookout spot with several spectacular columns behind us. He dismounted, then used my phone to take a picture of us, grinning like loons as we sat on our mounts, the vivid formations rising behind us into a stark blue sky. We'd reached Bryce at last, and the hoodoos were worth it.

CHAPTER TWENTY-ONE
COUNTING THE COST AT GRAFTON

I'd been saving quarters for the next trip to the laundromat, a periodic evil on any extended road trip. Every night, I collected the change from Mike's pockets and my wallet into a Ziploc baggie, keeping it handy in the glove box. The day we left Bryce, I tried to pick up a quarter at a gas station—only to find it had been glued onto the pavement.

Scattered around the parking lot were several more quarters—a dime and a nickel too. All glued down.

Color rose in my cheeks, that furtive embarrassment that happens when you've been pranked. I glanced around to see if anyone was laughing at my attempt to pry the quarter off the asphalt, or if there was a camera pointed at me. The area appeared deserted. The gas station staff likely needed a few laughs, and after a moment of being shocked by the meanness, I tried to shrug it off.

This trip had been full of money contrasts: saving quarters for laundry but spending two hundred a night on the National Park Lodges whenever we were lucky enough to get them. Eating hundred-dollar dinners and blowing up mattresses in campgrounds. Drinking a nice red wine by the fire and refilling used water bottles from a fountain.

I felt a constant push and pull worrying about how much we were spending, even as logic told me that a few thousand dollars extra wouldn't make a difference in the long run—but it would in our quality of experience.

Mike and I got married when I was twenty-one and had dropped out of college; he'd never finished. We worked service jobs in those early years: I as a bank teller, he in construction. Later, after the babies were born, we settled down in a tiny rental cottage in Kapa`a and did swing shift parenting: I worked breakfast and lunch shifts at a hotel while he took care of the kids, then he worked at a fine dining restaurant nights, while I cared for them.

When Tawny and Caleb were three and five, a settlement from a car accident Mike was involved in came through as a windfall. We decided to go to the Midwest and finish college with that money, with the intention of returning to Kauai to have real careers. We sold everything but our trusty Honda Civic, shipped it to California, and drove across the USA with our kids in the back seat. With the much cheaper cost of living in the Midwest, we were able to buy our first house for forty-six thousand dollars in a seedy part of Mishawaka, Indiana.

With two young children in tow, it took us seven years to finish our degrees while working jobs similar to those we'd left on Kauai —but in 1999, Mike and I both graduated from Bethel College together, cum laude.

We'd always intended to return to Kauai, but Maui was where we found jobs, so we sold our Midwest house, packed up the kids again (now in fifth and sixth grade), and relocated back to Hawaii. We bought our house on the sunny side of Haleakalā, and we've been there ever since.

Through all of those years, money was tight. We had what we needed, but not a lot extra. There were things to pay for every time we turned around: student loans, braces, drama lessons, doctor bills, a new set of tires. This road trip to the national parks was the first time we'd ever taken a vacation together in close to thirty years. So, even though we'd decided we could afford it and would pay it off afterward, I still found myself breaking a sweat over the stack of charge receipts thickening my wallet.

I'd grown up poor, much poorer than our kids, who liked to reminisce about the lean years when we were both in college: We ate bread from the day-old bakery and chicken thighs prepared different ways most nights of the week. Mike had grown up blue collar, but his mom had stocked the fridge with frozen potpies instead of tofu and homegrown sprouts, as mine had.

"There is enough; there always has been," I muttered aloud, leaving the glued-down quarters and heading for the rental SUV. We'd worked hard to get where we were, and a little splurge now and again, like spending the night in the National Park Lodges, was okay.

SHAKING MY BAG OF CHANGE, ESTIMATING HOW MANY LOADS IT would cover, reminded me of one of my counseling students. Amy had been a runaway, living on the streets of Lahaina, panhandling for change until she was caught and placed in the alternative education program I was working in at the time. The old plantation building was held up with termite spit and dirt-colored paint, and I worked there as a clinical supervisor, problem-solving program issues and helping with therapy part-time.

The morning she came in to see me, the pockets of her Goth style black jeans were jingling with chains—and coins.

"Hi Amy," I said.

"I need counseling. I don't want to work on that shit."

Mrs. Tamaguchi, the teacher, stood behind Amy. A little sparrow of a lady, she made amazing cream-filled almond cookies for the students, and worked hard to create a homey, welcoming atmosphere for them, along with teaching. She didn't deserve the attitude she was getting from Amy.

"Right now's not a good time." Mrs. Tamaguchi wrung her hands. "Amy needs to do her studying. That test is coming up."

Amy crossed her arms over her chest. Self-injury scars were laced up her arms. Her pierced lip protruded belligerently.

"Maybe Amy's time would be better spent working on whatever's bothering her right now," I said, smiling at Mrs. Tamaguchi in understanding. "I'm sure she'll try to catch up later."

Mrs. Tamaguchi withdrew, and I gestured to a nearby table. "Have a seat, m'dear, and tell me all about it."

"I haven't seen you in a while," she accused. "Months." Amy often suspected the adults in her life of abandoning her, while doing the best she could to reject them first.

"I have another school to cover. I wish I could spend more time here. Besides, you were gone too."

"Oh. Yeah, I was."

Amy fiddled with one of her string bracelets. Her hair was brown and curly on one side, bright blue on the other. This accentuated her unusual eyes—one was green, the other brown, and they were both a little too wide set, as if they each wanted to wander off and do their own thing.

"So. You said you needed counseling. What's up?"

"I don't, really. That study shit is just boring." She tried a little glare, with just one eye—the green one.

I laughed. "Pretty bored myself, until you came in. How about you catch me up on what you've been doing since I saw you last?"

I'd known Amy since sixth grade, when her bipolar disorder was beginning to manifest and she was doing her first stint in a foster home due to drug-addicted parents. I still remembered the social worker's comment to me: *They were living like wolves, eating out of cans and sleeping in an abandoned car.*

I'd learned to just say what I'm thinking with kids. "Your eyes are amazing. It's like they each came from another planet and decided to join your face, just to make it more interesting than anyone else's," I said.

She laughed, a rusty bark like it didn't get used much. "Since you saw me last, I've been in and out of the hospital. And I was living on the street."

"How was that?"

"Scary." She looked at me with both eyes, and the effect was intense. "Hawaii isn't what people think. All kinds of shit happened. I got raped, and robbed, and had no food . . ." Her voice trailed off. She looked down and jingled the coins in her pocket. I had a feeling she always carried them with her, just in case. "I'll take the hospital or jail anytime, over the street."

"Seems like you figured something out through that."

"Yeah. Want to hear a song I wrote about it?"

"Sure."

Amy dug in her backpack and pulled out a dog-eared composition book. She flipped through the pages to a poem, much crossed out and rewritten, then opened her mouth and sang.

The sweet strong clarity of her voice, the incongruity of the situation, the total surprise of witnessing this, froze me in my chair.

The song was about running away, about longing for her mother, about insanity; it was clear and pure and gut-wrenching. Tears sprang to my eyes and rolled down my cheeks; I could no more stop them than the rain.

Amy closed the notebook. "I want to be on *American Idol.*"

I sniffed and wiped my cheeks with my sleeve. "Damn, girl. That would show 'em." We didn't need to clarify who "them" was: her parents, the system, the world.

Amy relaxed and smiled. She showed me more poems and drawings. Hair-raising stuff. She let me see her scars. She told me stories from the street and the hospital. "But I like where I'm at right now."

Mrs. Tamaguchi stuck her head in. "Your ride's here," she said to Amy. "Your foster dad came to take you to a doctor appointment."

"Bummer," we both said.

"I'll see you again," I promised. "I'm helping out with this program now."

"You better," Amy said, and gave me a little poke—more of that suspicion that I was ditching her on purpose. I walked her out to the car, a dilapidated Chrysler. Her foster father, a worn-looking man in a blue work shirt, was behind the wheel.

"Amy's awesome," I said, after shaking his leathery hand through the window. "I'm so glad we got to spend some time together today."

"She wants to be a singer. We're getting her lessons," he said proudly.

Amy smiled and nodded. She clearly liked the foster dad; that was a relief. Maybe she wouldn't run away this time.

"That's great. Amy has a beautiful voice."

She got into the passenger side. A chunk of rust fell out from under the car as she slammed the door. How much did those singing lessons cost? How long could this family afford to get them for her? I waved goodbye as they drove off.

Mrs. Tamaguchi met me at the classroom door. "She was so irritable," she said. "What was the matter?"

"Amy wanted to tell her story. She'll be fine as long as she stays with that family and keeps singing," I said.

I donated money to the foster parents anonymously to pay for the singing lessons, but in the way of these things, I was transferred to cover a different school and lost touch with her. I like to imagine Amy on American Idol, singing her heart out and blowing away the world.

TODAY WAS A "MELLOW DAY"—ALL WE HAD PLANNED WAS A SCENIC drive up to Kolob Reservoir on the top of a nearby mesa, and then meeting a Facebook friend, Jacqueline, in person. She lived near Bryce and wanted to show us the ghost town of Grafton, Utah, where scenes from *Butch Cassidy and the Sundance Kid* had been filmed.

In honor of interacting personally with another human, we both cleaned up in our room before checking out. Mike shaved for the first time on the trip, complaining of having to use my pink "lady razor," and I put on makeup.

Or tried to.

I put the mascara on first, then tried to put on eye pencil, and gummed up both. I turned to show Mike. "Look at this."

This man has an incredible eye for noticing, but never seems to register anything about my appearance. I always look "fine" to him no matter how fat, thin, zitty, or frazzled I am (and that's probably a good thing).

Mike squinted at my face, but even he couldn't miss the raccoon eyes that I'd somehow drawn on. "What happened?"

"I've become Camping Woman. I forgot how to put on makeup."

"You look fine, but you better start over."

"Why? If I'm so fine." I batted crusty eyelashes at him.

"Well, if you like the Tammy Faye Bakker look."

I snorted. "Just what I was going for." I used hand cream to clean my eyes off and started over again, remembering the right order: sunscreen/moisturizer on face. Cover-up on eye bags and red spots. Eye pencil. Eye shadow, *then* mascara.

Voila! I hardly recognized the glam queen in the mirror, I'd gotten so used to Camping Woman's face.

We drove out to Kolob Reservoir and saw a few wonderful things: a field of grain blowing in the wind, with red butte formations in the background. A blue reservoir like a wind-ruffled gem with a couple in a bass boat, fishing—a painting come to life. A lot of real estate signs on summer cottages decorated the tiny community of Kolob.

We had an excellent lunch at a roadside lodge boasting an alarming taxidermy museum, complete with polar bears and wolves taking down a moose, all realistically posed and creepily dead. The taxidermy animals put me off a bit, but the pie was excellent. Afterward, we set off to meet Jacqueline at the turnoff to Grafton in a village called Rockville.

"Cherokee Jak" was a smiling-faced woman who drove a VW van from the sixties with a tricky starter. I presented her with a sheaf of grain I'd cut from the picturesque field and big Hawaii hugs. We left her van at the junction and took off in our SUV to view the graveyard where her four-times removed uncle was buried, and then the ghost town of Grafton.

The sun was directly overhead when we arrived at a plot of terra-cotta-like gravestones handmade from river clay embedded with pebbles. A large black lizard was parked on one of these, and Mike tried to photograph it—to no avail. The lizard zipped from tombstone to monument in the blink of an eye at every click of the shutter.

"That's a whiptail," Jak told us. "Fastest lizards around." We admired her several times removed uncle's picturesque plinth, beautifully carved and embedded with those ubiquitous river pebbles.

The nearby ghost town of Grafton had originally been built and settled by hardy and determined Mormons. Bricks dug from red mud on the banks of the North Fork of the Virgin River made for sturdy construction that was standing the test of time, though the town had been wiped out by flooding and an Indian attack in the 1800s that took significant life, including that of Jak's uncle. After these disasters, the remaining settlers, disheartened, pulled up stakes and moved on, leaving a deserted village of sturdy buildings standing intact. Stepping inside was a little eerie, like walking through a movie set.

"Look at this," Mike said. We chuckled as he tried to exit the front door of one of the homes; at six-three in height, he couldn't step through without the low doorjamb hitting him in the nose. I took a funny picture of him standing there, a head too tall for the opening.

The desert heat seemed to have preserved everything, even the wood. As we walked among the dwellings, admiring the workman-ship of the pebble-embedded bricks and hand-hewn porches and doorways, there was a constant sense of trespassing—any minute, one of those long-bearded, hardy farmers would ride up on his mule and demand we get out of his house. Even so, we enjoyed wandering through the hamlet, glimpsing a lifestyle that proved that people were both smaller and tougher a hundred years ago.

CHAPTER TWENTY-TWO
CULTISTS AND SHAVE ICE

Mike, Jacqueline, and I walked along an abandoned road trimmed in Queen Anne's lace and cornflowers outside of Grafton, looking for a barn Jacqueline remembered and thought my husband would want to photograph. As we went, we passed a blackberry field where a family of women and children ("polygamists," Jak called them) were picking the fruit.

They looked lovely, like something out of a movie—the girls and women were wearing the long pastel dresses and traditional bonnets I'd seen in a big *People* magazine article on a group that was a subcult of Mormonism, while the boys wore normal modern clothing. A jarring note of current times was the big white twelve-passenger van the family had parked in the middle of the field.

Mike already had his camera out to photograph the barn, and when the cultists saw that, the whole group of them ran and hid from us behind a big clump of bushes. It was weird to be someone they were afraid of when I was observing a group I disapproved due to their sexual practices with young girls and violation of children's rights.

Something about the dry grass, the rundown buildings, and the kids being dealt a hand they could not choose or free themselves from, took me back to a day ten years ago when I was working for the Hawaii Department of Education.

Deep in the sugarcane fields, the alternative campus for "emotionally disturbed" kids was approached by driving on a dirt road through the processing mill, marked by a smokestack belching steam at all hours of the day and night and a series of gigantic metal buildings emitting loud, clanging noises and smelling strongly of molasses. Everything in the mill area was coated in rust and the iron-rich, red soil characteristic of Hawaii. My car at the time was white, so every trip to the campus was documented by the dirt that invaded every crack and cranny.

Once I made it through the mill area, often pausing for the massive cane trucks rattling with chains and sprouting mountains of unruly stalks, I drove by a mountain of gently steaming bagasse fermenting on the far side of the mill. Bagasse, the refuse product of stalk fiber left over from the cane processing, was efficiently used as fuel for the mill.

Bumping on down the potholed track and over a wooden bridge spanning the irrigation ditch, it always appeared, at that point, that I was driving on into trackless twelve-foot-high seas of swaying sugarcane—but that's where I hung a left on an unmarked dirt road and navigated back to what had once been a thriving, pulsing center of island life: the cane workers' village.

Those crumbling cottages, the church, and other buildings had been repurposed for various indeterminate things, but the central school, now used to house Maui's administration, stood shabbily proud, a pretty art deco design reminiscent of the 1920s when it had been built. Giant monkeypod trees cast much-needed pools of shade over outbuildings that hadn't been updated since the fifties, one of which housed the Alternative Learning Center.

I parked in the least dusty spot I could find, behind a tall oleander bush, and got out, shooing several loose chickens away as they ran up, hoping for a handout. I crunched across dead, wind-blown grass toward the same decrepit building where I'd met with Amy.

The kid I'd had a phone call about and his educational aide were standing on the steps. Earlier in the day, the boy had accused his mom of beating him, and Betsy, the counselor, had to call Child Welfare Services to report it. Later, however, Kamuela had recanted his accusation and confessed that he was just angry with his mother from a fight over breakfast—or lack thereof. Now, she'd failed to pick him up after school.

"Hi, Mom!" Kamuela hollered. *Why was he calling me 'Mom'?*

"Hi, Kamuela." I reached them.

Queenie, the stately Hawaiian aide, sat down on the steps beside Kam, her gold bracelets jangling, frowning with irritation. "Da boy sassy today. He calling everybody Mom."

"F-ing Mom," said Kam. Lean and tan at thirteen years old, his clothes ragged, his eyes bouncing around like ping-pong balls, Kam had early-onset bipolar and some kind of developmental disorder caused by in utero drug exposure.

"You're mad at your mom," I observed.

"F-ing whore is late," he snarled.

Queenie put her large hand on his arm. "No swearing," she said. "Watch your language." Kam shook her off, and Queenie opened her mouth to chastise him some more.

"Let's call your mom and find out the problem," I said quickly.

The counselor put her head around the door. "Oh hi, Ms. Toby," she said. "Hey, I just called Kamuela's mom. She's out of gas over at the Salvation Army, so she can't come pick him up."

Kamuela kicked the post of the porch, hard. Bits of termite shit rained down on our heads.

"Well, we'll just have to take him there," I said. "I want to talk to her anyway. See what she says about the fight they had this morning."

Queenie reared her shapely bulk up off the step. "I stay done wit' dis," she growled. "Hope you in one better mood tomorrow, Kamuela." She went inside.

Hope you're in a better mood too, Queenie. I leaned my elbows on the railing beside Kam. I'd seen the boy around my neighborhood for years: graffitiing at the park, riding a too-small bike at all hours around the community with no supervision, and most recently, ripping open packets of sugar and pouring them into his mouth at Starbucks.

The counselor joined us on the step. Betsy was young and pretty, paying her counseling dues right out of her Master's degree. No one wanted to work in this program, including me most days. "I can drive us to the Salvation Army."

Kamuela looked at me, his jumpy eyes settling on me for a nanosecond. "You coming?"

"Yeah. Do you mind?"

"Whatever." Kam clearly wanted Betsy to himself—probably had a crush on her. Something to keep an eye on.

He bolted off the step, zigzagging across the grass, a misguided arrow. We followed, trying not to raise too much red dust. We got into her hot little car, and I let the kid sit in the front, which I could tell he enjoyed by his happy glance at me as I settled into the back.

"How come you're so tan, Kam? I used to see you riding your bike around town and you were never this tan," I said.

"We living at the beach," Kamuela said. "I go in the ocean every day after school."

"Yeah, his family has been homeless for a couple of weeks," Betsy said. "We're going to ask your mom for a towel and change of clothes, right, Kam? So you can take a shower at the program if you need one."

I remembered the stained shower surround in the staff bathroom, filled with rust stains and cockroach droppings. *Yuck.* "I didn't know the staff shower worked. Does it have hot water?" I asked.

Kam swiveled his bouncy eyes toward Betsy. "I hate cold showers."

"It's not pretty, but it works," Betsy said. With her smooth blonde hair and slim brown legs, she'd look perfect in a twinset and pearls —in some other place. Instead, she wore a T-shirt and khaki shorts, a whistle and keys clanking around her neck on a lanyard.

"So, what's your mom doing at the Salvation Army?" I asked.

"What do you think?" Kam snapped. "They get food there. Sometimes they hang out and watch TV." He fiddled with the radio.

Betsy commented on his rap music choices as we drove to the rundown area where the Salvation Army was located. We pulled over to the side of the road behind a battered van, and a woman got out.

Mary, Kam's mom, had the same stringy arms and legs as her son, but with the solid barrel midsection they say makes one prone to heart attacks. We walked over to her, and Betsy introduced me. "This is one of our supervisors."

I stood to the side, trying to be unobtrusive. My job was to help Betsy do her job, which partly meant processing with her later about whatever she could have done to improve the outcome. I was curious to see how she handled this situation.

Betsy opened the conversation. "Kamuela told me you had a fight this morning."

Mary turned to Kam, who had picked up a handful of gravel from the side of the road and was throwing it at a junked car.

"Stupid kid called me one prostitute," she barked.

"Whore," says Kam, with perfect diction. "I called you a *whore*."

"Who your faddah?"

"Dad."

"Who your maddah?"

"You."

"There are no *whores* around here, only one smart-mouthed kid." Mary put her balled fists on her hips. "And I never beat you, even for that!"

Betsy interjected gently. "Kamuela, can you see how that name hurt your mom's feelings?"

Kam threw another rock. "There was no breakfast," he said. "Parents should be able to make breakfast for their kids."

"I doing the best I can," said Mary. "That's all I can do." She folded her arms over her stout middle and tried to look angry, but her lips were trembling.

"It's okay, Kam, you can eat breakfast when you get to school," Betsy said. "Please don't call your mom names or tell lies about her when you're angry."

The kid threw another rock. *PING!* "Sorry, Mom," he mumbled.

"Okay," Mary said. "I sorry too. I just so stressed out. Let's go get your faddah. He inside, watching television."

Mary looped an arm around Kam's thin shoulder. He leaned into her as they walked toward a low cinder block building painted institutional green.

Betsy and I headed back to her little car, letting the hot air whoosh out as we opened the doors. We got in. Betsy turned the vehicle on and we headed back to the program's depressing campus.

"It was really nice how you interpreted what was happening for them," I said.

"I just wish I could do more," Betsy said. "It's hard to leave him, knowing they have nowhere to go."

"Focus on making sure Kam gets his needs met when he's at school, and you can't go wrong," I said. "You're not responsible for everything."

Betsy burst into tears. I patted her back as she pulled over to the side of the road, weeping. I listened to her cry: about how hard it was for the kids in the program, how much crap they endured at home and from the world, how their pain got to her, too. Her blue eyes were blurry and her nose was pink when she finally wound down.

"It's okay," I said. "You do the best you can, and that's all you can do."

There I was, saying the same thing as Mary at the end of the day.

~

WATCHING "THE POLYGAMISTS" HIDE FROM US BEHIND THE blackberry bushes, I again wondered if I was doing the right thing, leaving mental health for my dream job of writing.

I'd made a difference as a therapist. I'd helped—made things better, even if it was only a little bit, in a tiny corner of the world. Most days I'd loved it, even when it broke my heart and left me bruised.

Now I was walking past girls in pastel dresses, doomed to be married at thirteen. I've included a mention of them in this book; maybe by doing so, someone else can do something more for them. I hope so.

We walked back to dusty, deserted, sunbaked Grafton. After making sure Jak's van would start, we gave her many thanks and hugs before driving on toward Page, Arizona, where the famous slot canyon at Antelope was our next destination.

I leaned my forehead on the window and watched the arid countryside roll by, feeling a melancholy brought on by the ghost town of broken dreams, and the unsettling experience with the polygamists.

They thought we were the enemy, trying to take pictures of them like animals in a zoo, while we judged them as child-abusing fanatics. All of us were separated by our beliefs, walking past each other, missing a chance to build a bridge instead. I was saddened by the encounter.

As evening stretched the shadows like taffy, we pulled into Springdale, a little town outside the west entrance to Zion National Park, where we'd decided to find a motel.

My low mood was cured by discovering a real Hawaiian Shave Ice stand.

A traditional Hawaii treat, "shave ice" is made by a spinning blade scraping ice off a frozen block. The shavings are packed into a paper cone and doused liberally with tropical colored syrups. Shave ice, Hawaii style, is never to be confused with an ordinary ground ice "snow cone."

The lovely lady who served us said that the stand's owners were from Volcano Park on the Big Island and were real Hawaii folks. That alone was enough to banish the homesickness I'd been fighting all day. I chose lilikoi, mango, and coconut, and dug in with my spoon, closing my eyes to let the flavors of Hawaii melt on my tongue.

I was here in Utah now, and it was epic and memorable. I'd be home soon enough.

We checked into our roadside motel and set up for dinner out on the tiny deck, where we drank wine out of paper cups and ate sandwiches from the cooler.

Mike aimed his camera on super slow shutter speed at the spot where Google said the moon would rise above the shoulder of a nearby mountain. That round silver orb appeared right on time, sliding out from behind the jagged silhouette like a coin trick, into a warm night filled with bat song and a smell like cotton candy that our friend Jacqueline had said was a native tree that bloomed by the Virgin River.

I wrote about the day and began to make sense of my jumbled emotions through the process. I write to know myself better, to understand, to gain insight—in hopes that, by sharing, others might as well. Maybe, that too is a form of helping.

CHAPTER TWENTY-THREE
HORSESHOE BEND AND ANTELOPE CANYON

Late in the afternoon of the next day, I was sitting in front of a wheezing air conditioner in the Best Western overlooking the gigantic power plant dam at Lake Powell in Page, Arizona.

It was a grim view, and we'd paid extra for it.

Land the color of a moth-eaten African lion sloped down to meet the starkly blue lake without any softening of vegetation. The air shimmered with heat, as if oil were rubbed on the window. I suppose some people found this sight interesting, but the huge slab of the dam with its wire-sprouting carbuncle of a power plant didn't seem worth fifty extra dollars to gaze upon.

We'd driven all day. I was hot, tired, and miserable with that itchy rash on my hands flared up, when we finally arrived. I had no one to blame but myself, because this side trip was my idea. I'd seen those pictures of Antelope Canyon on Instagram, and had pushed to go see it.

Mike had booked us a 10:00 a.m. "photographer's tour" for the next day that he'd researched on Tripadvisor. To go on that tour, I would have to carry a DSLR camera and tripod.

As the AC gradually cooled me down, I realized I was nervous about the next day: worried about handling the "real" camera and doing the place justice. I had resisted all Mike's attempts to get me shooting with a DSLR camera before this because I was almost phobic about the technology aspects: downloading, archiving, editing, etcetera. I knew I had a good eye, but I didn't like all the hassle and responsibility of a full-sized camera.

This expensive side trip might not be worth it, and I hated looking at the dam and the coal plant nearby. They reminded me of all that was wrong with humans and what we did to the planet. I was thoroughly grumpy, and just wanted to take a cold shower and go to bed.

Mike left me to cool off and siesta as he explored the town, but when he came back he lured me out of the room with the promise of sweet potato fries (a treat I'd never tried), and "something amazing you have to see."

He took me for an evening hike through a cooling breeze, over sand dunes to the edge of what I'd thought was Lake Powell; instead, we arrived at a famous spot called Horseshoe Bend

The great green snake of the Colorado River almost doubled back on itself there, curving around a spire of striped Navajo sandstone bigger than the Empire State building, an astonishing natural

wonder that made our eyes bug and jaws drop. The edge of that bend down to the Colorado River was one of the steepest and highest cliffs we'd yet approached.

A human, properly placed in a photo, adds context, tells a mini-story, and is something to measure size against. Mike's newly shorn silver head (he'd found a barber in Page) hanging out into the scene worked nicely to do that in my photo of him as he lay on his belly and stuck his tripod out into space, working his camera with a remote trigger to get some really great bird's-eye shots.

Some of the other tourists really seemed to have a death wish, though, scrambling about and taking repeated snaps of themselves against the breathtaking drop, their hair blowing straight up as gusts of wind hit them from thousands of feet below.

Annoyance filled me, watching the antics of the young. A more appropriate response than giggling, jostling, making victory signs, and spitting over the edge might have been one of awe and respect. Snapping gum and yelling at a friend while working a phone seemed like something that could be done anywhere.

I flashed back to growing up on Kauai. Both of my parents had a keen aesthetic sense, and Pop had insisted on quiet contemplation to deeply experience nature. I'd found it hard, when I was a kid, to rein in my natural exuberance; but being taught to truly inhabit a moment of observing was a lesson I'd appreciated a thousand times since.

Funny how time brings us full circle, and we realize that our parents knew more than we gave them credit for.

OUR ANTELOPE CANYON ADVENTURE BEGAN INAUSPICIOUSLY THE next morning. The lobby of the Best Western was mobbed by tour bus groups, all trying to eat, check out, and board buses for the very place we were headed. They foraged like hungry billy goats, loud and aggressive, through the complimentary breakfast bar. We tried to breach the horde several times to grab food and make our escape, to no avail. The crowd never seemed to lighten, and finally we ran out of time and had to get in line with the rest to check out and get breakfast elsewhere.

"Guess where all of these tourists are headed," Mike said grimly, yanking down the brim of his hat. "Into Antelope Canyon. With us."

Because Antelope Canyon is on the Navajo reservation, all access is supervised by Native American tour guides, and the fees were solid. I was happy to pay to be able to see what all the buzz was about. We drove just past the coal power plant, belching photogenic gray smog, turned right, and, somewhere out in the desert, parked by an awning with a sign on it that said, "Adventure Photo Tours."

That outfit consisted of a stocky older Navajo man with a braid down his back named Joe, and his young, hipster nephew in slate-colored skinny jeans and a fauxhawk. Our group was small—five serious male photographers strung about with much gear, and me, holding Mike's spare camera. We piled into the bed of a giant, beefed-up pickup truck with wooden benches and a roll bar, and took off.

The ride out across the desert at top speed, churning up and down hills and swales of sand, was enough to get me squeaking with excitement as we bounced on our bench, the wind in our faces. We eventually pulled up and parked at a narrow, dark slit in the sandstone wall of a mesa; by then I was hyperventilating with nervous anticipation.

Navajo Joe led us inside the slit in the rock in single file, his nephew bringing up the rear. We were immediately submerged in a cool, dim, subterranean environment lit by lances and bars of light so bright they hurt the eyes and seemed to burn the sand the sunlight touched into mercury pools.

The effect was like what Mike and I had experienced when we explored Fat Man's Misery in Zion, but Antelope was so much bigger and deeper that it became its own world. Steep, sinuous, incredible contortions in the striped stone revealed the movement of water long gone, its path frozen in time.

Our guides would toss a handful of dusty sand into the light beams, and drifting forms coalesced that reminded me of "dancers, angels, ghosts," as I heard my fellow visitors call the ephemeral visions wrought of particle and sunbeams.

Joe and his nephew did a great job sheep-dogging us from corner to view spot to curve, holding us back and letting other groups through so we all got time alone in each splendid turn of the canyon. "We're just waiting for this beam," the nephew would say. The two squinted up to the slit of sky far above until just the right moment, when some incredible new light effect would occur, and they'd move us forward to see it.

The two of them had that route totally memorized, and in spite of sometimes stifling crowds, a fine rain of sand that blew down from the opening overhead, and a good deal of jostling to get the best photo, two hours flew by in a place that really defies words.

I was caught up in a frenzy of photographing, filling almost two memory cards with the DLSR and taking thirty pictures with my iPhone. I stuck the huge camera under my shirt like a bulbous pregnancy to protect it from the drifting sand that periodically drenched us, and I elbowed my way like an aggressive news reporter to the front to get the best view, plonking open my tripod right into the middle of various feet and bodies with hardly an "excuse me."

Trying to get the pictures of each incredible sight was like getting caught up in bidding at an auction, gambling at a slot machine, or grabbing for the tastiest bits at a seafood buffet. Our trip through the tunnel was a surfeit of delight, with a limited time in which to capture and enjoy it. Every moment, we knew that this was likely our only chance to see, and capture, this fleeting, ever-changing spectacle.

Afterwards, laughing with our new photographer friends as we swerved and slewed our way back across the sand dunes in the truck, we were all on a dopamine high, exchanging business cards and promises of future photography adventures together. I was able to post four of my iPhone pictures as soon as we got back to civilization, assuaging my acute need to share the experience.

Letdown set in as Mike and I drove out of Page; the feeling was the psychological equivalent of the crash after a sugar binge or the hangover that follows New Year's Eve.

We both sank into exhausted silence as we drove toward Mesa Verde, Colorado, our next national park destination, unable to even speak of the profoundly beautiful things we'd seen that day.

CHAPTER TWENTY-FOUR
MESA VERDE AND DURANGO

We drove for hours through monotonous dry Arizona backcountry in shades of crumpled suede—buff, moss, peach, and beige, peppered by lumps and knobs of unprepossessing stone. We saw nothing but crows and buzzards in the bleached sky, and eventually pulled into the gritty little town of Cortez, Colorado at 7:30 p.m., about an hour outside of Mesa Verde National Park.

At a local restaurant called Jimmer's, we devoured a couple of pounds of different kinds of barbecue. The restaurant was filled with great original woodwork and many stuffed moose heads. I especially liked the pump bottles of different kinds of barbecue sauce offered at the self-service counter. The *huli-huli* chicken in Hawaii is good, but nowhere near as tasty as the grilled delights we'd begun sampling in the Southwest.

Mesa Verde National Park was a surprise after the monotony between Page, Arizona, and the Four Corners location we'd passed through, the junction of Arizona, Utah, Colorado, and New Mexico.

A huge mountain, all by itself, rose out of the plains. The park was supposedly somewhere near the top of it. I didn't know much about Mesa Verde, and was surprised by the elevation, coolness, and grand vistas as we drove up, and up, and up. We pulled into the appropriately named Far View Lodge at the pinnacle of that mountain at almost nine p.m.

Charming, built in the 1970s, and never upgraded since, the park's lodge was clean and comfortable. It felt great to finally wash the Antelope Canyon sand out of our clothes and hair, brush it out of the cameras, and close the curtains on another gloriously over-stimulating day.

I DID MY MASTER'S IN SOCIAL WORK INTERNSHIP IN NARRATIVE adventure therapy under a charismatic, visionary, and idealistic young man back in 2004, my good friend Loren Lapow, MSW. He'd since relocated his Maui Hero Project operation to Durango, Colorado, where he worked with Native American youth in addiction prevention and character education. When I contacted him to tell him that we'd be in the area (only an hour separated Durango from Mesa Verde), he offered to take us on a "river float."

I texted him back. *"Beginner level only. We want to photograph the whole thing."*

"No worries," came back. *"I know you."* I grinned at that. He *did* know me. During the internship, he had challenged me to climb cliffs, take ten twelve-year-olds into the bowels of a lava tube, endure a sweat lodge, and jump off a fifty-foot waterfall.

Loren knew I was a sissy when it came right down to it, anxious as an egret in a hat shop, but that I'd always try something when challenged.

Unfortunately, rafting in Durango meant we wouldn't have long to explore Mesa Verde National Park.

Mesa Verde is most notable for the ancient Puebloan village sites carved into the living cliffs. As we set out to explore, we discovered that all of the sites were only accessible via guided tours, which we hadn't had time to schedule. We tried to get another night at the lodge after our rafting trip, so we could return to do a tour the following day, but both lodge and campgrounds were full due to Memorial Day weekend.

Discovering that we were going into Memorial Day, the official kickoff of summer, threw me off. I'd been immersed in a calendar-free Camping Woman zone, where days of the week didn't matter.

Clearly, Mesa Verde was one of the parks where it would have been beneficial to make reservations in advance before visiting. Its location was so remote that driving in and out for activities was a lengthy time commitment. With no self-guided tours of the main sights available, the best visit of this park would include at least two days of hiking, and the hikes were pretty rugged, with steep elevations and not much accommodation for folks with any kind of mobility issues.

Out of options to stay longer at Mesa Verde, we ate one of our picnic dinners while enjoying the sunset. Daylight flowed away like honey draining away from the walls of the pale pueblos carved into living stone, a haunting sight.

The park brochure we picked up told us that the Ancestral Pueblo people, formerly mesa dwellers, began building beneath the overhanging cliffs of the mesa sometime in the twelfth century. Their structures, made of stone and clay, ranged in size from one-room storage cubicles to interconnected villages of up to 150 rooms. By the late thirteenth century the population began migrating south to New Mexico and Arizona, and eventually the settlements were completely abandoned for unknown reasons.

We slept well and got up early, packed up from the Far View Lodge, and did a whirlwind drive-through of the park. Photographing the Puebloan village from vista points, perfect and tiny as Egyptian ruins dug deep into the mountains, I was plagued by questions.

Why did they live so high in the cliffs? What was the advantage, other than defensibility? Admiration colored my thoughts: these were some badass, tough, hardworking people. I got winded by the elevation just going down to the lookout points, let alone climbing on the hand-and-toeholds cut into logs and cliffs that they'd used to get around.

We drove on to Durango with a sense of unfinished business at Mesa Verde—not the only park that we'd felt that way about. "We'll be back," I told the empty village in the cliffs as we drove away.

"I hope so," Mike said, as if I were talking to him.

～

LOREN WAS SUPPOSED TO MEET US AT A CITY PARK IN THE MIDDLE OF Durango. A raging brown flood churned past the park, and the minute I saw it, my heart went into overdrive.

"I'm not doing it if that's the river we're going on," I told Mike, my hands sweating as I got out of the car. I rubbed them on my jeans. "There's a reason I've never gone river rafting, or even wanted to." Early experiences with the frequent flooding on Kauai had imbued me with a deep respect for how dangerous rivers could be.

"Sure, honey, it's your choice." The twinkle in Mike's eye told me he was too smart to argue with me.

Loren, looking as youthful and fit as ever, pulled up in a big Silverado pickup truck with a camper on the back containing a hard-core mobile man cave full of sports equipment. That he was still single was evident in the camper and its contents, but his footloose lifestyle made me feel more middle-aged and washed up than ever.

We hugged, and I said, "How do you stay so young?"

"I keep moving." He grinned.

"I hope that's not the river we're going on." I pointed a trembling finger at the churning chocolate-colored torrent nearby.

"Let's take a walk." Loren spoke in the calm but compelling voice he used to hypnotize nervous or rebelling teens. We proceeded along a path beside the river, and he showed us a ledge of rapids at the edge of the park. "This is a class three rapid called Smelter. It's the heaviest section we'll be doing today. This is just a mellow float."

"No way. I've never gone rafting before. I was thinking, like, a mellow, jade-green river, looking at the sky, taking pictures . . ."

"I know what you were thinking, but it's spring, and we've had some recent snow melt. You'll be fine." Loren's unwavering gaze implied a confidence in me I didn't share.

"Let's go!" Mike was bouncing on the balls of his feet with excitement. "That looks like a blast."

I was still terrified, but I remembered the reason I was taking this trip. *Would the Toby I used to be miss out on this once-in-a-lifetime chance to go rafting with a good friend in Durango?* Of course not!

I decided to reserve judgment, and if it really seemed like too much, I'd bail at the last minute.

We were meeting some other friends of Loren's for this supposed "float," and everyone was running behind, so we took Loren to breakfast and got a taste of the arty-culture-cowboy-athletic vibe that is Durango. Afterward, we met our rafting companions on the banks of the Animas River several miles upstream from where we'd "eddy out." Not one of them was over thirty, and most of them wore nothing but bathing suits. I felt like I'd been shuffled into one of those games of "find the thing that doesn't belong." Any minute now, someone was going to call a halt to this nonsense, and I'd be spared.

But that didn't happen.

The launch site was a madhouse. A high-energy, festive feeling filled the air as seemingly hundreds of young people milled around prepping to go downstream. Mike and I were the senior citizens of the bunch.

Everyone seemed so casual and upbeat. I couldn't chicken out. After all, what was the worst that could happen? But I was too well able to imagine that . . .

"You got this," Loren said with a grin, catching my eye as I hesitated before climbing aboard the small raft he was piloting with just the two of us as passengers. We were traveling downriver in a group with two more rafts filled with his cute twenty-something friends.

Even a "river float" isn't a passive journey, by any means. Mike and I, rendered chunky by PFDs (personal flotation devices) sat side by side in the bow, each holding a paddle, while Loren sat in the stern with a pair of long oars. We pushed off into the foamy brown flood.

Loren turned out to be a great captain. He gave clear directions: "Forward two strokes! Dig deep!" Mike and I paddled in sync well, and I remembered that long-ago tug-of-war when we'd first met—our bodies, so different, instinctively knew how to work together.

Our little raft made it without incident through the class one and two rapids leading up to Smelter, eddying out to the banks a few times for the young people to fuel up on beer and flirting, and then we ran the big rapids across from the park.

The feeling of riding the rapids was remarkably similar to taking off on a wave when surfing.

Paddle, paddle, paddle as hard as you can; a drop into the wave; turbulence; water everywhere in a wet roar; the excitement of making it as you come out the other side. I found it a surprisingly familiar feeling—and the three of us got all jacked up on adrenaline, whooping and hollering as we spun to the side and waited for our traveling companions.

Much further down the river, and when we'd safely eddied out at the pickup point, Loren told us that it was the first time he'd piloted solo. We had been the guinea pigs for his maiden voyage captaining his own boat, and I yelled and punched him in the arm.

Loren's like the little brother I never had, mischievous and challenging. He also has a great gift of leadership and keeps a cool head that I'd learned to trust through years of working professionally with him and hundreds of teens.

We hugged Loren goodbye. "Live your myth!" Loren said, the motto of his program; and it felt good to know we were figuring out how to do that, too.

CHAPTER TWENTY-FIVE
OURAY AND BLACK CANYON NATIONAL PARK

We were tired after all the excitement when we got on the road, headed for Black Canyon National Park to the north, where we planned to camp for the night.

On the atlas page, the route was a relatively straight line, but we found ourselves going higher and higher into snowcapped peaks as the afternoon wore on. Forests surrounded us with gushing waterfalls and snowmelt creeks bursting their banks, and there was no sign of civilization anywhere.

Despite a hat and tons of sunscreen, five hours of direct sunshine had taken its toll on this fair redhead. I was severely burned, an effect amplified by the medication I was taking for the weird rash that had plagued me on and off. As the drive wore on, a pounding headache increased to dizziness and nausea.

"I think we took a wrong turn somewhere," Mike said, the wrinkle between his brows deepening. "Just try to rest."

"I can't." Tears crept out from under my puffy lids. The rash was a riotous flame of itchy pain swirling up my arms and across my neck and chest. "I feel yucky, Mike. I just want to stop and go to bed. I don't feel good."

But there was nowhere to stop.

The road, still going up, hardly had a shoulder to pull over on, let alone a handy motel. We wove on through the stunning wilderness, but I was too tired and tearful to enjoy it. I fantasized about getting a plane home from the nearest large town.

Finally, as dark was catching up to us, I had to get out the atlas to find out what we were contending with—and discovered that we were inadvertently traversing the San Juan Mountains, which neither of us had ever heard of.

"We're crossing a freakin' mountain range by accident!" I cried, and gave way to a meltdown of exhausted tears as we crested another peak.

Mike pulled over, and we both got out at a vista point to stretch our legs and regroup—and that's when we spotted an oasis of beauty below us, a perfect little picturesque town nestled in a cup of green, snow topped mountains, the setting sun in the background.

"We'll go down there and find a place to stay, and you can spend all day tomorrow in bed, if you need to," Mike promised.

We consulted a travel review app once we had a signal in the quaint Victorian village of Ouray, which billed itself as "the Switzerland of Colorado," and worked our way down a list of availability until we found a room at the Twin Peaks Lodge.

The Twin Peaks sported fan-folded towels, a natural hot spring bathhouse, tons of amenities, and great service people. I immediately took a shower and slathered myself in cortisone cream while Mike fetched some takeout from a nearby restaurant. After eating, we crawled into bed with the blackout curtains drawn.

We were both, despite the "wows" we continued to be surprised by, overwhelmed and road-weary.

One look at my bright red, rash-covered, baggy-eyed face the next morning told Mike that I hadn't yet recovered from overdoing it.

"Let's take a couple of days off and stay here," he said. "Ouray is pretty, and you can walk around if you feel like it or stay in bed all day. I'll explore and do some fishing by myself."

Ouray was a break we both needed; me especially. I stayed out of the sun and napped most of the first day. The following one, we visited a lovely church called Ouray Christian Fellowship for Sunday service, and did a gentle walk and photo exploration of nearby and dramatic Box Canyon Falls.

Even though we'd both begun to have "beam me up Scotty" fantasies, there was no easy way to get back to Hawaii from the mountain-bound heart of Colorado. Next on the travel plan was Moab, Utah, with Arches and Canyonlands National Parks, and I couldn't miss that.

~

WE PACKED UP FROM THE TWIN PEAKS LODGE FOR THE LONG DRIVE day to Moab, Utah with the machinelike, nonverbal efficiency we'd developed over the last three weeks: I could now pack or unpack in five minutes flat.

Unpacking: wheel carry-on size suitcase into room, unzip and put bathroom bag on counter. Plug in phone and laptop. Take all pillows and fancy crap off bed, put my own pillow out of suitcase on my side—whichever one has a lamp—and lay out my row of skin unguents and e-reader on the bedside table. Voilà—unpacked.

Leaving was a reverse of this process.

Setting up for camping was more involved but consisted of both of us putting up the tent. I fitted together the support poles while Mike staked out the floor. We could put that together in about five minutes, and then I'd inflate the bed inside the tent with a battery-operated pump while Mike unpacked the SUV and set up a cooking area. Sleeping bags and clothes in, and we were done in about twenty minutes.

Once underway from Ouray, we did a drive-through of lovely Black Canyon National Park outside Sunnyside, Colorado. This was the destination we'd been attempting to reach when we stopped at Ouray, but it was another hour beyond that. I'm so glad we paused in Ouray, because Black Canyon, while pretty, had no facilities other than outhouses. We would have had to camp for sure, and I was in no shape for that physically.

Black Canyon National Park's main attraction is a steep, rocky valley containing the Gunnison River—wide, smooth and green.

"See, this was what I thought a river float was about," I told Mike, pointing to the calm, translucent jade stretch of water bordered by willows.

"Thank God that wasn't what it was," Mike said. I smacked him, laughing.

The freeway leading out of Black Canyon toward Moab, Utah was rough. The state speed limit was seventy-five mph, and at that speed, the rental SUV levitated when it hit lumps and bumps in the asphalt—yet, if we went slower, big rig trucks hauled up and rattled us unnervingly as they passed.

Mike held the wheel and speed steady as best he could while I leaned my chin on my hand, bored by the desert plains, and reflected on a newfound affection for Walmart.

Anyone who knows me knows that I am not a fan of Walmart. I dislike the company on principle, as a big-box store with cruel employee practices, and I oppose Walmart specifically on Maui. They've hurt the economy of small, local stores on our island, and often their products are lower quality. Worst of all, there are too many choices on their aisles, and I end up wasting time when I shop there.

I've never liked shopping. Shopping clutters my brain, taking up mental bandwidth with annoying decisions, like what kind of tampons to buy. Scented or unscented? Small, medium, or way too big? Plastic applicator or environmentally friendly? Brand name or generic?

Buying just that one item uses up so much mental effort. Costco is better for that reason alone. Even though it's a mega store, the products are good quality, and they try to help local and third world manufacturers. Most importantly, there is only one kind of each thing, thus reducing decision-making to: *Do I want it or not?*

But despite my bias, on this trip, Walmart was a godsend.

My attitude first began to change in Prescott, Arizona, when my rash started acting up. I *knew* Walmart, with all its variety of products, would have an answer. I went in and found the pharmacy section down the entry aisle and to the left. There, I discovered several types of skin potions, all cheaper than anywhere else.

Disliking decision-making and unsure which one would work, I bought them all.

Later, in Utah, we needed snacks, drinks, and batteries, and spotted a Walmart. We'd reconnoitered that section in another store in another town in another state, and we were now able to make a beeline to what we needed. Even if Walmart is huge, every store is laid out much the same, and for road-weary travelers, this is a boon —along with the fact that they will allow travelers to park overnight in their parking lots.

We stopped in Sunnyside, Colorado after our brief visit to Black Canyon National Park, and I ran into a Walmart for more rash cream.

I felt confident going into this known entity, turning left, and finding the skin stuff right next to the cold remedies—just like at the Walmart in Prescott, and just like every Walmart everywhere else.

One of the toughest things about a long trip is that our brains get tired of assessing, choosing, and deciding about every little thing, all the time, as we have to do when experiences are new— hence the proliferation of chain restaurants and franchise inns on travel routes.

We crave the familiar because it's less work for our overloaded systems.

Walmart is also the "community outing" destination for many elderly and disabled people during the week. Cruising the aisles with me at nine a.m. on a weekday were handicapped folks, their caregivers, and elderly people driving wheelchair shopping baskets. As I entered the checkout line, a woman with a clubfoot was discussing an upcoming gastric operation with the mostly deaf clerk in shouted detail.

Instead of impatience, I felt right at home. Going into Walmart was always a cross-section of the human experience, and I was braced for it as a woman with a toddler shrieking "Gimme candy! Gimme candy!" moved into line behind me.

Familiarity no longer breeds contempt. When traveling, familiarity breeds fondness.

I finally understood why Americans ate at McDonald's while in Paris.

CHAPTER TWENTY-SIX
ARCHES NATIONAL PARK

We rolled into Moab in the late afternoon, going against a heavy flow of Memorial Day departure traffic, plonked our stuff into a random motel, and zoomed to Arches National Park to catch the sunset.

"Catching the sunset," when with my photographer husband, was a form of hunting; it meant a rapid assessment of the whole accessible park area for proper lighting angles, then targeting where we'd go for the actual shoot, all of it done with a sense of pressure and exhilaration—we had to chase the light before it was lost.

Arches National Park's wilderness is made of red sandstone in brittle, grainy layers like a hard sugar frosting. Each of Utah's parks has a unique character and feeling to it—and the feeling of Arches is *celestial*.

We pep-stepped down a sandy desert trail to view the famous Delicate Arch from a viewpoint lookout. We were so far away that it looked like a crude cement bracket on a bare hillside.

"Let's do the longer hike to that formation tomorrow," Mike said. "All we have time for now is Windows."

The arches, or "windows," framed wide-open deep blue sky, as if the rust-red stone shapes were settings for the most beautiful jewel of all—the Utah heavens. Like Zion, Arches was immediately accessible and immensely gratifying. Anyone could get out of their car, walk a few hundred feet, and stand inside vast stone rainbows and feel immersed in the experience of the place.

The same craze that had overcome me at Antelope Canyon took over again, as the visual feast of exotic shapes against the blue backdrop was highlighted by the changing sunlight. I bounded and clambered over boulders and along multiple gigantic slickrock and sandstone protrusions, trying to capture the beauty of the place as its formations kaleidoscoped through the waning light.

Mike was somewhere in the area too, equally frenzied.

It's hard to explain the need to capture, the drive, the compulsion—an urgency that pushed me to hang out over ledges, grapple with unsteady footing, and climb where no human my age or physical capacity should go. Other photographers understand it. Maybe plein air painters, and I've seen surfers, sailors, birders, fishers, and hunters get pretty intense in pursuit of their quarry.

Once I was able to capture some decent pictures, I began to calm, breathing in the warm, ochre-colored air as my gaze traveled happily over rounded, visually pleasing, naturally occurring sculptures in brittle red rock: obelisks, spheres, triangles, ovals, pyramids, spirals, and, of course, arches.

The Arches National Park website told us more about the geology resulting in the unique landscape: sixty-five million years ago, the area was a red rock seabed. Slowly, that landscape began to change as geology wrinkled and folded the sandstone like a giant rug. As the sandstone warped, rips broke through it, creating the potential for the shapes that would emerge. The tectonic plates moved, the entire area rose, climbing to thousands of feet of elevation, and then eons of weather carved layers upon layers of rock away.

Once they were exposed, those pressurized buried sandstone

layers expanded, creating even more fissures and cracks that became places for rain and wind to drill deep into the rock and shape it more and more.

Nowadays, erosion by water is the main influence on the land. Rain dissolves the rock and carries sand and particles all the way to the Colorado River. Winter snowmelt pools bore into cracks and expand them. Gradually, this geologic process breaks down the layers of these unique sedimentary deposits into cliffs and flanges called fins, and those eventually erode, creating formations we now recognize as arches.

Satiated at last, I climbed a bulky ridge and sat overlooking the whole area, feeling like a *Menehune* on the shoulder of a friendly giant. A dry breeze carried the scent of desert flowers and sage to my nose. The sunset unfolded in a cloak of saffron, crimson and mauve that settled over the towers, peaks, and crenellations rising from the dusty floor. The other people had melted away, and all I heard was the sweet song of a meadowlark echoing off the naturally amplifying formations.

I sat there until the first stars came out, and finally Mike joined me on the giant's shoulder. "That's my girl." He extended a hand to lift me to my feet. "I knew I'd find you up here."

I just nodded, and we walked down into the dark holding hands.

MORNING DAWNED GLORIOUSLY, BUT CLOUDS SOON ROLLED IN AS Mike and I took off from the dusty town of Moab to find Canyonlands National Park.

We'd been under the impression that both parks were close to Moab, but only Arches actually is—Canyonlands turns out to be about sixty miles south of the town, or thirty miles north. It is so big it can be reached either way!

We decided to go south, because we wanted to see Newspaper

Rock, a famous collection of petroglyphs along the way. Fueled up on drive-through coffee, we took off.

Our pattern had been to do something early in the morning on coffee only, have a later breakfast around ten, lunch around two, and dinner even later, orchestrating everything around sunrise and sunset photo planning. "We'll find somewhere to get some breakfast on the way," Mike said, as we drove out of town.

But once we left Moab, there was nothing but sage, early spring daisies, and great red sandstone protrusions—no breakfast to be found. By the time we pulled into Newspaper Rock, conveniently located near the road, we'd been reduced to eating stale trail mix and beef jerky I found under the seat.

Accessible sights are wonderful, and Newspaper Rock is just that: pull off the road, park, walk ten feet, goggle and click with the other visitors to the shrine.

I loved the humorous, gossipy feeling of the petroglyph site, a huge wall of red sandstone inscribed with animated stick figures and animal drawings. Just like its name implied, early people came through this place and added their carvings to a group mural, creating a tapestry of artwork imbued with a feeling of humor and delight in the human condition. Modern graffiti here and there seemed to add a note of *now* to a continuation of some timeless, ongoing dialogue that made me feel connected to all who'd gone before.

Even prior to the official entry to Canyonlands, we realized that it was a gigantic park; we weren't going to get to see much of it if we were still going back to Arches to do an evening hike to Delicate Arch.

We spotted a horse herd grazing loose, and I was spellbound by the paint, Appaloosa, and pinto band wandering through green grass beneath a big orange butte. The scene was like something out of an old Western—I kept pinching myself at its iconic beauty.

We pulled over, and I called and whistled to the horses, but they were on the other side of a metal trough, and only looked at me.

"Let's get closer." Mike hoisted his camera and headed toward the horses. I followed, feeling naughty but thrilled by the possibility of getting a close-up photo of the uniquely Southwestern-looking animals standing in the shadow of the butte.

As we approached, picking our way across the bunchy grass, the horses came trotting over to greet us, rubbing us with their velvet noses and posing for pictures. They surrounded me with their delicious fragrance, a scent that's always made me happier than any cologne.

"We can go back now. I got my photo of the day." I'd been able to get a portrait of one of the paint ponies with a backdrop of massive striped butte and sky. I wished I could stay longer, surrounded by the gentle, beautiful animals, but we had an actual park to explore.

Once inside Canyonlands itself, we took a hike through some of the cavelike butte formations scattered around like gigantic gray-white mushrooms.

Canyonlands is not easily seen in the way Arches, Bryce, or Zion are. My word to describe that park is *convoluted*. It's a huge, sprawling maze of massive, corrugated valleys, and to really explore it properly requires long hikes or horseback riding. Many of the formations reached easily looked like toadstools with crowns of grayish sandstone and softer layers beneath that are scaling away, creating caves and hollows in the rock below.

We hiked around one sandstone outcrop whose underscoring completely surrounded the bottom of a massive turtle-shaped outcrop. Especially interesting was an old cowboy camp inside, the wood of a crude bunk brittle but intact, the cave's walls stained by fire smoke and marked with cave paintings left by people who'd lived there well before the cowboys.

We drove back to the motel after exploring Canyonlands and napped hard, arising around five p.m. to do the strenuous three-mile hike to famous Delicate Arch for the sunset.

Tanked up on more iced coffee, we drove toward Arches Park. I was surprised to see that the overcast skies had churned into heavy-bellied, yellowish clouds trailing spatters of rain. "What the heck? I thought this was the desert!"

We hurried, energized by the storm clearly brewing and worried that it could steal our sunset in the park. I kept up with Mike until we reached a vast mountain of slickrock where we had to ascend about three hundred vertical feet. I started getting a stitch in my side and stopped to catch my breath while Mike cranked on ahead, clearly in photographic "get the shot" mode.

I was more interested in the storm whipping up around us.

The clouds swirled, near enough to touch, and a rough wind blew me from behind, almost pushing me up the massive slope. I was acutely aware of channels that ran water off the big rock mountain, worn in a series of steep dry hollows and runnels along the cracks. There was no lightning, but spits of rain cooled my hot cheeks. *Were nylon shorts and a light cardigan over a tank top going to be enough coverage from the elements?* I already knew they weren't.

I was exhilarated and nervous at the same time—I loved the drama of the weather, but, unfamiliar with the dangers here, I worried about lightning, flooding, or falling—perhaps all at the same time. My imagination was once again in overdrive.

The hike was beautiful, steep, and varied, as all worthwhile hikes are. Sidling around a corner of the great sandstone knoll to a large arena-like bowl, I dropped to my knees on the rim in awe. I soaked in the splendor of the churning sky, the expanse of red rock, and the Delicate Arch itself, fragile and unlikely as a giant unicorn standing alone in a field.

The weather had greatly thinned the usual sunset crowd. Right in the middle of the rock amphitheater was Mike's tall form, rendered ant-sized by the scope of the place as he set up his shot. I took one picture, two pictures, and then it started raining. *Really* raining.

I pulled back into the shelter of the knoll's crown, wondering what to do. Mike moved his gear back into a more sheltered area and covered it with a plastic hood. I walked down a way and shouted, "It's getting dark. I think I'd better go back. Want to come with me?"

"I have a headlamp. See you at the car." He tossed me the keys.

"Don't get hit by lightning." I left, turning my face into the fierce wind and slicing rain and tightening my thin cardigan around me. There were several photographers remaining besides Mike, none of them moving an inch except to cover their gear with waterproofing.

I felt exultation rise, and my heart sped with excitement as I set out alone.

I've always liked storms. On Kauai, where I grew up, they usually involved wind, rain, and surf. Heavy weather was a frequent visitor to that northernmost of the Hawaiian Islands. On Maui, we don't get enough rain on our side of Haleakalā, so we welcome storms. We seldom wear rain gear, let alone carry umbrellas in Hawaii, so I felt right at home in my skimpy, wet clothing as I walked briskly along the carved stone walkway and around the knoll, the wind supporting me like a friendly helping hand. Farther down, I stopped to take a picture of the path ahead as I trekked down the giant slick-rock slope, creamy and smooth as the side of a vast dinosaur egg.

"You're enjoying this, aren't you?" Another hiker, a man sensibly attired in proper gear, carrying a trekking pole and wearing a parka, had followed me from the arch's dramatic setting.

I smiled at him. "I love storms." I pocketed my camera phone to keep it relatively dry. "We get a lot of them in Hawaii, where I'm from." We hiked the two and a half miles back to the parking lot together, and I enjoyed the company as we chatted about the parks and our travels. We waved goodbye at the lot, and I got into the SUV. I shut the door and turned on the engine to engage the heater. The rain fell in a steady pour outside as darkness fell.

As always, just a little past when I wished he'd return, Mike loomed out of the rain, grinning and unfazed, blue eyes alight, and tossed his backpack of gear into the backseat.

"Did you get the shot?" I asked, handing him a bottled Gatorade.

"I got what I could. That was fun." He pushed his damp hoodie off his silver head and drank deeply.

"The colors are going to be so bright tomorrow after this wash-down," I said.

And in the morning the rocks and desert did shine bright, as every plant sang a song of thanks to the heavenly flush they'd had. We packed to get on the road to Nevada.

THE RASH THAT HAD BEEN PLAGUING ME ON AND OFF THROUGHOUT the trip had worsened overnight and spread to my other hand, burning and stabbing like hot needles. I was intent on packing and checking out of the Moab motel, so it wasn't until we were wolfing down breakfast in town that I showed Mike my hands. "I think the rash is worse."

"What do you want to do about it?"

"It's time to go to a doctor." I'd taken two Benadryls the night before and slathered on cortisone cream twice, only to have the hives multiply, more painful than ever. I was both frustrated and alarmed by the persistence of symptoms. Whatever was going on was becoming chronic; it seemed to me like an allergy, but none of the antihistamine supports were doing a thing.

We searched for an Urgent Care on our phones. There was one in Moab, and an emergency room too, but it didn't open for another two hours.

"Let's get on the road," Mike said. "There are a lot of towns between here and Great Basin National Park, where we're headed next. Someone will have an urgent care."

We drove for hours across barren plains and another unexpected mountain range. I listened to my affirmations recording to stay calm and positive. Mike used his phone to look for doctor's offices, dismayed to find that the one in Moab was the only major one for about three hundred miles in any direction. In a town called Salina, we eventually found one. But inside the lobby, a sign was taped on the door: *"Doc on Vacation."*

At a nearby pharmacy, a woman directed us to a clinic in the next village. We pulled up at another office only to find the door locked, even though the business hours were correct.

I was ready to cry. I bit my lips on bursting out with, "I just want to go home!"

I was having a medical problem while traveling. These things happen to everyone; I had to find a way to handle it without making both of us miserable about a situation that could not be helped. We persisted in looking for treatment because there was no other choice. My hands were not improving on their own nor with anything I'd tried, and the pain was no longer tolerable.

Finally, in the booming metropolis of Delta, Utah (pop. 3554) we found a family clinic that took me as a walk-in. Two hours later I had a new prescription, a totally different diagnosis, and a culture pending. I felt a little better about the situation, in that I'd been doing all I could to deal with what appeared to be a subcutaneous staph infection; hopefully it would improve now that I had the right medication.

We got back on the road for our final hours of driving to Great Basin National Park in Nevada, and after some time on the unspeakably beautiful and empty Route 50 we'd chosen over the more well-trafficked Highway 80 from Salt Lake City, we both began to get our groove back.

I wrote some impressions in my battered spiral notebook as we followed a ruler-straight, two-lane highway through the high desert, with B.B. King's blues keeping us company on the stereo.

Passage across the Great Basin on the Loneliest Road

They call Highway 50 the Loneliest Road, but I think it's the loveliest. It's raining off to the north and heaven's trailing a bridal veil over the plain. Cobalt clefts lie among dusty mustard velvet tea-napkin hills fringed by a border of silky tasseled grass tossing in the wind of our passage.

Salt flats gleam the glossy bone-white of the moon, set off by the smudged turquoise of an inland lake. Cloud shadows race across the open land, an ephemeral dance of light and dark. Ahead, the next range of mountains glow Prussian blue and violet, beacons of snow on their peaks.

The road is so straight that oncoming cars appear gradually, shimmering into being from miles away, mirages coalescing into form. A cop light pulses miles ahead, some poor soul getting a ticket, a visually strident signal that's a discordant note in a country of gold, green, and blue.

A peregrine falcon flies beside us on cushioned wings, white and innocent underneath, stroking the air silently and dropping a bolt of death on the plain.

The wraith column of a dust devil whirls and falls, collapsing as if it never were.

A coyote trots away from roadkill, his coat rough and sides still lean from winter.

There's a carmine-pink shiver as wind ripples the firegrass alongside the gray asphalt. As we ascend a mountain, the clouds are close enough to pluck like silver cotton candy and eat with a taste of rain.

The ridgeline climbs, frozen waves of dark olive stone lashing the lapis sky.

We pass the crumpled glove of a dead squirrel, rolled aside by careless wheels moving too fast.

CHAPTER TWENTY-SEVEN
GREAT BASIN NATIONAL PARK

Nestled on a mountain, Great Basin National Park, Nevada, was unexpected after the long, flat drive through desert on Highway 50. The smell of cypress and pine filled the air. The birds had gone to bed, leaving only the rushing sound of a chilly snowmelt stream and the crackling of burning logs as we made a fire and set up tent camping.

I was utterly content in that moment, sitting on a log, gazing at the fire. A dinner of ribs, corn on the cob, and salad with a mango for dessert settled in my tummy. Cooking over an open campfire gives a unique flavor that makes every bite delicious.

"These are some of the darkest skies in the United States," Mike said. "I've been looking forward to shooting some stars out here."

Kissing him goodbye when he left to find a good spot for his star capture, I was proud that I knew what he meant: there was no light pollution to interfere with the stars' brightness because there were no settlements, anywhere, in any direction.

I looked down at my blotchy, red hands: they were getting better already with the new antibiotic cream. I sighed with relief and gratitude as I settled into my camp chair to write in my journal and watch the flames.

Mike soon returned, and we put out the fire and zipped the door shut on another long but satisfying day.

~

TEMPERATURES, PLEASANT WHEN WE ARRIVED AT THE PARK, TURNED bitterly cold as the night grew deeper. Perhaps the elevation (7500 feet) and nearby patches of snow should have clued us in, but we were unpleasantly surprised. Our sleeping bags were rated for forty degrees; that was nowhere near warm enough, even though we eventually donned multiple pairs of pants, shirts, socks, jackets, and even our boots. Mike and I tossed, turned, and shivered, unable to get comfortable enough to sleep through a well below freezing night.

Exhausted, stiff, and cranky, I only crawled out of the tent the next morning when Mike called that coffee was waiting. He'd gotten the fire going, too. I staggered over to it, fell into my camp chair, and put my frozen boots up on the metal rim of the camp's pit. I wrapped my bloodless hands around the hot mug he handed me.

"I love you," I said, grateful for the coffee and the fire. "What a night from hell."

"That was miserable. I was hoping you were a little warmer than I was. I don't think I ever really slept."

"No," was all I managed to say.

Once the sun came out, though, the park burst forth with the glories of spring. Singing birds of all sorts surrounded us, industrious woodpeckers pounded away, wild turkeys did a mating dance nearby, and deer with fawns wandered through our camp.

We decided to try our luck at fishing in the alpine lakes at the top of the mountain and took a short hike, carrying our fishing poles, into a chilly blue-dark pine forest leading to the glacier (*surprise!* A glacier?) but turned back when a sign informed us there were no fish.

Mike had gone out for a sunrise shoot before I woke up and discovered a mountainside covered with daisies. On the way back from our fruitless hike, he drove me to see them. "You're going to love this."

Acre upon acre of bright yellow black-eyed Susan daisies covered an entire side of a hill studded with silvery granite boulders. Every now and then, a juniper or fir tree added a geometric note—and the moon was still up, smiling in the blue sky above.

I took several pictures, shaking my head at my paltry technology's inability to convey the magic of the scene. Mike tromped off toward the stream below in pursuit of several interesting-looking songbirds to photograph, and I waded through the flowers and sat down on one of the boulders.

Looking out at the sea of yellow blossoms, I wished my mom, Sue, could see this amazing sight. She *loved* daisies. Nothing made her happier than a cheerful bouquet of handpicked roadside blooms.

All of a sudden, I missed her, and Hawaii, and my kids and dogs and sisters and friends.

Overcome with exhaustion from the long cold night and a surfeit of beauty and homesickness, I lay down flat on the boulder and had a good cry.

I'd also begun my monthly during that miserable night—*surprise!* So my underwear was packed with paper towels because I'd forgotten feminine supplies.

I eventually mopped my streaming eyes with my none too clean shirt from yesterday. I sat there, soaking in the sun, until Mike returned.

I pointed to a sign on the road below me, featuring a fat animal shape. "*Marmot Crossing.* What's a marmot, exactly?"

"Some kind of woodchuck, I think." Mike stowed his camera and got in the SUV. I joined him.

"What's a woodchuck?"

Neither of us was sure what that was, either, but our phones had no signal to look it up.

Mike fired up the SUV and we pulled forward, only to see a fat brown animal roughly the dimensions of a beaver, napping asprawl in the sand-graveled road.

"Marmot! Crossing!" I exclaimed.

We looked at each other and burst out laughing.

Mike reached back to grab his camera and stalk the beast, which looked like a giant guinea pig in buff and brown with a brushy whisk of a tail. The marmot let him get about twenty feet from it before it leapt to its feet and waddled rapidly away, ducking into a hole beside the road. We continued on and met several more marmots, either lying in the road sunbathing or spread like fat fur rugs over boulders.

We'd read that there were some very intricate underground caves to explore at Great Basin, so we decided to go to the visitor center and see about a meal and one of the ranger-led tours of the caves. I looked up *marmot* on my phone using their Wi-Fi, because, even having met several, I still wasn't sure what they were.

Turns out that we'd flushed a Great Basin yellow-bellied marmot, a subspecies of ground squirrel, of which there are thirty-five subtypes. These were not small animals: they were twenty pounds or more of big-ass guinea pig cousin with a tail, and they were waking up from hibernation and enjoying the sunshine as much as we were.

The underground Lehman Caves at Great Basin were a surprise, too.

After the humid spring sunshine, the cool, damp environment of the caves felt good. A scent like mushrooms and lemon water surrounded us as we walked a sloping path approximately eighty feet down into a maze of limestone caverns.

We didn't go through the whole two miles of caves, due to some passageway repairs being undergone, but enjoyed the unusually rich formations, dense with stalactites, stalagmites, popcorn, and shield formations as the ranger leading us pointed them out. Experiencing the absolute pitch darkness when our guide asked us to turn out our lights was an exercise in sensory deprivation. The dark felt like a substance, Jell-O-like, encasing me. I immediately lost touch with my extremities and felt dizzy and disoriented. *Would blindness be like this?*

Sanity wouldn't last long if I were locked up alone somewhere in the dark, and I decided to include cave or lava tube settings in some of my upcoming books. (Recent thrillers *Wired Dawn* and *Wired Ghost* have underground lava tube scenes based on my experiences.)

We broke camp and got on the road after lunch, with another long drive ahead, 387 miles to Carson City, Nevada.

Back on the Loneliest Road for a while, Mike pulled the car over at my shrieks of excitement. "Wild horses! Wild horses!"

A black stallion, head and tail high, stood on a grassy knoll, watching over a herd of peacefully grazing mares and foals.

We whipped a U-turn and drove back to get closer so we could try to get a picture of the horses, pulling off onto the shoulder of the road.

The stallion was having none of it once he spotted us. He whistled up the herd, racing down to join them and circling to bunch them together. We were treated to the sight of the band galloping away, the mares clustered protectively around long-legged foals, all of them raising a flurry and causing the ground to shake with their thundering hooves.

We rolled slowly along the road, in no way pursuing, but staying parallel.

The stallion turned to face us as soon as we stopped our vehicle. He mock-charged us, eyeing us down, his tail raised and mane flying as he stomped his feet and neighed to warn us off. He seemed quite capable of charging the SUV and taking us on.

Mike backed up respectfully onto the asphalt.

The Black (because that's what he immediately became to me, a fictional stallion I'd loved obsessively as a girl) neighed and stomped one more time, then whirled and galloped off after his family, taking them inland and out of sight in a swirl of dust.

These things can still happen on the Loneliest Road.

CHAPTER TWENTY-EIGHT
THE CARSON RIVER AREA

I had a memory of Carson City that kept us driving well past the point of discomfort, all three hundred and eighty-seven miles from Great Basin, Utah.

In this memory, I was twenty-two, and seven months pregnant with our son Caleb. We had spent a romantic weekend in a great big Victorian bed-and-breakfast, surrounded by towering lilac bushes, and we fished the streams surrounding the area. There was even a photo anchoring this memory in our family album: me in front of the bright green Volkswagen Karmann Ghia we drove back then, grinning like a jack-o'-lantern and holding a stringer of trout draped over my giant belly. "Oh, Carson City is so beautiful," I rhapsodized. "Maybe we can even find that darling B&B and get some breakfast there or something!"

However, the place we rolled up to late in the night was not the cute Victorian village I'd mythologized in the annals of memory from thirty years before. The real Carson City, Nevada, was large, modern, and gritty—a series of frighteningly tacky casino/hotel combos and big-box stores.

Mike was particularly disenchanted, as we'd gone through an

arduous process getting Nevada fishing licenses at a roadside casino, and he'd hoped that "the lakes all around on the map" would be good to explore.

We were crushed with exhaustion and disappointment by the time we found a room at a motel and crawled into hard beds with rough sheets. But at least the room was warm and we had showers, an improvement over camping in subfreezing temperatures the night before.

Mike left early the next morning to ascertain if the area was indeed as lacking in charm and activities as our first impression. He returned at seven-thirty a.m. to find that I was up and packed, wicking a Lipton tea bag up and down in a Styrofoam cup and trying to get it to flavor lukewarm water from the room's carafe.

"Nothing here," he said grumpily, confirming my worst suspicions.

We hardly spoke as we left; I did some research on my phone and discovered that the location I'd "remembered" as Carson City was actually Placerville, a quaint gold rush town halfway between Sacramento and Lake Tahoe.

"I remembered wrong," I said.

"No kidding." Mike was still grumpy.

"I was correct about everything else," I said. "Just not the name of the town."

"Wouldn't have made much difference. We still had to do that drive, and there wasn't much to see or do after Great Basin."

"The hope of it kept us going, though. That was a really long day."

"Maybe today will be better."

And it was. Half an hour after we left Carson City, we discovered Lake Tahoe's immense, deep blue presence over a nearby ridge.

We bought new California fishing licenses at a fly fishing shop whose helpful employee directed us to Markleeville, on the Carson River, and a little place called Sorensen's All-Season Resort. "Great fishing and cute cabins," he told us.

THE CARSON RIVER OUTSIDE OF TAHOE WAS A FAST-MOVING TOPAZ joy to fish. We started casting by a bridge, later hiking across a meadow thick with new grass forcing its way through last season's snow-burnt dead mulch. Tiny purple crocuses enhanced a riverbank studded with silver-shot granite boulders, and willows were budding over clear water that glowed golden in the back swirls behind rocks or in shadows undercutting the bank—places where hungry trout waited.

Meadow larks and swallows darted and called, flying intricate patterns around our heads, while a pair of plovers, alarmed by our proximity to their nest, began an elaborate injury-related drama to draw us away. Off in the distance, jagged snowy peaks reminded us that winter had only recently surrendered her grip on this area.

I tried a variety of lures, but the one the fish were biting was a small, gold, barbless Panther Martin, with a slow reel and slight jigging motion as if the lure were a temptingly injured minnow. To challenge myself, I tried to aim accurately on the cast, landing just short of the opposite bank, behind a rock outcropping or under a branch.

Clambering over rocks, rolling up my pants and taking off my shoes to ford feeder streams—all of it induced a mental peace that reminded me that we were born for being in nature, not apart from it. I could hear my ancestors, still alive in my DNA, rising up and crying, "Yes!" They made their presence known in the deftness of my hands, in the silence of my steps, in the accuracy of my cast, reveling in being alive again.

I never noticed them, these unknown forebears, quite as much as I did outside in nature. That makes sense when I think about who they were: hardy intellectuals who lived outdoor lives. Teachers, missionaries, entrepreneurs, town founders, explorers: tough, adaptable, intelligent folk who succeeded in difficult times.

I hope to write someday about the ones who went before: those resilient ancestors who survived long enough to pass along their genes (particularly here in the United States where everyone but the Native Americans are immigrants) and gave us the foundation of who we are today. If we get in touch with the grit that made us, their fortitude and drive could help us solve the complex problems we face, like climate change, in the twenty-first century.

After we settled into our cabin at Sorensen's, a sweet collection of cottages clustered around a central restaurant, Mike took off for more exploring and I settled in to absorb the atmosphere. I spent the afternoon in a hammock, watching the new spring leaves of quaking aspen shiver in the light breeze overhead, and thought about not much.

I eventually went into our cabin and napped in a good bed with great sheets.

I woke up and stared at the hand-plastered ceiling of the cabin and thought some more about not much.

I looked over at my laptop and battered notebook and thought about writing but had nothing to say. Instead, I snuggled in bed and read a wonderful book of Southwestern nature essays I'd bought myself as a treat at the Canyonlands Park gift shop: *The Anthropology of Turquoise* by Ellen Meloy. Her funny, challenging, lyrical nature essays absorbed me for the afternoon. I learned much about the flora, fauna, and geology of the area and found a kindred spirit in the sensitive, quirky Meloy with her keen powers of observation.

Looking on the back flap for the "about the author" section, I was shocked to discover that she had passed away in 2004. Meloy's literary voice was so immediate and engaging that she felt alive to me, like a friend I'd hoped to continue getting to know through her writing. She had grabbed my heart in her fist through her beautiful, passionate descriptions of the unique nature of the Southwest; I was changed because of reading them.

I felt a pang of deep grief, and tears sprang to my eyes.

Holding the little volume of essays in my hands, I was shaken by a small but profound personal earthquake. This was the kind of writer I wanted to be: someone whose voice on the page was so fresh, vital and compelling, that it became a form of eternity.

CHAPTER TWENTY-NINE
MARKLEEVILLE AND WRAP-UP

Mike blew in as dark fell. He grinned at the sight of me, tucked in bed with my book. "I turned the heater on," I said, by way of fulfilling my wifely duties.

He laughed, plonking a stringer of fish into the tiny sink. "I wondered what you'd be doing. I thought, maybe Toby will make up the fire in the fireplace or start dinner. Then I thought, *nope*. She'll be in bed with her book, and the heater on." He knew me that well, yet still he loved me.

"You're welcome to join me. The bed is excellent." I arched one eyebrow suggestively—my favorite party trick. "But you have to clean up first."

He came over, growling and pretending to grab me with his fishy hands, making me squawk—but then kissed me instead, and headed for the shower.

~

IT FELT LIKE UTTER LUXURY THAT WE HAD ANOTHER WHOLE DAY AT the cabin before we had to drive back to the Bay Area, spend a few days visiting family, and then fly home to Maui. I went fishing with

Mike in the morning but spent the afternoon alone at the cabin, watching the resident marmot that lived under the porch, and mining my journal for some nuggets of insight from the trip.

1. **Pick well when you marry.** All other decisions, like education, jobs, where to live, what to do—none will have as much impact on overall happiness as who you choose for your life partner. Yes, partners can be traded in or swapped out, but not without some damage along the way.

2. **You don't actually need much stuff.** I discovered that one carry-on and a little backpack can hold all I really need to get through a whole month of living—and probably the rest of my life.

3. **Nature is essential to joy.** Humans weren't designed to spend our days cooped up in cubicles and our nights locked in buildings. Walking along paths, fording streams, swimming, climbing, sitting and watching, exploring and discovering . . . these activities are in our genome.

4. **Creating art is a way we can live forever.** Mike and I were feeling our age on this trip—but our words and images will outlive us to inspire for years to come.

5. **Take care of your body so you can really live in it.** The body is our vehicle to experience. It's hard to do anything when you aren't physically healthy, and as best we can, we must take responsibility to keep that engine running.

6. **At any given moment, really be in the moment.** I learned to turn off busy mind chatter, to use all of my senses to be present in whatever moment and place I was in—looking through the bug-spattered windshield at desert streaming by, sitting on the sun-warmed sandstone shoulder of a giant formation, standing in line at Walmart. I learned to concentrate and focus any or all of my senses to have a deeper experience of each individual moment of

what remains of my life. (This will also be good for my writing.)

7. **Sharing your experience or adventure with others deepens it.** Choosing to write about and photograph this trip to share it was an ongoing discipline—yet I found it helped me deepen my experience to write about the day. I noticed more as I looked for moments and elements that would be interesting or moving to write about. Being alert for pictures to take enhanced, not detracted from, my own experience. In writing about what we did, I embedded my memories more deeply. Creating this book is a way I crystallized those memories, polished and honed them, and I reexperienced them by sharing them.

CHAPTER THIRTY
SEATTLE OR BUST

Two years later, we continued our National Parks exploration, taking our second major road trip.

We'd planned this journey as a month-long route beginning in Seattle, driving and taking ferries all the way up to Alaska, then looping back to the United States through British Columbia, finishing up in Olympic National Park and the San Juan Islands before heading back to Seattle.

After the plague of the mysterious rash on our adventure, I went through a long, arduous diagnostic process to get to the bottom of what was causing it. I'd explored every option available through our health insurance, including a consultation with an allergy specialist in California; but it was a naturopath on Maui who did the blood testing that uncovered the substances I was having histamine reactions to.

We discovered that a host of foods and additives caused a histamine reaction (allergy) that presented as hives. The hives had become inflamed with a secondary bacterial infection under the skin on our Southwest trip.

I now had a long list of foods, drink, and additives to avoid. I had done so, and the rash was finally under control.

After that fateful annual physical, I'd been on a mission to reclaim my health, become more fit, and lower my stress so that I could go into the second half of my life with more energy.

I'd lost twenty-five pounds since our first trip by avoiding my allergy foods. My skin was now clear, and I was limber, with much more stamina. "The proof of the pudding is in the eating," they say, and my pudding had fewer ingredients now. We don't know why I suddenly developed reactions to things I'd been fine with for years, but the doctor who finally unlocked the puzzle suspected it was the change in hormones as I went into menopause.

"I've seen this before," the naturopath said. A tanned guy who looked like a young Jack LaLanne, he was not someone I'd have sought out when I was trying to be 'normal,' until nothing traditional Western medicine had to offer provided answers. "The allergies may back off after you're on the other side of menopause. It's something to hope for."

I was so miserable I'd have done anything—even give up *coffee*, which turned out to be one of my histamine reaction foods.

A word about becoming a tea drinker: I was a reluctant convert.

I loved coffee. I mean, really loved it, and had my entire adult life. I liked the smell. The preparation ritual in the morning. I even loved the little green trees with their glossy leaves that grow so well in Hawaii; the red berries and the crunchy brown beans you could eat covered in chocolate. But somehow, in the way of the weird body chemistry problems I'd developed, it had become one of my main allergy triggers.

I'd been "off" coffee for a year, and I missed it. At home, Mike made his morning pot super early so I wouldn't smell it perking and moan and groan with longing. Occasionally, I'd indulge in a cup to see if I was still allergic—and, within hours, I'd develop that familiar rash around my lips and on my hands.

I was much healthier than on our first trip, but my transformation was the result of dogged and persistent pursuit of answers, and some of those answers had come through reclaiming things I'd experienced growing up wild on Kauai. I'd returned to that lush and powerful island to uncover answers about diet as medicine, by attending a ten-day yoga lifestyle retreat at an organic farm in Anahola called Hale Pule ("House of Prayer," in Hawaiian).

The experience had begun with a daunting e-mail three weeks before my departure date: *"Please prepare for your retreat by ceasing all alcohol, smoking, and other substances, refined flour/sugar, meat, and caffeine, so you don't spend your retreat time in withdrawal from these things."*

Mike was out of town when I quit everything, which made it a little easier to withstand temptation, but I still had to undergo withdrawals from everything but smoking—and it was ugly. Somehow, I soldiered through with only a few falls off the wagon and arrived at Hale Pule's lush Kauai grounds in the shadow of Sleeping Giant outside of Anahola, grumpy from caffeine withdrawal, apprehensive, but determined.

Myra Lewin, the head of Hale Pule, was a radiant woman somewhere between sixty and eighty. She and her assistants, two lovelies both coincidentally named Kelsey, welcomed me and showed me to a cozy little hut that would be my home for the next ten days.

The schedule was not for the faint of heart: we rose at 4:30 a.m., did a Vedic fire ceremony with chanting in the yoga studio at 5:00, meditation for an hour until 6:15, then a yoga class until 7:30, and finally breakfast—before doing assigned work on the farm.

Once that was done, free time until lunch, and again in the afternoon.

Meals were highly anticipated events that took hours to prepare. Myra, her staff, I, and the WWOOF (Worldwide Opportunities on Organic Farms) farm workers, or "woofers" for short, gathered to reverently partake of unbelievably fresh organic meals seasoned by nature, Ayurvedic herbs, and sunshine, carefully prepared to maximize nutrition.

Ayurvedic eating is all about strengthening the digestive system (*agni*), which is seen as the source of health. When the body is digesting and benefiting from healthy food, it naturally wants to heal and support itself and can handle various stresses better.

The Ayurvedic lifestyle emphasizes balance in all things. My health problems were seen in this perspective as being "out of balance," with too much *pitta*, or fire element; so, in the afternoons I had treatments, mostly wonderful hot oil rubs, that were designed to calm my fire and help me restore balance—which was exactly what I was craving.

Improvement took a while, however.

I had a horrible first night in my little hut without any chemical sleep aids (which I'd been taking for years), and I had a nightmare that I was dying when I finally did fall asleep. I staggered through the next day, hardly able to stay awake, but was advised not to take a nap because we were working on restoring my natural, unforced circadian rhythm.

The next day and night were better, but still extremely hard. I was anxious, exhausted, and achy, and there was no chemical or other escape. All the sitting cross-legged and upright, from meditation to meals, was killing my (weak) back, and there was no aspirin to be had. I longed for escape, some easier softer way, but there was no way out but to go on.

Nuggets of goodness and insight began to emerge by Day 3.

I loved the farm work. Being among the plants felt restorative. I became interested in the others there with me—I was the only one on a personal retreat, but the four yoga-practicing farm workers, there on a work-for-trade situation, were incredibly thoughtful, beautiful young people that welcomed me as one of the oldest people on the property (besides Myra). Next to them, I felt like a barnacle-encrusted booze bottle washed up on the beach among beautiful shells: lumpy and uncoordinated during yoga class, unable to sit through meditation hour. My inner light (if I even had one) had been obscured by years of mental and physical scar tissue.

Vanity died as I gave up makeup, shaving, and any sort of hair styling—what was the point? I was stripped to my chubby, nondescript, fifty-something essence. Degrees and accomplishments meant nothing in this setting. I cried randomly—during yoga class, during yard work, during meditation—and didn't know why. "It's just energy that's been stuck moving around," Myra assured me, which was comforting.

With my remaining will, I resolved that, no matter what I was challenged with, I would say YES, and fall forward in the direction of trust.

Night 3 I was rewarded by a full, blissful, chemical-free night's sleep. And then on Day 4, I woke up at 4:30 a.m. feeling ready for the day, WITHOUT the alarm! I was completely off all my medications and supplements for the first time in forever.

But the real change happened on Day 5, when my cognitive functions came back online. I was suddenly inspired to work on my memoir during free time, a project I'd brought along but had little hope of actually tackling.

Day 6 I went to the beach alone and walked vigorously and swam (on top of the already rigorous schedule), testing my energy level—and it was steady and strong throughout the day, without the highs and lows of my previous pattern.

Day 7 I got the complete plot of the next *Wired* novel downloaded into my brain during meditation hour and had to run out and frantically write it down in my journal in the fifteen minutes before yoga class started.

I loved the meditation because I wasn't told to empty my mind or do a mantra. Instead, propped against a wall because of my back, in the sandalwood predawn dark I prayed, listened, and Spirit gave great ideas.

Day 8 an allergy rash erupted—but in a place where it had never been before, and looking different than usual. I was crushed at this "defeat," and went to Myra for a consultation.

"Did you eat any fruit?" Myra asked, her sea-blue eyes concerned. Slender and flexible with wonderful skin and luxuriant, long silver hair, Myra's what I'd love to look like in my latter years—and she can do a headstand, too.

"Yes, but not any of my allergy fruits," I said. Testing had showed histamine reactions to pineapple and cranberry, as well as to a host of other things. "I only ate papaya."

"Did you test for papaya?"

"No." That hadn't been on the food test, no doubt created on the Mainland somewhere. "But I ate a lot of papaya growing up."

"No more papaya for you. Here's some salve, and we'll cool you down with aloe juice at meals."

At Hale Pule, I learned a new way to deal with my rash without cortisone cream—and also that fruit was probably not my friend, at least while my digestive tract and gut biome were rebuilding. Healthwise, things continued to improve. The day I left, I dressed in the same clothes I'd worn ten days earlier for the plane, and they hung on me. My skin felt soft and dewy from all the oil rubs and clean living. My hair was bouncy, my eyes bright, and I felt an inner calm.

"You're glowing," said Julie, the family friend who picked me up from the retreat and took me to the airport.

At home, I continued to implement the changes I'd committed to following. I did my own yoga routine in the living room. Then I'd eat a simple breakfast, walk the dog, and write—and not until I got at least a thousand words completed on my current work in progress did I open e- mail or social media. Burnout and extra weight sloughed off like old skin, and emotionally, I felt healed from some of the extreme diet and lifestyle things I'd gone through growing up.

I'd made peace with the colonics and food elimination diets Mom had put us on. I saw what they were in a new light, appreciated the good intentions behind them, and even implemented some of them for myself.

I wasn't wedded to "normal" anymore, and it was a good thing.

Insights I gleaned from the retreat:

1. *A consistent routine calms anxiety, depression, lack of focus, and mood/physical symptoms.* Set up a daily schedule that includes reflection time, regular meals, physical activity, time with others, etc., and stick to it.
2. *No (phone or other) electronics until after daily writing and breakfast* to minimize timewasters and distractions and increase productivity.
3. *Simple, natural, nourishing, easy-to-digest foods* can help the body heal itself. As the digestive tract improves, inflammation decreases.
4. *Your body WANTS to be healthy and whole.* Use intuition AND science to listen for its inner wisdom.
5. *Don't be afraid to take some risks in your quest* for answers, especially if the risks are in a healthy direction: i.e., giving up caffeine, refined sugar/flour, meat, diet soda, alcohol and substances, and over-the-counter medications. Maybe you won't even need further intervention if you do that.
6. *Slow down. Be present for more moments of your life* by turning off the noise and cutting back on activities. Let the brain wander. Sometimes it needs a rest.
7. *Renew your circadian rhythm/sleep pattern* through regular daily exercise, no napping, finishing eating, drinking, and electronics by 6 pm, and going to bed by 9 pm. Tough the first few days, but then . . . Nothing like a good night's rest!
8. *Spend time working and playing in nature* every day. This will renew both mind and body. Humans did not evolve indoors.
9. *Treat food and mealtime with respect*, because food is medicine and the body's building blocks. When talking with others, stop eating and talk. Then, eat while they are talking, or just take your time for the whole meal. Don't shovel in mouthfuls of food while talking—neither activity is quality if you do.
10. *How to lose weight and stay slim forever:* Serve yourself no more than two handfuls of food (no matter what kind it is) and

chew every bite until liquid. Stop when you first feel a slight pressure in your tummy, the "first burp." **You will never eat too much again if you stick to this method.** *The burp is a signal that your stomach is full. If you ignore it, letting out the burp and continuing to eat, the stomach makes a little more room and expands past what it really needs.*

11. **Waste time gloriously, not passively, on occasion.** *You'll know the difference—one afternoon on the retreat, I lay on a blanket under a flowering avocado tree buzzing with bees and read a vampire romance. It was glorious, not passive, time wastage.*

12. **Curious about something?** *Follow that feeling and dig deeper. Curiosity leads to creative ideas, and creativity to fun and abundance.*

13. **Sit in silence** *(preferably dark) and pray, breathe, imagine, and let the mind wander and settle. If it gets too busy, go to paying attention to the breath and counting slow inhales and exhales. This is a hugely beneficial practice for the whole body, not just the brain.*

◦≈◦

TRAVELING WAS GOING TO BE A CHALLENGE TO THESE PRINCIPLES, BUT I vowed to do what I could to maintain my commitment to health.

Departure from our home on Maui went smoothly, with friends Ken and Cindy arriving to housesit. The dogs were excited to get plenty of attention from this canine-loving couple, and Mike and I left a little early, eager to get our trip through the Pacific Northwest underway.

My new health program was put to the test before we even left Maui, as I sat down in a booth at the airport restaurant for breakfast. I perused the menu and was dismayed to find almost everything on it contained "forbidden" foods.

I'd known that this kind of situation would be an issue; I just hadn't anticipated it so soon. The waiter, a kind Filipino man, helped me talk through the choices on the menu until we figured something out that I could eat.

He ended up bringing me a plain bowl of lettuce and an unadorned burger patty, since I couldn't have sugar, eggs, coffee, or dairy.

I stared down at my unappetizing meal, then glanced over at Mike digging into a large, cheese-laden chili omelet.

"How many times is this scenario going to play out in the next thirty days? I hate being that fussy customer. I hate it," I said passionately.

Mike reached over and laid his warm hand over mine. "I know you do."

The compassion in his eyes made me cry. I snuffled briefly into my paper napkin—Mike believed in and supported me. He knew I didn't like needing special attention and hated having "something wrong" with me, and that helped lift the onerousness and embarrassment of my restrictions a little bit.

The flight to Seattle was smooth and mellow. We watched a movie on a rented tablet, sharing the earbuds like a couple of teenagers. I noticed how blue Mike's eyes were. I hadn't noticed that in a long time.

Something about traveling together, outside of our usual routines, made me more aware of all the little details that had drawn me to him thirty-plus years ago: the shape of his shoulders, one of them made of titanium now. His long, strong legs. His rugged, skillful hand, and how it looked and felt, holding mine.

As we descended into Seattle, I was impressed by the majestic, snow bedecked, volcanic mountains all around the city. Arterial waters, lakes, and possibly the ocean were all swirling in a mysterious blue mist around the sprawling metropolis, and it was still sunny and bright at eight p.m. "I had no idea this place was so gorgeous!"

"That mountain," Mike said, pointing at Mount Rainier, a

singular snowcapped peak framed by the plane's window. "Wow."

We were picked up from the airport in a hotel shuttle van driven by a Mr. Singh. He wore a large lavender turban and, after dropping us off at a Ramada Inn, bobbed his head with dignity to our thanks and tip.

Our room smelled of cherry rug cleaner and was decorated in clashing multiple patterns. We could see high-rises in the distance, what must be the heart of Seattle, but we were in an area that looked like typical American urban sprawl: multilane thoroughfares bordered by nondescript strip malls, with an occasional scrawny tree to break things up.

At nine-thirty p.m., we walked along the slowly darkening road looking for somewhere to eat. We passed a brightly lit doorway in one of the strip malls that seemed like a restaurant, but as we approached, we discovered it was a religious gathering of some kind, to judge by the signage in unfamiliar writing over the door. Everyone exiting was dark-skinned and wore light-colored, draped clothing. Scarves were wrapped gracefully around the women's heads. I was a little disoriented by having no idea what country the tall, slender people streaming out of the building were from, or even what religion they practiced.

We eventually found an open restaurant in another strip mall and went in: Juba was a convivial place with a welter of foreign voices chatting while semi-watching a large TV in the corner. I picked up the slightly greasy, laminated plastic menu and, once again, looked for something I could eat with my many allergies.

So far, we were the only white people I'd seen since we'd left the airport, and I wished I'd read up on Seattle more. I'd had no idea it was so multicultural. We have many races in Hawaii, and I recognize all of them: I know how to navigate situations with Japanese, Koreans, Hawaiians, Chinese, Tongans, Micronesians, Filipinos, Caucasians, and blends of all of the above. I know their dialects and foods.

Here in this ethnic corner of Seattle, however, I was clueless—an uncomfortable but fascinating feeling.

The friendly waiter approached, but repeatedly nixed our attempts to order things from the menu. "No more. We don't have that today."

"What do you have left?" I finally asked.

He had goat meat, and beef something-or-other. We ordered that, along with pasta and pita, which were words we could recognize.

I'd never eaten any sort of African food before except an Ethiopian dinner prepared by our friend Jody Brown on Maui, who was an adventurous cook. Juba's East African cuisine was entirely new, and everything the waiter brought us was delicious. My beef dish came with flat bread and a thin soup and was basically a pile of chopped, spiced steak.

I made little tacos out of the flat bread and dipped them in the soup, while Mike chewed on a hind leg of goat along with a towering pile of thin, spicy, red spaghetti. The mango smoothie he'd ordered was amazing: a sweet, tangy blend of real mangoes and probably tons of sugar. It tasted better than any mango smoothie I'd ever had in Hawaii and was only a couple of dollars.

I looked around as we ate. There were no women in the restaurant, not even waiting tables or working in the kitchen. "Where are all the ladies?"

Mike shrugged. "Maybe they're home with the kids."

Probably. It was almost ten p.m., and the women I'd glimpsed coming out of the religious gathering had been traditionally dressed.

Walking back to the Ramada, holding hands as we looked for stars in a sky that had finally surrendered to sunset well after ten p.m., we passed a grocery store with signs posted in many languages and gazed into a lit barbershop filled with people talking in foreign voices that reminded me of bright confetti floating on the air.

If this had been Maui, it would all have been shut up tight hours ago. The adventure had officially begun.

CHAPTER THIRTY-ONE
SQUAMISH, BRITISH COLUMBIA

Mike left early the next morning via taxi to pick up the van we'd rented for the month as I contemplated my carry-on bag in the Ramada Inn. What was appropriate to wear for a day of upscale socializing in downtown Seattle, ending in a cabin somewhere in British Columbia by the close of day?

I decided to wear my new Columbia hiking T-shirt and my first-ever pair of ripstop nylon hiking pants with zip-off legs, along with a cardigan and a bright scarf to dress it up. I put on the outfit, turned to and fro, and felt official: a real traveler, wearing multipurpose clothing.

I'd never worn high-tech hiking clothes before, and the pants sounded slithery when I moved. I whisked and swished, but the outfit, dressed up with the scarf, looked professional.

Mike returned with the van, and we drove into the city to meet three of my writer friends in Seattle for breakfast. Kim Hornsby and Christine Fairchild wrote suspense novels, and my daughter's childhood friend, Heather, was also a writer. We talked books while I had a delicious Mexican concoction with avocados substituted for eggs. After breakfast, we said goodbye to Kim and Christine. Mike, Heather, and I drove to the fabulous Chihuly Garden and Glass museum, where another writer friend had bought tickets and left them as a gift for us.

Dale Chihuly, who looks like a real-life pirate, is a pioneer in the art of glass. In 1968, after receiving a Fulbright Fellowship, he went to work at the Venini glass factory in Venice. There, he observed a team approach to blowing glass, which became a critical element of his conceptual art process. His work is set apart by enormous, organic shapes in every color of the rainbow. Chihuly cofounded the Pilchuck Glass School in Washington in 1971, and since the founding of this international glass center, Chihuly has led the world in the advancement of glass fine art. His work is included in more than 200 museum collections worldwide. He has been the recipient of many awards, including twelve honorary doctorates and two fellowships from the National Endowment for the Arts. Seattle's Chihuly Garden and Glass is the most extensive permanent exhibit of his work, encompassing an entire building and its grounds near the famous Space Needle.

The little pamphlet accompanying the tickets contained a Chihuly quote: "I want people to be overwhelmed with light and color in a way they've never experienced." Basking in a flood of brilliant light that shone through the graceful glass forms in a ceiling installation overhead, I felt rinsed, as if I'd dived into a spectrum waterfall.

Pictures just don't do the Chihuly facility justice, but Mike and I took a lot of them anyway, compelled to try to capture the otherworldly experience of the museum.

If you only have time to do one thing in Seattle, visit the Chihuly Garden and Glass!

~

WE WERE ON THE ROAD OUT OF SEATTLE AT LAST, WITH "CLASSIC Vinyl" rock playing on the rental van's satellite radio. Getting out of the city by two p.m. had been hectic, but with Lady Google the GPS to guide us, the navigation was relatively painless. The large van we'd rented for the month had a smooth ride, a juicy engine, and, most importantly, a roomy back area for sleeping in.

As we went farther north into bear country, I didn't want to sleep anywhere, like a tent, that those beasties could get into.

I was determined, however, not to let fear get the better of me—a premise for both of the road trips. I wanted to rediscover the brave girl I'd been, and while I'd made progress on that quest, I still had a long way to go. I have two animal phobias: cattle and bears. If you read *Freckled*, there's a story in that book that describes how this phobia got started.

Bears, while I'd never been exposed to them, had been generalized by my brain as extra smelly, jumbo-sized cattle with claws and fangs—*not good*. Extrapolating from there, cows at least were usually fenced. Bears? They could be anywhere and get into anything, in the regions where we were headed. Having a hard-sided shelter to sleep in gave me a little more peace of mind, and Mike was willing to accommodate my worries. "Last thing we need is you tossing and turning and poking me all night because you think there's a bear outside," he said.

We were behind schedule when we got out of Seattle, though, so by the time we got to Bellingham, Washington, where we were picking up a load of preordered camping gear, we didn't have as much time as we'd planned to spend with my friend, novelist and fellow Hawaii lover Janet Oakley. Janet and I talked writing as we roamed the aisles of the sporting goods store with a shopping cart, looking for the right rain jacket, bug spray, paper towels, butane fuel, and more.

The van finally loaded with supplies, we bid Janet goodbye and headed for the ominous-sounding town of Squamish, somewhere outside Vancouver.

All was well until we hit the Canadian border, where we lost our beloved Lady Google and the Verizon data plan on our phones stopped working.

That meant navigating the old-fashioned way: buying and checking a map, looking for badly marked street signs, and generally getting lost and annoyed near the end of an exciting but energy-draining day. Americans heading north—*buy a Canada data plan ahead of time!*

Still, considering the challenges, we didn't do too badly making our way through Vancouver, a very clean city but with oddly angled glass windows on the high-rises that had a jarring visual effect.

"It's like all of the buildings were designed as a nineteen-fifties take on what mid-twentieth century architecture should look like," I said.

Mike speculated more practically that a single contractor with a lot of glass to get rid of had won a bid to do the whole city. Many find it attractive, I'm sure, but something about Vancouver's architecture seemed odd to our visual palates.

Once outside of Vancouver, Highway 99 was a sensuous, sultry ribbon unwinding along lush mountains overlooking a stretch of water lit with the dim gold of an extended sunset.

A bald eagle flew by. Veils of blue mist teased us with glimpses of layered views of mountains still robed in snow, while fiery light stroked over the glassy water before us. As the day waned in an extended foreplay of extravagant beauty, we drove along a road bordered by harsh cement girders with no turnouts, pullouts, vista points, or other places to capture the stunning sunset.

Only another photographer can fully appreciate the palpable frustration of driving along a stunning stretch of road with a fantastic sunset happening and being unable to get the shot. Mike pulled off the shoulder several times, defying death to run across the freeway with his camera in hand, but it was an exercise in futility.

Mike was growling with frustration by the time the sun went down. "I'm writing the Canadian tourist board," he said, only half-joking. "I'm an unsatisfied customer."

"Just be here now," I said, quoting Ram Dass as much to myself as to him. "Let's try to remember it."

He shook his head. We'd both noticed how hard it was to remember things as we aged. Our photography serves as a shorthand to access those memories.

I couldn't quite believe that Canada was a foreign country; other than the weird windows in Vancouver, it felt like home. But without the GPS working, the cabin we were supposed to be staying in was highly elusive in the dark, and we were hungry. We stopped at a casino outside of Squamish for dinner and directions. Without our phones working, even that was difficult—not just for us but for the waitress trying to help by drawing a map on a napkin.

We'd had quite a journey from the Chihuly and lunch at the Space Needle, to the log cabin we eventually found and settled into in the wildwood of British Columbia. As we dropped into our bed in the cabin, we looked at each other in weary triumph. "We made it!"

One day down, twenty-nine more to go.

CHAPTER THIRTY-TWO
SQUAMISH TO LIL'WAT, BRITISH COLUMBIA

I woke to find Mike gone, scouting for fishing and photography opportunities in a preternaturally early dawn after a strangely late sunset now that it was midsummer. We were heading so far north that, when we reached Alaska, we'd only have a couple of hours of real darkness per day.

I enjoyed getting up at my own speed. If we were a caveman couple, I'd be warming up the pot of roots and grains over the fire, and he'd be off catching game to eat.

Instead, I did the morning routine I'd developed in the last two years as a way of recovering my health: meditation, five sun salutations, making tea, and journaling.

I'd decided to make blog posts out of my journal entries along the way to keep my readers engaged, though I wasn't working on fiction books during the trip.

Another major area of growth in the last two years, besides my health, was my writing. I'd added considerably to my library of books written, from five in my first series to close to twenty in two related series (Paradise Crime Mystery and Thrillers). I'd doubled our income from royalties, bringing us to a comfortable place financially. Blogging the journey justified charging the trip to book research, which it most definitely was.

I still had a small, private therapy practice back on Maui, one day a week when I saw clients and kept the dust from collecting on my licensure—but I'd worked through a lot of the guilt and angst about leaving my career in the Department of Education. Readers swore my stories helped them in new ways, and I was learning to be content with that.

And even one day a week as a therapist taxed my soul on a deep level.

ONE OF MY NEWEST CLIENTS WAS THIRTEEN YEARS OLD. A provocatively dressed pocket Venus, rounded and golden, Hoku had a mouth like a split plum and highly sexualized behavior that made it hard to see her as the child she was.

She had been referred to me after bouncing out of the offices of several therapists on Maui, and I coordinated with her school counselor, too, so she couldn't tell each of us different stories. She had an Axis II diagnosis of Borderline Personality Disorder, a stubborn and intractable addiction to personal drama that's notoriously resistant to treatment.

None of it was her fault.

Witness to domestic abuse, abandoned by an alcoholic father who was in and out of prison, at age twelve Hoku had been violently raped by a forty-year-old neighbor, who was now rattling around the local parks, out on a technicality and awaiting trial, at which Hoku was going to have to testify. The perp was probably doing shit to other homeless people, let alone any little girls he could get his hands on, and that he wasn't safely in jail ate at my stomach.

I'd been working with Hoku for several months, and it was eight months since her discharge from the hospital on Oahu where she'd spent six months for a suicide attempt following the rape. Each week, our sessions were filled with tales of sexual exploits with boys at school, running away from home, fights with other girls, drugs, and cutting herself.

The more I tried to reflect choices or present alternatives to these self-destructive behaviors, the more agitated Hoku became. "You just don't understand, Ms. Toby!" she yelled, when I tried to help her problem-solve about what she could do differently. "Stop lecturing me!"

She refused to take any responsibility for the current disasters she was creating in her life. I felt like a paid audience at a circus; she'd cast me in the role of spectator to her drama.

Yet she kept coming back. Week after week she came, which was more than she'd done with her other therapists. She wanted something from me: to witness her reckless pain and ongoing misery, and somehow bear it with her.

Her sessions were torture. I felt my own unresolved hurts, losses, and daddy issues clamoring about my head as I struggled with anger at her heedless waste of herself. I made an appointment for supervision with a therapist I trusted and discussed the case. He told me that I was doing all that was possible with a client like this. He did have one additional bit of feedback, though.

"Get her to calm down. Get her grounded in her body. Help her feel safe, so she can hear something from you and see that she has some personal power in her life," my mentor/therapist said, stroking his white beard sagely. He didn't have any ideas how I could do that, though. He told me to trust my intuition. "You've got plenty of skills. Something will occur."

Great, thanks. I paid him and left. I was dreading Hoku's next appointment.

Sure enough, she came in like a hurricane, pacing around in agitation as she told a story of sneaking out and going to a party with "much older kids" where she drank, took Ecstasy, and had sex with several of the boys.

As I tried to redirect her, worrying about pregnancy, STDs, and weirdly, the boys she was initiating into sex (some of them the age of my son), Hoku finally sat down on the couch.

Her language was foul, her affect angry. She seemed to want something from me, refusing to stop talking as she described "giving head" to the boys.

I *had* to take a different approach. I went with my gut. Instead of sitting across from her in my therapist chair, I came over and sat at one end of the couch while she occupied the other. She was startled, big brown eyes wide, and for a second, she looked thirteen.

"Hoku, you seem cold. Put this blanket on." I covered her (too scantily clad as usual, she was shivering in the air-conditioning) with a super soft, fuzzy microfiber blanket that hung folded on the arm of the couch. "I want you to relax and just be, in this moment. Is it okay if I touch your feet and give you a foot massage?"

"Yeah," she said hesitantly. She'd worn rubber slippers into the office, as most Hawaii people did.

"The minute you feel uncomfortable, just say so." I covered her bare feet with the fuzzy blanket and tucked it firmly around her. I set her covered feet on my knees and squeezed them hard, with deep pressure.

From my work with autistic kids, I'd learned about the importance of "deep pressure" and "heavy work" as a way to give sensory input to a person with difficulty processing information from their bodies. Though she wasn't autistic, Hoku's trauma and emotional wounds had effectively disconnected her from her body.

I kept squeezing her blanket-covered feet slowly and deeply. "Breathe in with me through your nose. Now let's exhale together very slowly . . . Count to five on the exhale . . . one . . . two . . . three . . . four . . . five . . ."

By the time we'd done three of these, she was limp as a puppy, mercifully silent at last.

I set her feet down and led her through a guided visualization of golden light healing her body, healing her heart. Making her body a safe place, a place she could trust. Her body was hers. No one could touch her without her permission. Her body was a place she could feel good in, feel safe in, a place she could trust, love, and appreciate. Her body was a good place, and hers alone.

Ten minutes later I went back to my chair, struggling with a niggling worry that she'd accuse me of something inappropriate for touching her feet, as BPD clients are wont to do.

I pushed the thought away. Nothing else would have done for this damaged child but that deep pressure and the cozy warmth of the blanket, physical input to her jangled system, meant to heal, not hurt.

I had to live with the risk.

"I feel better." Hoku was calm. Her eyes were clear. There was a feeling in the room like the freshness in the air when a rainstorm has passed.

"Good. I want you to notice what it's like to be in your body, to know it's good to feel. I'm going to teach you some techniques to ground yourself." We rehearsed what she could do to calm herself down when she was upset before she saw me next. For the first time ever, she cooperated with the exercises.

Finally, I hoped I might be able to get somewhere with her. I was exhausted, but in a good way, like I'd emotionally taken a hill at a run. As soon as she left, I called Hoku's mom and described what we had done in the session, in part to protect myself but also to share the technique so her mother could use it. "Try some deep pressure hugs. Shoulder massages. Sit close to her. Hoku is craving healthy, healing touch."

Hoku's mom was thankful for the input and promised to try my ideas. I made careful notes and decided to record our next session to protect myself in case of any backlash.

The next week, Hoku arrived agitated again. I turned on my tiny tape recorder to make sure we were on the record.

Hoku had cut herself, deep parallel scratches on her arm, after a phone exchange with her abusive, abandoning father. She wanted to run away from home because her long-suffering mother wouldn't let her smoke pot in her room. She had not tried the breathing, skin brushing, or tapping I'd suggested.

I was more assertive with her this time. We did the relaxation exercise and visualization, and when she was calm and grounded in her body once more, we discussed cutting—why she liked it, what she got out of it, and how the pain, followed by a rush of endorphins, put her back in her body.

I gave her ideas about how she could get more physical sensation and endorphins without hurting herself, and I wrung a commitment out of her to call a friend to talk about the problem before cutting. We brainstormed a list of safe people she could call and get hugs from.

"I want to call *you*, Ms. Toby." Her eyes were tearful. "You're the only one who really helps me."

"I'm sorry, Hoku. We can only talk during our time together." Clients with her diagnosis often try to push professional boundaries, and then would turn the tables on those who allow it. I feared that very thing myself.

"What about texting?" Her mouth trembled.

"I don't text with clients," I said gently. "We talked about who you can contact."

"You don't care. You just pretend to care for pay." *She sure knew how to stick a knife in my soft parts.*

"Hoku. My job is to help you learn ways to feel better on your own, not to make you dependent on me. I wouldn't be doing my job right if I didn't have good boundaries."

"Boundaries are just an excuse." Her eyes overflowed; her core wound blinded her to anything but rejection. I reached over, took her hand, and give a big, hard squeeze, looking her in the eye.

"I care. But you have to wait until our sessions to talk to me," I said firmly. She needed physical input to feel connected; it made work with her extra challenging. I handed her a wrapped present. "Open this."

Hoku unwrapped the pretty, jewel-encrusted journal with a little lock and key I'd bought her. "I'm going on a long trip. A whole month. And while I'm gone, you can write me all the things you want to tell me."

Hoku was anxious that I'd be gone, but she loved the journal, and that it had a little lock on it. "Nobody can see what I don't want them to."

"Exactly. Just like your body, your journal is all yours."

We did a writing exercise together. She wrote a raw, gut-wrenching poem in her new journal and shared it with me. My heart lifted; writing was going to be another way she could heal herself.

At the end of the session, Hoku locked the journal and strung the tiny key onto the chain around her neck. She was only thirteen again, in that moment.

Hoku's rapist was convicted and given a fifteen-year sentence. Hoku made good progress in therapy over several years. The deep pressure intervention I had begun with her became a regular part of her services program, supported through the school under Occupational Therapy, and she continued to write and compose songs and poems as a part of her healing.

I TOOK A WALK AROUND THE SUNWOLF RESORT CABINS IN SQUAMISH, of which ours was one of twelve or so mostly unoccupied units. During my ramble, I found a trail through greening woods along a turquoise river, its crazy color attributed to glacier melt, according to my reading. Purple hollyhocks grew wild among fields of white daisies accented by columbine, and big, fat bees, bigger than any in Hawaii, worked the flowers busily.

I drifted along in an almost dreamy state. The setting was Technicolor yet peaceful, with no one around but butterflies. I discovered wild blackberries and raspberries and had a breakfast of sorts among the daisies.

But filling my hands and pockets with the berries reminded me this was Bear Country.

Bears might like blackberries (and redheads) for breakfast, so I didn't wander too far off the road, especially since literally no one in the world knew where I was—a strange feeling.

I pictured a bear roaring out from behind a tree, smelling the berries—*HIS BERRIES.*

The massive grizzly of my imagination took one look at my strange red hair and freckled skin—I was clearly an alien invader, and I was stealing his food. He charged and embraced me in his terrible, powerful arms, cutting my flesh to ribbons with four-inch claws as he smothered me against his potent-smelling chest. And then he bit down on my head, and my skull crunched between his massive teeth. My brains oozed between his writhing black lips, and he spat out their foul taste. The bear dropped me to the ground, and then clawed open my pockets and took back his berries.

My imagination has been both friend and enemy. Before I knew it, I'd pep-stepped back to the cabin, crushing the remaining berries in my overwrought state.

Mike returned and we got on the beautiful, empty road. We drove through miles of vistas featuring rugged mountains and lush foliage. We stopped in Whistler, the winter ski resort, and refreshed ourselves with a walk around the shops and a cup of tea before driving on.

Somewhere outside Whistler, we took a wrong turn, which we only realized was a wrong turn when the road literally dead-ended at a lake. A friendly local directed us back to the main road, and we discovered we'd gone an hour out of our way.

Recouping from that serious detour involved telling each other funny stories of other wrong turns we'd taken and stopping for gas at a tiny rundown hamlet called Lil'wat to fuel up and confirm that we were back on the right track.

The Native American gas station owner was kind to us and gave us free coffee and directions. I had no idea what the politically correct term for Native Americans was in Canada. After much debate, Mike and I decided to call the locals "indigenous tribal people."

My favorite sight of the day was two elderly tribal ladies in wheelchairs, decked out in beads, shawls, and moccasins, selling raffle and bingo tickets and tracking their enterprises on iPads as they sat on the deck of the gas station store.

I bought a lovely beadwork barrette from the store's dusty display counter of "special items" in thanks for the help. Bright red beads were interspersed with rows of black, yellow, and turquoise in a showy blossom pattern sewn onto leather, and *Lil'wat First Nation* was inscribed on the metal.

Aha! Now we knew what indigenous tribal people were called in Canada, and I loved the way First Nation sounded proud and strong.

CHAPTER THIRTY-THREE
LILLOOET TO SMITHERS, BRITISH COLUMBIA

On we went from Lil'wat, taking a break for fishing at the only river we found that wasn't thick and chalky with runoff glacier melt. Mike caught the first fish of the trip, a tiny German brown trout. Bushwhacking through the river willows, we met the famous mosquitoes we'd heard so much about.

These helicopter-sized monsters were three times as big as Hawaiian mosquitoes, so big I could feel their weight when they landed. We were glad we'd taken everyone's advice and hosed down with bug spray.

Back on the winding, two-lane road, we somehow took *another* wrong turn—which we didn't realize until the road turned to dirt, bordered by miles of purple and white flowers.

In the morning, that would have made a gorgeous photo and a fun area to explore, but it was getting late at seven-thirty p.m., and we hadn't eaten since breakfast. Food we'd stashed in the cooler was sloshing in melted ice at the bottom.

I was frustrated by still being three hours away from our campsite due to wrong turns, and Mike was fed up with not being able to get out from behind the wheel and go fishing.

We argued about how long to continue down the dirt road

toward a lake and a campground whose location we were unsure of, and eventually compromised by backtracking to the nearest town, a rugged mining village straddling a couple of mountains called Lillooet. Mike dropped me off at a motel and took off to find the lake he was sure was just over the next mountain.

This humble establishment smelled of pine rug cleaner and was decorated in painted cement block and shiny imitation Laura Ashley. I unpacked, took a shower (sighing with relief to wash off the bug spray), and later walked down the wooden sidewalk to eat tasty, fresh Greek food at a nearby restaurant. I ordered takeout for Mike. Back at the room, I continued my personal debauch and ran myself a bubble bath. Mike ended the day the way he liked, a fishing pole in one hand and camera in the other.

Hopefully, we'd be a little more on target with our destinations tomorrow—after all, we had a ferry to Alaska to catch in four days.

We left Lillooet at the first gleam of dawn the next morning, heading for Barkerville, a historic gold mining town that has maintained itself in total period authenticity. We'd bought a map at the Lil'wat gas station run by the industrious First Nation ladies, so the day went much more smoothly in general. We found a beautiful place called Marble Lake on the way out of Lillooet and fished the glassy green waters, enjoying the haunting cries of a family of loons nesting in the reeds.

The route was gentler after the mountains we'd just passed through with their thirteen percent grades and "Check Brakes" and "Avalanche Zone" signage—which, even in summer, had led to a certain nervous jumpiness on my part.

Mountain breezes continued to cut through the "jacket" I'd ordered online for the trip. That item had turned out to be more of a sweatshirt, and the sky was heavy with cloud. We were traveling through an area that was consistently cold enough to still carry winter clothing in June, and at a sporting goods store in one of the villages, I was relieved to find a serious-weather Viking jacket with a hood and liner that the saleswoman recommended as the kind of parka she wore herself. Mike purchased a pair of lug-soled all weather boots, replacing the hikers that he'd melted on the Big Island.

As we left the store, the clouds opened overhead. Heavy drops splatted the windshield of the van like exploding water balloons. The great weather we'd been blessed with came to an end, and our driving speed slowed to a crawl.

We rolled wetly into the historic gold rush village of Barkerville, where Mike had booked a room for us at the St. George Hotel, the B&B in the center of town. We discovered that we couldn't park the van near the inn where we were staying—no cars were allowed inside the village's perimeter, because nothing was permitted that would break the period spell (all the staffers were in costume, as well.)

We eyed the authentically muddy central street, peppered with horse manure and streaming with rain.

"The security staff can drive your luggage up in the buggy, or you can bring it up yourself in the hand cart," the ticket-taker said, snapping his suspenders.

"We'll take the cart." Mike and I spoke in unison. We'd begun to have what I call Mind Meld, sending each other texts at the same time and finishing each other's sentences.

I put on my new weather-resistant jacket, tearing off the tags at the entry gate, and Mike worked his stocking feet into his latest boots. We were grateful for the waterproof gear as I pushed the metal cart loaded with luggage from behind and Mike hauled from the front. We made our way uphill through the mud, being commented upon by roaming bands of schoolchildren in raincoats swarming over the place.

"Whose idea was this?" Mike panted, as we finally reached the St. George Hotel, a former saloon and bordello in continuous operation since 1880, squatting in semi-restored bawdy charm amid buildings of similar era.

"Yours," I said with a triumphant grin. By having Mike plan the whole trip, I'd subconsciously hoped to avoid responsibility for any disasters that might ensue—a fact that he'd called me out on during the argument the day before. We had agreed that we wouldn't grumble about anything that happened, no matter what it was or whose "fault" it was, from that point on.

We were met at the door by our landlady, complete in mobcap and pinafore over long skirts. Tracking mud and apologies, we banged our way, toting our bags, up an impossibly steep and twisty set of stairs and were installed in a tiny room.

"People must have been smaller back then," Mike observed, ducking under a lintel that caught him mid-forehead.

"Oh, what these walls have seen." I glanced around at the Victorian wallpaper, pressed-tin ceiling, and gold-cherub lamp of the former bordello bedroom, so small only the bed fit in—but then, that's all it had needed.

Barkerville is definitely worth visiting if you come through British Columbia. The staff are wonderful, the costumes fun, the businesses full of authentic and hard-to-find merchandise. If you stay at the St. George Hotel, be aware it's a bit of a hike with your bags and better done by the staff. It's also a sociable B&B environment, with a very knowledgeable innkeeper.

Mike left at dawn the next morning, looking for photography opportunities. I slept wonderfully in the cold room, buried in hamster-like bliss under a mountain of heavy down. I woke up around seven a.m., having adapted to the ridiculous amount of daylight by wearing a sleep mask, but took one look at the chilly rain pattering down on the muddy street outside the window and pulled my eye mask back down for another hour.

Mike woke me on his return, and we went down to the dining room for a personally made breakfast with our fellow guests. I was delighted to have my very own silver pot of tea and delicious homemade granola as we visited with the other visitors around the table. I'd given our hostess a bookmark the night before, and this morning, she told me she'd read my books.

"I love your mysteries. Found you on BookBub," she said, referring to an e-mail promotion list I use. It was amazing to find someone familiar with my stories in a place like this, and I handed out a few more bookmarks to other guests who'd overheard and asked for them.

After checking out and hauling our luggage back to the car, we walked around the whole village and took a hike into the forest above. I was enchanted by starlike dogwood blossoms punctuated by whisks of Queen Anne's lace and set off by the tatting of new ferns against the dark conifers.

Wandering the period town, I was reminded again of how hardy people were a hundred years ago. I'd likely have died from the appendicitis I got at sixteen if I'd lived back then, or with the complications I had with my first child. It's humbling to remember I owe my life, several times over, to modern medicine. Not only that, choices for women were slim to none back in that day: drudge, whore, or wife, though drudge was probably a large part of any role.

It was fully eleven a.m. by the time we'd left Barkerville and were driving toward Tyhee Lake Provincial Park, supposedly a good fishing area. That destination was at least six hours away if all went well—and it didn't.

We'd hardly left Barkerville, with me at the wheel, when I noticed a shimmy the van developed at around seventy kilometers an hour. Unfortunately, this was the speed that the highway, filled with mud-spattered, impatient Ford F-150s and loaded logging trucks, demanded we maintain.

We pulled over. Mike walked around, checking the tires, but couldn't see anything wrong. A few miles later, we pulled over a second time. The problem didn't go away. In fact, it began to get worse, until the tires were wobbling so badly that they seemed in danger of flying off.

We called the rental car company and discovered that they had no satellite offices outside of the U.S. Their sister company had an office in the upcoming metropolis of St. George, but the place would be closed until Monday.

Today was Saturday, and we were soon due at the docks in Prince Rupert for our prepaid ferry to Alaska.

We sat on the side of the road and talked through various scenarios.

We could wait until Monday in St. George, change out the car, then drive like heck to get to Prince Rupert in time for the ferry, forfeiting the prepaid cabin and campground we'd planned on.

We could drive on to Prince Rupert, hoping the suspension would hold, and plan to get another car there.

We could abandon the car in Prince Rupert and take the ferry to Alaska without a car—after all, our plans there didn't call for one especially. Then we could come back to Prince Rupert and rent another car for the drive back to Seattle through B.C.

"Let's just try to get it fixed in St. George," Mike said, but neither of us felt optimistic that we'd find an open garage that could service something this serious.

We limped into St. George, a modern sprawl on the fat artery of the Fraser River. Without Internet on our phones, finding something open seemed impossible. We felt as if we'd been rendered blind, fumbling and feeling our way across these new challenges without the information stream we'd come to count on.

Asking for help at a car rental place in St. George was the beginning of the solution. In a series of tiny miracles, we were able to get the van into a tire place. The alignment, thrown off by an accumulation of mud,was adjusted while we ate lunch at a nearby Japanese restaurant.

The Canadians impressed us, from the attendant at the Enterprise rental office, who had no obligation to help but found a mechanic open and made us an appointment, to the hardworking mechanics who put our van up on the hoist and surrounded it like a pit crew, even taking the vehicle out onto the freeway to drive it at seventy kph to test if it was fixed.

Mike and I also did well through the challenge. "We solved the problem and didn't even fight! We must be growing up or something," Mike said.

We drove on for another six hours, over velvety fields of hay and alfalfa, through rippling groves of aspen, past miles of various kinds of pine. We passed farms with fat cattle and rusting tractors, and we breathed the sweet pungent scent that is newly cut wood, the smell of tree death, as we circumnavigated mountains of logs, hillocks of two-by-fours, and train cars loaded with golden mounds of wood chips.

We drove through rain and sun and rainy sun, as the sky played out high drama overhead through peekaboo layers of cloud and teasing glimpses of rays.

Tyhee Lake, our destination for the day, turned out to be a weed-choked expanse of boat-only fishing filled with noisy families and clouds of mosquitoes. Our site was in a grove far from the water, and there was nothing of interest to see or do. Feeling a pang over the twenty-seven dollars we'd spent on a reservation, we drove on to a town called Smithers. This place was at least stationed on a river, and Mike perked up at the idea that we might yet find some fish.

To our surprise, the first four motels we went to were booked. Eventually we found refuge at the Fireweed Motel, a roadside carbuncle surprisingly updated with blond wood furniture and white matelassé bedding.

Mike left with his fishing pole clutched hopefully in hand. I sat at the Ikea desk in the dark, having unplugged the lamp in order to plug in my laptop—but the smell of the place was gloriously neutral. There was good WiFi, the van was working, a cup of tea was imminent, and I was headed for another bubble bath: the best possible end to the day on a road trip.

CHAPTER THIRTY-FOUR
SMITHERS TO CASSIAR CANNERY, BRITISH COLUMBIA

We got on the road early again, not finding much to explore in the utilitarian town of Smithers, and were delighted to discover that the intervening miles and hours between it, and our destination of Prince Rupert, were some of the most spectacular of the trip so far.

We experimented with videos taken with various cameras and phones on the dash of the van, and Mike got some great footage in various formats of the clean, curving road, the towering pines, and blue, snowcapped peaks.

By lunchtime, we reached a town called Terrace, and determined to keep to our resolution to eat at "local color" restaurants, we drove around until we found the Bear Country Inn and Restaurant, mobbed because it was Father's Day. We were able to sneak onto a table for two since most of the locals eating there were large family parties.

"Happy Father's Day, honey," I told Mike, guilty that I'd forgotten about the holiday; it was always one that triggered sorrow about the distance I still carried from my own father.

"Thanks." Mike was distracted by retrieving texts and messages now that we had Wi-Fi.

I fiddled with my napkin, looking around the place, filled with multigenerational parties. Would we ever live close to our children like these families? That seemed unlikely, with us in Hawaii and the two of them at opposite ends of California, just beginning to settle into life with significant others.

I missed Tawny and Caleb suddenly and acutely, so painfully I had to stanch sudden tears with a paper napkin.

Nobody had ever told me that when your kids grow up and leave, you never stop missing them. I was still clobbered by that heartbreak when I least expected it, a ghost-limb pain I tried not to spend time with because everything had gone well raising them. They seemed successful and well-adjusted; we'd done our job, and they'd grown up and left us. Wasn't that the goal?

I blew my nose and dabbed my eyes, but I needn't have worried Mike would notice my upset. He was studying his phone intently, his mouth curved in that almost-smile he hid behind his silver mustache.

"They remembered," I said.

He looked up, his eyes very blue, happiness in the crinkled corners. "They did."

My husband had been a great dad; as someone who hadn't been close to my own father, I vicariously reveled in how reliable and involved Mike had been with our kids while they were growing up. Not much for roughhousing or games because he was too serious for those activities (they had me for that), he was a loving disciplinarian when he needed to be, doing his part with the hard stuff like doctor visits, braces adjustments, piano lessons, supervising chores. The soul of integrity, a man of his word, and always a solid provider, Mike was there with me to witness and celebrate every first step and accomplishment. I couldn't have asked for a better father to our children.

We were served by a lovely woman who genuinely seemed to care that we liked our meal. The homemade lemon cream pie we shared for dessert was *onolicious*. I'd never eaten anything quite like its fluffy tart goodness. Even the crust was crispy.

"Do you miss your dad, on days like this?" My father-in-law had passed recently.

Mike nodded, his gaze on his plate. "He was a good dad. I'll always miss him."

"Me too." A man of few but pithy words, Everett Neal had loved a good glass of wine and a game of poker. He'd had a dry humor that revealed the sharp intelligence in his brown eyes. He'd been sparing with praise but always quick to help anyone in need, and he'd passed on his obsessive love of fishing to his son.

Mike spotted a provincial park (the Canadian equivalent of a U.S. state park) alongside a stream, and we pulled over to take a break. We had a delightful hike through the forest, and I caught the biggest trout of my life on my first cast into a crystalline pool—a three-pound Dolly Varden. The fish fought like a hero, and I didn't want to kill him, and because we were uncertain about our cooking arrangements, I let him go, though I second-guessed that decision several times the rest of the day.

We arrived at the small, picturesque town of Prince Rupert . From here, we'd be taking the ferry to Alaska; in the meantime, it took some doing to find our lodgings, a restored cabin Mike had booked for us at a place called Cassiar Cannery on the Skeena River.

"You're going to love this spot, Toby," Mike promised. "It looked great on the website—a beautiful place where you can take a day off and hang out, while I go find bears."

"Bears! I'll stay at the cabin, thank you very much."

"Good. Because I'm taking an all-day boat tour to an island sanctuary for grizzlies, and I only booked a ticket for one. I knew you wouldn't want to come." Mike clearly couldn't wait to get as close as possible to the animals. "Bears are perfectly adapted to their environment. Really magnificent animals."

We pretty much had opposite reactions to the mighty creatures.

We drove to the end of an exceptionally long country road bordering the mighty Skeena River and entered what was clearly an old cannery. A big gate on an arm swung open, and two gorgeous dogs that looked like slender huskies with long legs trotted out, howling an unearthly greeting.

Our hosts, an energetic young couple named Mark and Justine, met us when we parked.

"Those dogs are awesome," I said, watching the beautiful animals trot beside us with a fluid, slinky movement I'd never seen before.

"That's Betty, and this is Veronica," Mark said. "They're husky-wolves."

"Husky-wolves?"

"Yeah. Half husky, half wolf. The husky part means they're a little more domesticated," Mark explained. "Full-blood wolves tend to wander off to be with their kind."

I was immediately enamored of these mesmerizing beasts. "How do I get one?"

Mark laughed. "They're hard to come by, as you can imagine."

Mark and Justine showed us to our adorable cottage, literally built out onto the huge, tidal river. They told us the story of how they had bought the cannery, which closed in the 1980s, from a biker gang. The gang had lived and hung out there for years, collecting wrecked cars, motorcycles, metal scrap, and growing dope. The property was in such disrepair that Mark and Justine bought it for a song—and then put in years of hard work clearing, cleaning, and rebuilding.

The couple had a brochure with a little historical information about the place:

In 1889, Alfred E. Green put a $16 deposit on a property in the Skeena Slough to participate in the salmon boom of the late 1800s after Inverness, the first cannery, opened in 1876. Green sold to the Cassiar Packing Company (Caspaco) in 1903 and Cassiar Cannery was in business, fully operational for over 80 years and holding the record as the longest consecutively operating cannery on the West Coast. By 1905, there were 12 canneries operating near the mouth of the Skeena River.

The Grand Trunk Railroad connected the Skeena canneries in 1914 offering a new method of transport from the traditional boats or walking and connecting Prince Rupert with the rest of Canada. In 1959, the Department of Highways built a road terminating at Cassiar Cannery linking the canneries with Highway 16.

Northern salmon canneries were essentially small towns with every-thing needed available on site. Cassiar Cannery had a store, doctor, office, cookhouses, machine shops, bunkhouses, manager houses, blacksmith, ship-wrights, net lofts, all the canning and processing equipment, power produc-tion and more. Internally, the fishing industry operated without money – tokens or charges for food, nets, fuel and so forth would be levied against a personal account with the company one fished or worked for and it would be debited against one's paycheck. For a while, it was a time of plenty.

Beginning in the 1920s, the number of Skeena canneries began to drop and only the strongest remained. By the 1960s, only 3 operational canneries were left and by the 1980s, Cassiar Cannery was the last oper-ating salmon cannery on the Skeena River.

The property still included a gigantic dock where the main canning operation had taken place, and that had fallen into disre-pair. Mark tied up his boat there, accessed by a little boardwalk laid over the rotten pier. "We can't afford to restore that area," he explained. "We ask guests not to go out too far, because the wood is rotten."

Mark was a craftsman and boat repairman. He showed us his wood shop, sawmill, and tools, the entire upstairs floor of one of the former cannery workshops. The setup was enough to make my husband drool. Mark had built the furniture for the cottages with logs he pulled from the river, which is exactly what Mike would have done if he were twenty years younger and lived in this spectac-ular place.

Justine had a great design eye, and the restored cottages all had lovely modern color palettes and top-quality beds. "Justine's the reason this place looks so good," Mark said proudly as I exclaimed over the stylish linens in our pretty lodging.

We settled into Adirondack chairs on the weathered cedar deck overlooking the mighty Skeena. The river, ruffled with evening breeze, was an expanse of rich, silvery olive water, studded with logs lazily turning in the current. Beyond the edge of the deck, a tidal estuary of long, blowing marsh grass housed a variety of wildlife. A robin, fat and glossy, its red breast shiny and plump, hopped onto a patch of grass starred with tiny yellow daisies. A huge black crane flapped by with its long legs trailing, heading toward the pine-covered ridge above a muddy bank that defined the opposite shore.

My bones melted into the chair as I relaxed, scanning the river for bald eagles—according to Mark, there were several roosting nearby. The sunset played out in an extended, glorious dance over the water until we went to bed.

MIKE LEFT EARLY FOR HIS PHOTOGRAPHY BOAT TRIP TO A GRIZZLY BEAR sanctuary, and I woke up at a leisurely pace, investigating the kitchen for the tea setup. The advent of tea in my life had been uncelebrated—I had loved my morning coffee and was still trying to figure out how to get a buzz from tea that would give me the same caffeine jolt.

Canadians are tea drinkers, so the cottage had come with an electric kettle, an invention I'd discovered while visiting Prince Edward Island with my friend Holly the previous summer. The kettle was squat and utilitarian, without any sort of button or lid, just a plug to heat the water. I filled the kettle directly from a water dispenser, the water from the sink being somewhat peat-colored, and plugged it in. I took out the brown paper bag of highly caffeinated loose leaf Irish tea that I'd bought in Barkerville, and dumped a goodly amount of loose leaves into a china teapot (cream-colored with green flowers), and when I heard boiling, pulled the kettle's plug out of the wall.

My first cup of tea, poured carefully so that the leaves settled on the bottom, was delicious. I drank it out on the deck, listening to nothing but the trickle of water from an outfall pipe under the house, the buzz of bees, and songbirds filling the air with trills and riffles that echoed across the glassy morning water. A hummingbird, which we don't have in Hawaii, came by to investigate my bright hair.

Out on the river, giant fish leaped in the low water of the tidal banks, "shedding sea lice," Justine had told me. Three bald eagles, an osprey, millions of barn swallows, woodpeckers, robins, and squirrels passed by . . . but no bears.

This was worth noting because I didn't want to see bears.

My second cup of tea, thirty or so minutes later, was so strong and bitter it was undrinkable. Yikes! I forgot that Holly had told me four minutes per pot, no more, no less. Apparently, steeping longer only made the stuff bitter and not more caffeinated.

I made another pot of tea, removed the leaves, and saved the rest for reheating later. The Irish breakfast had more caffeine than a Lipton tea bag, for sure, because my energy and cognition improved noticeably.

I was ready to explore.

I went to find Justine and Mark, who were busily working on one of the cottages, their two-year-old son in daycare. Mark was installing tile, Justine was finishing the walls, and the aroma of fresh paint wafted around us as I asked about disposal of the smelly crab leavings from last night, where to do our laundry, and if it was safe to take a walk down the long country road through the forest.

"Do you have bears here?" I asked. "Do they come onto the grounds?"

"We definitely have bears," Mark said. "But the dogs keep them away. They have an understanding, the bears and our dogs."

Betty and Veronica lifted their heads, scenting the air, from where they'd been resting on the porch. They seldom made eye contact; they were so dignified and close to wild that I felt honored when one of them deigned to touch my hand.

I'd run away too if Betty and Veronica wanted to chase me off, just like the bears.

Mark offered me bear spray for my walk, which I happily accepted. "I usually take the dogs and carry a shotgun when I go." He pointed to the nearby railroad tracks. "To make noise, you know."

I nodded, bemused by the thought of walking down the railroad tracks in the wilderness with husky-wolves and a shotgun on my shoulder. Mark reminded me of Mike in his younger years—a tall, capable man who never stopped moving. "I can't wait to use my Father's Day gift—Justine and my boy got it for me." He pointed to a pile of firewood logs with a shiny new ax protruding from one of them. I grinned at the sight. An ax was the perfect British Columbia Father's Day gift.

Mark fetched the bear spray from their cottage; it was reassuring to see that the hefty canister was dusty from disuse. He blew it off and handed it to me. "I think you twist this thing here, point it at the bear, and shoot. But they say to be sure to shut your eyes; the stuff can blow back, and it's nasty."

"Ah." I chuckled nervously. "Now I'm as scared of the spray as I am of a bear." I accepted the can dubiously, and stuck it in my pocket. "Thanks."

I felt a little more confident setting off down the deserted forest road with the bulky canister protruding from the pocket of my sweatpants. I sincerely hoped not to have to use it, but I was determined to take a real British Columbia nature walk.

CHAPTER THIRTY-FIVE
CASSIAR AND BEARS

The road to Cassiar Cannery on the Skeena River in British Columbia was gorgeous. Narrow, smooth, and unpainted, the route was lined with bushes loaded with sweet, tart, orangey-red fat berries, a variety I'd never seen before. A bald eagle flew over me, so close that I could see a patch of feathers missing from its breast. The raptor emitted a croaking sort of cry as it landed on a nearby pine.

I picked a handful of the berries and wandered on, but here and there, I noticed large, crushed-down trails through the flowers and ferns bordering the road. Yes, there were bears here, and they were foraging for berries, because the salmon weren't yet running, so they must be hungry . . .

I forced myself to go a mile or so, then hurried back to the Cannery.

I was annoyed at being so timid, but I'd grown up in a place where there were no natural enemies in nature besides sharks. Nasty fellow humans were the only real dangers to be concerned about.

I returned the bear spray and held out my handful of berries for Justine's inspection. "What are these?"

"Oh, those are salmonberries, eh," Justine said. "A seasonal treat around here. They are called that for the color—so much like salmon."

Safely back on my deck, eating a yogurt sprinkled with the berries I'd picked, I settled into spending the day reading, writing, looking, thinking, and doing stretches and little walks around the place now and again. It was perfect.

Later in the day, Mark, Justine, and little Nicholas invited me to come with them to visit friends who lived out on one of the far banks of the river in an old settlement only accessible by boat. Mike was still gone when I excitedly donned my 'personal flotation device,' or PFD, and climbed aboard their sturdy aluminum river craft.

Justine and I sat on a central bench on either side of Nicholas, an adorable towheaded tot, all of us bunchy and thick in PFDs. Mark took the helm of his twenty-foot aluminum craft and fired up twin sixty horsepower Honda outboards that my husband had already drooled over.

The first thing Mark did once we cast off was to throw a chain around a log that was caught in the pier's pilings to try to tow it out from where it was trapped. "Got to keep the dock clear of debris as much as we can," he told me by way of explanation, hollering to be heard over the roar of the motors.

Intense tension translated through the rope and chain attaching us to the giant floating tree, and they hummed under the strain of the roaring outboards. We wove back and forth in the current, the engines revving to a scream, but the log wouldn't budge. I clung to Nicholas with one arm and the gunnel of the boat with the other, trying not to scream myself.

Justine and Nicholas had seen all this before and were unflappable; still, I couldn't help wondering how long any of us would last in that cold, murky, surging river should something go wrong.

The tree's roots were inescapably wound in the pilings. "I'll have to chainsaw it loose at low tide," Mark yelled, and threw the boat in neutral and unfastened the chain and its accompanying rope. The massive log, released from tension, swung around and crashed back into the pier, making the huge old structure wobble. I could see why he wanted to keep it clear. There were quite a few other downed trees rolling by in the current or fetched up against the supports. "We always have plenty of wood and never have to cut the trees ourselves," Mark said. "Tons of free lumber."

"Mark cuts the logs up for all kinds of projects," Justine added. "Not just firewood." She was clearly proud of Mark's many skills.

Their lifestyle was close to wilderness homesteading: how much more so would this river-locked place be that we visited next? I was wildly curious about anyone hardy enough to live waterlocked on this intimidating river.

Mark put the boat in gear, and we surged forward, racing up the wide tidal expanse, the wind in our faces, trees and olive-green water the only thing to see in any direction. We eventually turned into a tributary stream, where Mark tied the boat up at a dock, the first sign of human habitation I'd seen since the cannery.

Two older couples soon arrived to exclaim over Nicholas and meet me, and we trekked along a boardwalk laid over verdant, swampy ground to their house, a major renovation project.

Mr. and Mrs. French, who'd inherited the original cottage built a couple of generations ago, were finally retired from jobs "in town" and were adding on a second story to the ancestral home. The smell of fresh-cut cedar wafted around us because Mr. French, sixty at least, was milling his own lumber from trees he'd dropped himself.

"That guy works like a machine," Mark told me respectfully, in an aside. I got the feeling that was his highest compliment.

The Frenches showed us around the work in progress inside the house. The living room was finished and furnished with a huge flatscreen TV and lovely leather furniture.

"How'd you get that big couch out here?" I asked.

Mrs. French rolled her eyes. "Like everything you see here, we brought it on the boat. It was funny at the time, the couch strapped across the stern as we whizzed down the river."

They plied us with wine and Mr. French's homemade smoked salmon, a rich ruby-red filet fine enough to melt in your mouth, but even better layered on stone-ground crackers.

We talked about Maui, where all of them loved to visit. To my surprise, Mrs. French was even wearing a gold *honu* charm necklace that she'd bought on the island, and they promised to take a look at my books—only Justine, a mystery buff, had read them before.

As evening began its extended sunset pageant, we flew back down the river to the dock, where the husky-wolves were howling their haunting song, distraught that they'd been abandoned. Veronica demonstrated her devotion by leaping off the pier and swimming out to the boat. Betty went in halfway, then trotted around sensibly to meet the family where they tied up.

I returned to our cottage with a slab of the smoked salmon, a gift from the Frenches, to find that Mike was back from his adventure, sunburned and happy, sitting on the connected deck visiting with our new neighbors, guests in another cottage.

We drank more wine with these new friends, eating dinner side by side on the deck, and watching the resident bald eagle as he perched on a nearby pier post.

I was deeply impressed by the pioneer "get 'er done" spirit of the British Columbians I'd met so far, not to mention their friendliness and hospitality. I broke out the homemade salmon filet and told our fellow guests, a family from Edmonton who came often to Cassiar, about the remarkable Frenches. Mike described the grizzly sanctuary, an entire island given over to the great beasts just off the coast. As we watched the long sunset eventually release its hold, I was surprised at how deeply connected I felt—not only to the wild and wonderful river, but to the hardy people who lived there.

CHAPTER THIRTY-SIX
AURORA BOREALIS AND A LONE WOLF

After a long day on a boat taking pictures of eagles and bears, tired Mike was getting ready for bed when he got a message on his phone that the aurora borealis was possibly going to be visible in our area, due to a large solar flare.

Mike had set up the camera on the deck outside on time-lapse mode the previous night with no luck, and there was only a ten percent chance that the phenomena was going to be visible. Still, he took the extra time to set up the camera and point it up over the silhouette of the surrounding woods. We went to sleep in our snug little bedroom to the rhythmic clicking of the camera, set on automatic, outside the window.

Mike woke me up sometime deep in the short, dark night. "Toby! It's happening!" His voice was hoarse with excitement. "Wrap up. It's cold, and there are mosquitoes."

I pulled on socks and my hoodie, wrapped in a blanket, and stole out onto the deck, trying to be quiet because of the vacationers in the unit beside us.

At two-thirty a.m., there was already a lightening of dawn beginning to the east, but after a few minutes of letting my eyes adjust, I could discern thin, wavery tendrils of green light reaching up above the black line of silhouetted trees on the ridge line. "I can barely see it."

"Shoot. I think we just missed it," Mike said. "I can barely make it out. Hope the camera caught it."

We were engulfed in a thickening cloud of mosquitoes and no-see-ums. I had to spit a few of those out on my way back to bed, disappointed that the famous northern lights weren't more dramatic.

But the next morning, when Mike put together his time-lapse video, we were able to see how the aurora borealis had spun magnetic veils of purple, magenta, and green across a backdrop of spinning stars, framed by the dramatic, jagged black backdrop of the pine-covered ridge.

I gasped at the sight. So did Justine and Mark when we told them the exciting news that the solar event had happened and that Mike had been lucky enough to capture it. We brought them over to watch the video. "I had no idea that even happened in our area," Justine said. "Let alone in June!"

"Bucket list luck," Mike said.

SEATED IN OUR BRIGHTLY COLORED PLASTIC ADIRONDACK CHAIRS ON the dock, watching the river at low tide and sipping our morning beverages, a howl from the other side of the river lifted the hair on the backs of our necks. Long and low, echoing across the still water, the cry rose into the air like a ribbon of smoke, tickling our nostrils with a scent of primal danger.

The howling of wolves is one of those sounds imprinted on human DNA as profoundly disturbing—along with newborns crying and bumps in the night that might be bears.

Picking berries the other day had felt elemental, timeless, like my individuality was subsumed in generations of women driven to forage among the leaves and pluck these little jujubes of fruit.

Animals have instinctive drives and inherited memory—why not humans?

The song of the wolf on the other side of the river was another such timeless moment.

My skin prickled over my whole body as I sat up alert and began scanning, mentally reminding myself that we were safe, but imagining how I'd feel walking alone and unarmed on a forest path and hearing that song.

We looked for the wolf with naked eyes, binoculars, and the zoom lenses of our cameras and found it eventually—lanky and long-legged, almost invisible, its fur the brown of wood and gray of river mud. The wolf was nosing along the riverbank, stopping periodically to give its unearthly call.

"Where's the pack?" Mike asked.

"That's always the question, isn't it?" We chuckled nervously.

I was getting used to Betty and Veronica's "singing" at every guest who arrived at the cannery, and had thought I was relatively used to their spooky wolf-howl—but like a newborn's wail, no one can ever really get used to something when it's a DNA threat-level sound. Spiders, snakes, sharks . . . our nerves jangle ancient alarms anytime we reenter the food chain and see the web, hear the rattle, spot that triangle fin.

I follow a National Geographic photographer on Instagram, Paul Nicklen, who's also an environmental activist with nonprofit Sea Legacy. He'd shown the life of a wolf pack family on one of the small B.C. islands near our location, and his posts shared the coastal wolves' struggles to survive in the challenges of habitat loss and people's fear and prejudice. That has made me careful not to present an unbalanced picture of these creatures, respecting their place in the world—while sharing the truth of my experience with them.

I didn't know that seeing and hearing a wolf in the wild was another "bucket list" item until I did so.

∼

We left Cassiar Cannery with many hugs and promises to keep in touch—we hoped to house swap someday with Mark and Justine and visit the Skeena River again.

In nearby Prince Rupert, we ate a sublime breakfast at the famous Crest Hotel—highly recommended!

Our corner table had a view of the ocean we'd soon be traversing to Alaska. We watched bald eagles flap by the fishing boats and barges in the bay below, watching for scraps. We had some limited internet at the restaurant and were able to upload Mike's amazing aurora borealis video and share it with friends while we breakfasted.

I drank a whole pot of English breakfast tea, and between the sugary waffle I ate and the caffeine boost, I was ready to jog around town. Instead, we got in line for the long ferry ride to Alaska . . . and sat in the car waiting in line for *three hours*.

I fell into a food coma, curled up in the front seat as we listened on the van's audio system to Sara Malia Hatfield's audiobook rendering of *Twisted Vine*, Paradise Crime Mystery #5, which I had just published. I actually got tears in my eyes during one of the scenes. Who wrote that? It was gut-wrenching!

"So, do you like Sophie?" I asked Mike. This character had a major part in *Twisted Vine*, and that book was when I knew I had to write more books with Sophie as the main protagonist: hence the Paradise Crime Thriller series. "She's my next big thing."

"A computer tech specialist who looks like a model and does martial arts? What's not to like?" Mike said. That was the response I'd been getting from men. Women were a little intimidated; some had difficulty relating. I planned to show Sophie's deeper vulnerabilities in her own books, where I could really delve into her backstory. A domestic violence survivor, Sophie had overcome and escaped her sadistic ex-husband to hunt for justice. I was eager to embark on her character development arc through a series of fast-paced thrillers filled with spies, shady characters, action, and international intrigue.

People have asked why I self-publish; I always tell them it wasn't my first choice. My road to success began with bitter disappointment when my first agent retired on the cusp of selling my series. Rather than look for another agent, a process which can take years, I decided to self-publish *Blood Orchids*. This turned out to be the right route to readers for my work, because once I got started writing, I liked the fast pace and freedom of being an "authorpreneur." Turns out I'm good at the business end of writing, too. My entrepreneur Grandpa Jim's early lectures had not fallen on deaf ears after all.

I got out of the car to pee and was in the terminal building when Mike finally got signaled to board the giant ferry. I ran down the dock, chasing the departing van in a panic—but he'd told the gatekeepers I was coming, and everyone waved me on, smiling. I hurried down the massive gangplank into the bowels of the biggest ferry I'd ever been on, getting a cramp in my neck trying to see everything.

We'd booked a cabin on board the massive *Matanuska* since it was a 20-hour journey. Looking around the tiny space with its neat bunk beds, square porthole view, and closetlike head, I turned to Mike. "We're accidentally on a cruise, honey."

Another inside joke—we'd always sworn we'd never go on one.

"This is a Mike and Toby-style cruise." He kissed me, smiling. "No fancy food. No entertainment. Bunk beds."

I'd been on two cruises in my lifetime: one as a student, sleeping in a bunk in the bowels of a Latvian ship going through the Greek Islands, and a Disney Cruise to Mexico with my well-to-do grandma Gigi. Mike, however, doesn't like to be confined with a lot of people, overeating, hanging out poolside, or watching entertainment—and truth be known, neither do I.

We explored up and down the ship, for indeed that was what it was, and took naps in our little bunk beds. Eventually we bought some overpriced food in the cafeteria and watched humpbacks breaching from the windows as we ate our dinner in the no-frills dining area. "The whales remind me of home," I told Mike.

"They might even be the same ones," he said. We smiled; the whales connected us, from their calving grounds in Hawaii, to their feeding grounds in Alaska.

CHAPTER THIRTY-SEVEN
A LONG DARK TEATIME OF THE SOUL

We got off the ferry at Ketchikan, Alaska, the *Matanuska's* first stop, at nine p.m., and the light of day wasn't even close to over. Per usual, the shipping docks weren't the greatest way to see the area. When the cruise ships tie up in Kahului, on Maui, we see the pale, over-dressed tourists getting sunburned as they slog along our least-pretty streets down in the rusty, filthy shipping zone. (I hope that's not what they think Maui is like—nothing but gas storage tanks, whizzing cars, loose chickens, blowing dust, and a mediocre mall.)

We headed across the street from the ferry dock to a nearby Best Western and bought a glass of wine and a dark local stout so we could use the Wi-Fi in the bar. Mike uploaded a plethora of eagle and bear photos he'd taken while we were at Cassiar Cannery.

"Look at them fighting over the fish scraps, just like big seagulls." Mike showed me a photo with four bald eagles squabbling in the air over a tossed handful of fish offal. We were beginning to see why the locals treated them as pesky trash birds, but they were still fearsome to me with their glaring yellow eyes, snowy heads, and thick, powerful wings. Bald eagles make a harsh croaking sound, halfway between a crow and a bark—not at all like the skirling cries they're given in movies, which are apparently dubbed in from red-tailed hawks.

We poked around the village, but the stores were closed in the late evening (though it was still freakishly light out), and eventually we got back on the ferry, filing across the clanging metal gangplank. Once on the boat again, I climbed into my bunk and dropped into a womblike sleep. Something about the deep throb of the engine, the very slight rocking of the ferry, its steady sense of motion, took me back to a deep and quiet place of profound rest.

I slept through a stop in Wrangell, which I'd really meant to at least look at from the window since my friend Holly had written a magazine story about it.

I slept through a sunrise that Mike videoed from the bow of the ferry, too: "The longest sunrise I've ever seen," he said, showing me a blaze of orange and red, minutes long even in time-lapse, on his phone. "It seemed to go on for hours and hours."

When I finally did awaken sometime the next day, we were outside a collection of brightly painted buildings along the heavily wooded bank of a town called Petersburg. The massive ferry had been following a fishing trawler that didn't seem to know we were there and wouldn't get out of the way. As I came up on the main deck, the fishing boat was dawdling along just ahead of us, and the ferry's crew was gathered, speculating on what to do, as we drew ominously closer and closer.

Finally, the ferry captain blew the air horn—a blast that about levitated us off our feet. The trawler, which would have barely caused a ripple being mowed under beneath the mighty *Matanuska*, bobbled and wove, and finally pulled off to the side where our wake slammed its hull like tidal waves.

Drama safely over, we got in line for another indifferent cafeteria-style meal, enlivened by bickering between the grumpy short-order cooks behind the counter.

The short Asian cook in the hairnet took issue with the order taker and plate assembler, a rounded black guy (round brown eyes, round bald head, round belly under white apron).

"You said two eggs!" hissed the Asian guy, smacking down his heavy spatula on some pancakes to vent his spleen.

"No, clear as day, I told you ONE egg," the black guy growled. He looked up at us, fire in his eyes. "What do you want?"

"I notice a definite difference in service now that we're in the United States," Mike mused, tucking into his biscuits and gravy when we were safely ensconced in the eating area, looking out at more pine trees bracketed by snow-covered mountains.

"Let's see if it's just the ferry," I temporized, stirring yogurt into my fruit. "These guys have a pretty tough job, and it must get old fast." But we both had a feeling we'd gotten spoiled by Canadian politeness.

The sunshine of the first day had given way to a low ceiling of clouds and chilly spates of rain, as if God were randomly flicking us. The ferry plowed on through a tunnel of smooth, opaque green water and dark trees, heading for purplish mountains robed in snow.

As the hours went by, the journey assumed a Twilight Zone sameness.

The sun hardly seemed to move. I kept checking the time, but that was relatively meaningless because there was no sense of the day changing. Even though we were moving, I felt little sense of motion, and every time I looked out the window, it was an identical view: ocean, trees, snowcapped mountains here and there, perhaps a cabin or a dock as the only sign of humans. Sometimes these things were closer, sometimes farther away, but they seemed like a movie set background stuck on a feedback loop.

A weird scene in one of the *Pirates of the Caribbean* movies came to mind: the pirate ship was stranded in a huge desert, a half-light purgatory, and finally the stones turned to crabs that carried the ship to the edge of the world.

I was on that haunted craft, being pushed by the rotation of the earth to the edge of the world—on the longest day of the year.

What was this journey like on the shortest day of the year, when the *night* was this long? Just the thought chilled me, and I got out my crisp new Viking parka. I trekked through the ferry to stand right in the bow with the wind holding me up in a Kate Winslet *Titanic* imitation. The fun of that lasted thirty seconds, but eventually there was just nothing to do but go back to bed and sleep some more.

I WOKE UP AND LOOKED OUT THE PORTHOLE.

More hours had passed, but I had no sense of them. The ocean/strait/waterway we were on had broadened, but it was still the same: trackless forever stretches of trees, water, and snow-capped mountains.

For the first time, it sank into my awareness how far we'd come on this trip—and how far we were going. Mike had tried to show me, multiple times, on a large map, but my brain had refused to connect that little symbolic colored drawing with this vast, inhospitable wildness that we had the temerity to travel through.

A terrible, free-floating anxiety swamped me. I was unmoored, drifting across the cold wilderness, cut off from everyone I knew or loved except my husband.

Meanwhile, Mike slept on, snoring away in the little bottom bunk.

I left our cabin to get something from the cafeteria, hoping to calm myself by being with people.

It helped my anxiety to get into the cafeteria line, wedged between the apple-shaped woman in tight polyester with teased orange hair and the frantic young mother with the twin three-year-old girls, one tugging on her leg, the other on her hand. I existed in this line; I was one of these people.

I bypassed the grumpy cooks this time by choosing a premade

sandwich, then suffered through an agonizing checkout process with a new girl. "I usually make beds," she told me. "Sorry." She opened a laminated book of prices, ran her finger down the columns, and punched in my dollar-fifty cup of lukewarm tea and the sandwich. Every moment felt like I was pushing through molasses.

Sitting alone at a table, looking out the window at yet more water and trees, I squeezed mustard out of a plastic packet and went through the motions of preparing my sandwich. The dry, turkey-with-provolone-on-wheat was wrapped so hard in plastic that it looked and felt like a triangular throw pillow. I smeared mayonnaise on the fake-looking bread, took a bite, and chewed. *I am here, eating.*

I plonked my tea bag up and down in the cup as if it were an anchor.

I'd had these kinds of moments before, and endured them without telling anyone. I'd diagnosed myself with a kind of agoraphobia, fear of an openness that I felt swallowed by. The acute awareness of space and distance felt existential. I was a molecule in the universe, overwhelmed with the truth of my tininess, and the futility of it all annihilated me.

The first time I had a really bad attack like this, I was ninety feet below the water's surface, doing an open ocean scuba dive. I suffered a weird kind of reverse claustrophobia and burned through my oxygen way too fast, though I managed not to do anything stupid (like shoot for the surface) until the feeling passed.

In fact, I'd had an episode on our last road trip in Arizona, on the edge of the Grand Canyon, when I'd had to crawl to move and to simply lie down flat in order to look over the edge, totally overwhelmed by the depth and complexity of the space before me. I hadn't realized at the time that what I'd chalked up to a return of fear of heights actually came from the same root anxiety: overwhelm in the face of vastness.

My most recent attack of this had happened on top of Haleakalā under the Milky Way on an outing to photograph stars with Mike.

Gazing up into that spinning bowl of burning suns, I'd felt totally sure that I was going to fall out into space and end up floating among stars. I actually gripped onto the rocks so I wouldn't fall into the sky. I eventually had to turn over and shut my eyes.

And now, Alaska.

The place was just too big. The reality of the magnitude of our drive, plus its isolation from everything known, was setting into my psyche in a way I finally comprehended—and it totally freaked me out.

"I'm not in danger," I said to myself, dipping my tea bag up and down. "I'm having fun. An adventure. I wanted to do this. I like it here on the ferry." I did my breathing, staying present in the moment, just like I'd tell a client to do.

Nothing bad is happening.

Everything was nice and comfortable.

But I still couldn't wait to get back to our closetlike, enclosed cabin.

Mike was waking up as I come back in with half the sandwich. I held it out like an offering. "So. We're stopping in Juneau, then getting back on the ferry and going up to Haines even further north? And then, we're driving back to Seattle . . . through all of this? So many miles of trees and mountains?" I could feel how huge my eyes were, how wide and strained, and I tried to be funny with an exaggerated expression. Maybe I was a little successful, because Mike chuckled and shook his head. He caught my hand and pulled me in for a hug. I clung like a koala.

"I'm not letting you out of my sight," I said into his chest. "This is all too much for me. Too many trees. Too many mountains."

"I knew this was going to happen," he said. "It's sinking in—how big our road trip is. I tried to tell you. Multiple times. I asked you to get involved with planning, to tell me if it was too much. I even got mad at you that time because you refused to even look at the map."

I remembered that time he got mad, trying to get me to pay attention to the plan. I'd refused to do it. I didn't have a context to understand what we were undertaking, but I realized that, on some level, I'd known how it would affect me.

"I'm in it now, and I see how big it is," I said. "I had deadlines and my writing all the way until the day we left. I miss my writing!" Tears welled up. "I miss being in my stories. I miss being connected with people!"

Mike hugged me some more, pressing my body into his as if to take me inside him. "You can take a plane from Juneau and go back to Seattle if you want."

That seemed like the worst kind of cowardice. I hated being a coward. "I just have to get through this, one hour at a time, until it passes," I said. "Let's go on the observation deck. Stay with me."

The thought of holing up in a hotel in Seattle for a couple of weeks and writing *Bone Hook* while Mike drove all the way back through three thousand miles of British Columbian wilderness was tempting, though. We could then go to the cottage on the San Juan Islands together and meet our kids there for the family vacation we'd planned to end the trip.

Mike would be semi-safe and happy, adventuring.

And I would be safe and happy, alone, writing my book.

Out on the observation deck, we sat in swiveling chairs. The chill wind generated by the ferry's passing cooled me down. Everyone stood up, pointing and exclaiming, as we saw a humpback and then our first orcas, traveling alongside us in a swift-moving pod.

In the company of other people—a hipster young guy with a lime-green vest and fedora, a Mennonite man with a huge white beard and two female companions in kerchiefs and skirts, the apple-shaped woman wielding her binoculars—I was a person in real time. I existed among them.

But Alaska was awfully big, and I was not at all sure I could handle it.

CHAPTER THIRTY-EIGHT
JUNEAU, ALASKA

Juneau was a clean and lovely mix of green trees and steep, rugged mountains combined with modern, tasteful buildings and a shopping area near the cruise ship docks.

We were a bit cranky after my semi-meltdown. Tawny, our daughter, got through to us on the phone at a gas station where we were trying to buy a map after debarking the ferry, and offered some targeted suggestions to help us get our bearings. "Just hammer down some wine, Mom. You'll be fine."

We did need to eat, and one of my book fans who lives in Juneau had suggested the Red Dog Saloon. Sitting at a little table in front of a live country musician who looked like a cross between Willie Nelson and a gold miner, we ordered drinks and a plate of ribs. Accompanied by music and the kind of ribald, sexual, politically-incorrect joking that had gone out of fashion in the 1980s, we chomped down the ribs, thoroughly enjoying the rugged environment of the saloon with its sawdust floors, moose heads, and byplay between the waiters and the entertainer, who collected tips in a big white kettle labeled *VIAGRA*.

Refreshed in body if not in soul, we headed for the campground at Mendenhall Glacier. An eerily afternoon-like twilight lit the place even at ten p.m. as we entered the campground, and after a few glitches like being assigned the wrong campsite, we settled in. We made friends with our fellow campers, a couple roughly our age on a month-long safari for their thirtieth anniversary. We borrowed some kindling and fuel to get our fire started, and pretty soon we were sitting beside the firepit in our camp chairs, listening to night birds and shooing the few but mighty mosquitoes as we gazed at the great blue-white wall at one end of the lake: Mendenhall Glacier.

I'd never seen a glacier before, so Mendenhall became the yardstick by which I measured those I'd see in the future. Situated at the far side of a lake that was a puddle of its own runoff, the glacier jutted as high as the wall in *Game of Thrones*, a sheer cliff of white ice rived by blue melt lines the color of topaz. Like watching the lava on the Big Island, I was entranced by its unique and forceful nature, by its indifference to the schemes and plans of humans.

We locked everything remotely smelly in the bear-proof steel container provided by the park and took a walk in the gloaming of almost eleven p.m. I was still nervous about the prospect of running into bears, but we saw no sign of them, only beavers, ducks, herons, and sweet-singing songbirds. The park was painfully beautiful, with moss instead of grass providing a deep, soft base around the trees and interesting bamboo-like reeds and leafless plants that were some of the most primitive on earth, conquering the land left behind the glacier's melt and making it into forest.

We got set up for the night in the van and slept comfortably inside on a futon, tucked into the "Ozzie and Harriet" zip-together sleeping bag Mike had packed. Chilly rain pelted the van on and off all night, but it wasn't bad, considering that we were spitting distance from a live glacier.

We packed up early the next morning, eager to do a whale watch tour out of the harbor before we took a seaplane to Glacier Bay National Park, where we'd be spending a few days.

I'd been able to get enough reception bars inside town to book us a whale watch charter, and we ate a hasty and delicious breakfast at a place next to Auke Harbor before leaving. The restaurant offered nothing but waffles, with bizarre things on them and in them. Mike got the duck-and-brie waffle, and I ordered lemon curd with cinnamon and graham cracker crumbs. Other than the carbo-hydrate crash that I knew would come later, I was in foodie heaven.

If my character had been tested yesterday on the ferry, Mike's was today on the whale watch boat. A little Chinese woman with a video camera, refusing to follow directions from Chelsea, the nice whale biologist hostess, held us all up several times by ignoring directions to sit down, come inside, or otherwise follow the program.

She seemed fixated on Mike, and when we stopped to look for whales, she got right in Mike's personal space, reaching out around him and pressing against and in front of him, ignoring his glares and the many times he said, "Excuse me."

She was after his photography vantage points, and wherever he went, she went, too. With their height difference of close to two feet, the way she bird-dogged him was hilarious. When we returned to the cabin and our designated bench for a run after another pod of whales, Mike turned to me and said, "Come stand next to me. Keep her away. I'm tempted to drop her overboard."

"She looks like a Chihuahua taking on a Great Dane," I grinned. "Sure."

So, when we found the next spot where the whales were feeding, I wedged in next to Mike in a good visibility corner. Using our elbows, we were able to keep the woman back, but lo and behold, she inserted her arm between us and aimed that camera off the railing.

We both stared down at her, wedged between us like a tenacious gnome in her brimmed hat and colorful pantaloons. There was nothing to do but look at each other and roll our eyes.

At the time of our trip, only forty-eight whales in the world, all of them living outside Juneau, engaged in cooperative bubble-net feeding, a complex group behavior. A pod of whales encircles a school of herring, blowing bubbles and circling from below to force the fish close together into a ball. Then, at some invisible signal, the pod go deep beneath the "bubble net" and swim up through it in a close formation, their gigantic mouths open, and catch many more herring than any one of them could alone.

The spectacle would begin with birds hovering and landing on the water. After that we'd see whales circling and blasts of bubbles churning the water's surface. Then, all would go silent, a long and pregnant pause that stretched out for long, chilly minutes spent scanning the water.

Often, we'd be looking in the wrong place: the well-mannered British couple twittering beside us, the Chinese tourists crowding in —all of us on pins-and-needles to see where the cetaceans would surface.

Suddenly, a tight-packed group of giant open mouths would rise from the depths, emerging like a coordinated leviathan, their throats filling with fish like enormous black-and-white bellows.

The birds would shriek and dive, sometimes right into the whales' mouths, trying to grab fish. We'd be yelling, cameras going, everyone in a frenzy of excitement until, as suddenly as it had started, the whales would all disappear underwater again.

~

WE WHIZZED BACK TO JUNEAU, REPLETE WITH WONDER AT THE experience, and drove to the nearby airport, where a seaplane was taking us to Glacier Bay National Park, one of the most remote national parks in the United States.

The seaplane turned out to be a regular plane, but the smallest one either Mike or I had ever flown in.

Technically, I suppose five people could have wedged in, but they'd have had to be midgets, not the size of well-rounded me, tall and sturdy Mike, and the good-sized pilot. The three of us climbed in via one of the wings, entering butt-first to situate ourselves in the tiny space. I was so close to the pilot that his long hair blew in my face as we got underway.

Mike sat up front, his camera handy, but kept looking over at me to see if I was scared. I was determined not to be. I was adaptable and brave, dammit! I gave him a thumbs-up and showed my teeth in an attempt at a smile.

The thing revved like a mechanical bike, whizzed down the tarmac, jumped up into the air, and when it hit a bump, it just kept going, listing like a drunken dragonfly. Thankfully, there was no wind to batter us about, and the flight was smooth. We glided up over glorious uninhabited islands, verdant green forests, and mysterious waterways wreathed in scarves of filmy cloud. I loved every minute of the magical journey—but where would it end?

I'd never heard of Glacier Bay National Park, and now wished I'd read up on it. All I could see below was Alaska . . . and not one sign of humans anywhere.

∽

CHAPTER THIRTY-NINE
GUSTAVUS AND GLACIER BAY NATIONAL PARK

We landed on what looked like a parking lot in an area covered with pines. We crawled out of the tiny craft with little dignity, said goodbye to the pilot, picked up our minimalist bags, and walked into the tiny "airport" building. No one was around, but a huge, empty yellow school bus was waiting outside.

"Going to the lodge?" Mike asked.

"Sure am," the portly lady driver said.

We picked up our bags, carried them on, and sat down in the bus.

"That next Alaska Air flight has up to twenty passengers coming in," the driver told us. "We have to wait for them to land."

I could see the tops of Mike's ears turning red as the woman nattered on, telling us trivia about people we didn't know who worked at the airport. The bus got warm; ten minutes turned into twenty, then thirty.

"I'll go in and see what the holdup is." Off Mike went, determined to find a live body inside the apparently deserted building as I heard about the bus driver's grandkids.

A few minutes later, he came back. "The plane is delayed. Hasn't even taken off yet from Juneau. Can you run us out to the lodge? Please?"

"Oh, let me call and ask," she said, and then her phone got a fax tone repeatedly as she tried to call the lodge.

"Let me try on my cell." Mike called the number, handed her his phone, and we both listened eagerly to the front desk tell her to bring us in.

"Okay, we're off!" She pulled the handle and the doors shut. I had a distinct flashback to all the buses just like this I'd ridden as a kid—only now that I was an adult, the seats were too close together. Mike and I both had to take up a whole seat and turn to the side because our knees hit the seats in front of us.

We trundled along in the big, rattling bus down a board-straight road to nowhere, bordered by endless trees, at precisely the speed limit of twenty-five miles per hour. I reached over to the seat ahead of me and squeezed Mike's shoulder in thanks and acknowledgment. He'd succeeded in getting us moving, *and* had maintained his cool and good manners.

We pulled over at a clutch of stores in the center of the "town" of Gustavus and picked up several employees on their way in to work at the lodge, the bus now doubling as an employee shuttle.

Rain swept in suddenly, pattering on the roof and sliding down the windows in a way that took me straight back to the long ride on the school bus to Hanalei when I was a kid and it always seemed to be raining. Riding a school bus will do that, with its smells of diesel, Cheetos, and wet shoes.

Glacier Bay National Park was not much to look at, at least initially—a pebble-strewn shoreline we glimpsed through steady rain, and lots and lots of second-growth pine trees of exactly the same size. Moss and tall white flowers lit the dim gloom of the forest like tiny stars.

A debate about what the flowers were named ensued among the passengers.

"Cow parsnip," declared one of the Gustavus locals, a weathered-looking woman with round blue eyes and gray roots setting off an orange dye job. She had boarded the bus in town along with a handful of other hardy souls—college students who looked like they'd thought a summer in Alaska would be fun.

"I prefer Queen Anne's lace as a name for that plant," our chatty bus driver said over her shoulder. I agreed. Cow parsnip was not a good name for such a beautiful flower.

"No, it's not either of those. It's that bad plant, the giant hogweed," said one of the college students. "I'm a forestry major, so we learned about it. Don't try to touch it. There's a chemical in the sap that burns the skin."

The bus erupted in exclamations and stories about mishaps with hogweed. Apparently, this "Queen Anne's lace on steroids" is originally from Asia but is now spreading through British Columbia. I found it disheartening to hear that Hawaii wasn't the only place where invasive plants were gaining ground.

"What are those?" I pointed to a meadow area, where the endless twilight flared over some fluffy white blossoms in a swath that reminded me of snow.

"Wild cotton," said the weathered, blue-eyed woman. Wild cotton was exactly the right thing to call the poufs of white fluff on slender stems grouped in masses in the open, grassy areas.

Arriving at the lodge at last, we trekked down a series of boardwalks to a modular unit with a look of the 1970s about it. I whisked open the curtains for the purported ocean view we'd booked. Dark, forbidding spruce and hemlocks dripping with rain created an impenetrable wall in front of the window.

Mike still wasn't quite over the disappointment of our flight not being a seaplane and the hilariously annoying bus ride. He'd really wanted to splash down in the water among the icebergs, but the pilot had informed us "nobody does that anymore around here."

This bummer of an overpriced room was something he could try to fix, at least. "We paid extra for a room with a view," he said, hands on hips, eyes narrowed. "I'll go try to get us another one."

I shrugged and headed for the shower. I hadn't changed clothes since we'd boarded the ferry three days ago, and I couldn't wait to clean up and change into something fresh.

I'd just showered and gotten dressed, putting on extra layers against the deep chilly drizzle of the day, when Mike returned, shaking water from his parka and stomping his boots on the mat. "The rooms are all the same. Overgrown and run down. This lodge cost over a thousand bucks for the three nights, not including the airfare."

I was better off not knowing that. "Alaska's expensive, I guess. But there's nothing to be done. Let's just make the best of it."

After a scary-expensive but mediocre dinner in the dining hall, we were both so tired that our evening walk through the forest down to the dock overlooking glassy tidal waters took on a surreal quality. Six a.m., when we were scheduled to take a boat tour of the glaciers, was going to come really soon—and it was still light out at eleven when we drew the blackout curtains.

I WOKE UP AT FOUR A.M. AND COULDN'T GET BACK TO SLEEP, EVEN IN the darkness we had created with the drapes; I was feeling nervous about the boat tour, which was scheduled as an all-day activity.

I generally made it a rule never to be stuck on a boat for more than a couple of hours in case I got seasick, but this was a once-in-a-lifetime thing. Mike had promised I'd see puffins. I would put up with an all-day boat ride to see puffins; as a kid I'd loved how they looked like animated bath toys, and to this Hawaii girl, they seemed even more exotic than penguins.

I dressed in layers for the boat tour, knowing that we'd be on the ocean near some of the biggest glaciers in Alaska. First, my one pair of warm real wool socks, then my boots, the rustling ripstop pants, a long-sleeved shirt, and that weird gray thermal hoodie that had turned out to be my favorite garment because it was so versatile.

Over all of that, I wore the Viking jacket I'd bought in the town outside of Lillooet.

Carrying my backpack, I headed for the lodge, hoping for a quiet corner to write in and maybe to drink something hot and fortifying.

The building was buttoned up tight with a sign on the door that said it opened at six a.m., so I sat at a table on the restaurant's deck in the dim morning, wondering at how the sky managed to be the exact same shade of brightness as it had been when I'd gone to bed the night before.

The gloomy forest had begun to awaken with twittering birds as I went back to the room after writing my journal entry. Mike was awake and sorting his photography equipment for the day's excursion. Soon we were on our way down to the dock attached to the lodge and its outbuildings.

The boat, when we reached it, was a large, stable metal catamaran with three decks. I chose a window seat with a little table. Mike unpacked what we called the Rhino Chaser, a lens so big that it caused comment wherever we went.

"I think we should dub it *Size Matters*," I told Mike, after the fifth fellow tourist had commented on the nearly yard-long, foot-wide cannon of a lens mounted on a monopod because it was too large to hold steady by hand. Mike looked like a *National Geographic* staffer, holding the Rhino Chaser in his foul-weather gear as he stood gracefully on the deck, manly silver stubble covering his face.

The ranger on board did a good job of telling us interesting facts as the boat chugged toward the glaciers through calm, jade-green waters. "The size of national parks in Alaska is hard to wrap your head around," he said. "Glacier Bay National Park, just one of them, is bigger than the whole state of Connecticut, and the geography it covers is only two hundred years old. The spruce and hemlocks covering everything are so uniform in size because, when the glaciers melted and formed these island areas and deep bays and peninsulas, the plants and trees arose at the same time." He read a portion of Teddy Roosevelt's speech in authorizing the National Parks.

"Leave the wilderness unmarred. Man cannot improve upon its magnificence."

Truer words were never spoken.

Sea otters floated beside us, much farther out from the shore than I would have expected to see them, and I squeaked with excitement when I spotted the first puffin. "Mike! Oh my gosh! Get a picture of that cutie!" Puffins bobbed everywhere in the water around the boat as we approached our first landmark, South Marble Island.

The rocky knoll emerging from the sea was teeming with life. Layers of birds nested in the cliffs, from seagulls to kittiwakes to cormorants, and two species of puffins flapped and bobbed around us, unafraid of the boat. "True wilderness is untrammeled by humans, a place where man has no influence and leaves no footprint," the ranger intoned.

Humans certainly seemed to have no place in the abundant life that surrounded us.

Steller sea lions barked nonstop in reeking rookeries that covered rock outcrops protruding from the water. These creatures were unbelievably huge, the females up to eight hundred pounds and the males, maned in heavy, orangey fur, up to sixteen hundred. Their voices echoed deep and scary across the water, as the stench of bird guano whiffed up periodically to surround us with eye-watering ammonia.

After drifting along the island's shore, we picked up some speed and headed to a high, rocky cliff chiseled by frigid runoff waterfalls. The boat pulled all the way up to ground against the pebbled shore, and the crew let off five intrepid kayak campers, all women, setting forth on an adventure. As we pulled away, leaving those brave souls smiling and waving back at us from among their crafts and mounded up dry bags, I felt the beautiful vastness in such contrast to them; they looked tiny and out-of-place as we left, dots of bright red, yellow, and orange on a monochromatic gray-green shore.

I felt better about being a passive tourist, sightseeing from safety, when the ever-informative ranger told us, "Ninety percent of visitors to this park experience it from the deck of a cruise ship as it weaves through these bays. *You* are part of an elite ten percent of our park's visitors who actually fly to Gustavus, stay in the park, and get on this smaller boat to see and experience the wildlife up close. Those kayakers are some of the one percent of annual visitors who opt to go deep into the park to experience it—not so much for what's here but for what's *not* here. No roads, no buildings, no people."

I'd grown up in a place like that; I remembered the times when I was young and paddled a bodyboard down the Na Pali Coast into its secret bays in nothing but a swimsuit, and saw not another soul all day but the ones I'd traveled with. I swam and dove in the ocean and surfed without anyone else around. I hiked those mountains and experienced the Hawaiian wildness so much more than most—a gentler place, with fewer dangers than Alaska, but no less magnificent.

Miles further on, we drew close to some rugged cliffs thousands of feet high. "Look for mountain goats," the ranger said, and soon we spotted a lone white goat high on the cliff. My phone couldn't take any photos that showed anything, so I contented myself with binoculars to view a pair of twin baby goats, white as shaved coconut, leaping from pinnacle to precipice, banging their little heads together as they played. One of the kids was too aggressive, so the other ran to their mama and then turned back from the shelter of her side and her lowered, sharp black horns to confront its sibling. The little drama was utterly charming, partly because it was so unexpected to see this played out on the face of a thousand-foot vertical cliff hanging over the ocean.

The first major glacier we approached was named Marjorie. The ranger's lecture on the way glaciers behaved helped me understand how they shape the earth.

"Think of a hundred and fifty feet of snow falling on one spot and never having a chance to thaw. The snowfall piles and piles, compressing the molecules until the snow is packed into ice. It's heavy, and pushes down into the earth, pushing the earth up on the sides into mountains. And because it's heavy, it heads downhill, grinding up the stone into fine, silky sand along the way. Glaciers are moving rivers of ice generated by the accumulated snow of each winter."

We could see this in action as we studied Marjorie, a "stable" glacier. This meant that water lost off one end as the glacier "calved" was replaced on the other end as new snow packed down and pushed. The water directly in front of the glacier was sludgy, filled with silt and mineral. With the sound of a giant breaking bones—a terrible deep, cracking roar—a big section of glacier broke off in front of us and plummeted in a tumbling, chunky waterfall of slabs into the water below. The wound left behind on the glacier's face was the color of high-quality blue topaz.

Even hypnotized by the sight as we were, it was genuinely cold out on the deck, with a slicing wind. Neither Mike nor I were wearing mufflers, hats, or gloves, so I went back inside the boat, where the views were still good, if not as clear. But Mike never left the deck, instead reappearing periodically to warm his hands on a cup of coffee or to slide them under my jacket, making me giggle. He was energized and excited the whole day, a hunter with bountiful game off the bow and the Rhino Chaser to catch it with.

We saw three more glaciers, each a little different from the rest, and finally headed back toward Gustavus and the lodge.

I've never been overly fond of boats, and the vastness was getting to me again by the end of the eight-hour tour. I endured seasickness between wildlife phenomena sightings by falling asleep with my head in the corner.

Wildlife checklist from the day:

- humpback whales (numerous)
- white mountain goats (3)
- sea otters (8)

- Steller sea lions (infinite piles)
- puffins (2 kinds)
- nesting bald eagles (2)
- and a host of different kinds of seabirds.

It was worth being on a boat for eight hours to see all of that and the calving of a glacier, too.

After we arrived back at the dock, we needed to stretch our legs, so we took a short hike through the forest on a gorgeous boardwalk trail lined with flora we were becoming familiar with: mosses, lichens, ferns, early wild blueberry, spruce, and hemlock, which each have a role in the creation of new forest.

Taken by surprise at discovering wood ducks in a tiny pool of old glacier melt, we attempted some inadequate phone photos and tried to get some of wood tits and a squirrel—and that's when I found fresh bear scat near a ripped-up log.

"That's moose droppings," Mike said, seeing the whites of my eyes.

"Oh, no. Moose don't tear up logs looking for grubs." The bear poop was shiny, wet, and bright green. I started clapping and singing as I went along the trail, the strategy we'd been told was helpful to alert bears that humans were coming. "Never surprise a bear," we'd heard. "And never, never run from one."

I tried to imagine being able to stand my ground with a bear—and failed.

At dinner, I showed the photo of the green scat to our waiter.

"Oh, yeah. That's bear all right. Looks like he's been eating water weeds. The bears're all over the place now that the berries are coming out," the waiter said, Adam's apple bobbing with enthusiasm. Mike planned to go back with his camera now that a sighting was imminent, but I decided not to walk that trail again with anything less than an air horn and repellent spray.

After dinner, I went into the lodge's gift shop and found bear repellent in a canister as big as a fire extinguisher.

"It's forty dollars, and you can't take it on the plane," the helpful young woman behind the counter said. She was holding a dog-eared romance novel to her breast and wore rhinestone-edged glasses; I immediately liked her. "You can use the spray while you're here, and then donate it to the ranger station. They go through a lot of it."

I opted not to buy the stuff if I couldn't lug it along on the rest of our travels. The immediate area around the lodge seemed pretty safe, and I didn't have any plans for hiking alone.

THE NEXT MORNING DAWNED OVERCAST AND DRIZZLY, AND MIKE AND I trekked along the beach this time. "Beach" seemed like the wrong word to describe a scree of rocks of various different sizes and types. This beach was different from those I was familiar with, with stones still rough from their glacier grinding, not yet worn by water and waves.

The tidal surge in the area was about eighteen feet, and that morning, the tide was low, leaving behind a wake of seaweed, clam shells, and assorted other slime, but we saw very little actual sea life. A ceiling of clouds roiled overhead, and there was not another human for miles in any direction. I couldn't hear anything but bird-song and the crunch of gravel under our boots as Mike and I walked along the edge of smooth jade water that was Bartlett Bay, enjoying the refreshingly cool air and the fact that it wasn't actually raining.

Suddenly I heard that loud, half-swallowed, croaking cry I'd come to recognize, and a bald eagle circled us. Off to the left, in the water, a distinctive sighing blow sounded, the noise of a whale breathing. Fifty feet from land, a humpback rose, cruising in the shallows. This was probably one of the same whales that comes to Maui every winter, according to the naturalists we'd heard on the boat. Being so close to one of these giants from our warm waters at home as it appeared half a world away brought tears to my eyes.

We ran to climb a boulder to see the whale better, and it moved on. A pod of dolphins swam by next, and overhead the eagle circled us again.

We returned to the lodge, rented ocean kayaks, and headed out for a paddle on Bartlett Bay. The ocean was so calm compared to Maui. I was nervous at first, never having paddled a real sea kayak before, with all the accompanying gear: boots, waders, rain slickers, and a rubber skirt attached to the kayak and around my waist. The thought of tipping over in all that gear in freezing water made me a little sweaty underneath it all.

Mike and I paddled our craft out, hoping by some miracle that we'd see orcas; we saw otters instead. The adorable fuzzy creatures hardly paused in their eating and frolicking to pay any mind to us, yet somehow, without seeming to move, they were always too far away for us to get a really good look at them.

I felt the space, as I sat caught in my fragile craft between sea and sky—but it was not a formless void waiting to swallow me up. This vastness was wide, wild, and wonderful, and filled with all that should be there. *Was I making progress with the weird anxiety that had ambushed me on the ferry?* I hoped so. I wasn't going to give in to it, regardless.

CHAPTER FORTY
GUSTAVUS TO JUNEAU

Mike scouted around for a decent meal nearby and got us reservations in the hamlet of Gustavus for the world-renowned Gustavus Inn's five-course, locally sourced gourmet daily meal.

The Inn was a big old house in the center of the village, and we were dropped off for dinner there by the lodge's bus on one of its runs to the airport. The first thing that caught my eye was a giant garden behind the house, filled with flowers and a rainbow of lettuces, beans, peas, beets, kale, and more that provided fresh food for the Inn's daily meal. We ambled up and down, exploring it, until we were ushered in by the hostess.

They seated us family-style, and we made friends with a young couple who worked in Gustavus as kayak guides. The fact that locals made up most of the customers told us we were in for a treat.

We swapped adventure stories with the young people and devoured the dinner's courses as they were brought to us: fresh homemade sourdough rolls whose starter was a hundred years old, multi-green salad that had been growing outside mere hours ago, baby bok choy with carrots, Cajun-style fresh wild salmon, mashed potatoes with the colored skin on, and a finish of banana cream and crème de menthe pies, everything made that day by the Inn's staff.

The Inn had earned a James Beard America's Classics award a few years ago, and it was merited.

The staff called for a taxi to take us back to the lodge after dinner, and a plump, smiling lady showed up in a van with a magnetic sign on the door identifying the vehicle as Strawberry's Taxi Service. "Would you like me to show you the town?" she asked.

Mike and I glanced at each other. What could there be to this tiny village? Experiencing Mind Meld again, we both flashed back to our memorable "tour" of Kalapana with Stretch in his doorless van. We both said, "Sure!" at the same time, in no hurry to return to our dreary room at the lodge.

Gustavus had a lot more to it than met the eye initially. Strawberry took us by a homegrown golf course, carved out of the rugged fields with a mower; a busy dock where the locals battled seagulls and eagles on a daily basis to bring in their catch; a community garden, fenced so the moose didn't eat everything. She even took us to see the liquor store, decorated with a sculpture made of chain saws soldered together, which was owned by a fisherman who kept set hours: four to seven p.m., three days a week.

"There's always a line the minute he opens the liquor store," Strawberry said regretfully, as we pulled up in front of the slatternly building made of unpainted siding. The chain saw sculpture was definitely the property's main attraction. "There's a bit of an alcohol problem in this town."

A grocery store at the corner was still operating original gas pumps from the 1940s, Strawberry told us (they looked like it), and we found out that the ruler-straight roads had been built that way when Gustavus was a WWII support outpost, in case they were needed as additional landing strips.

Gustavus seemed to be a close-knit, warm, oddball community, with moose antler decorations on every lawn—and they sure knew how to eat.

~

THE NEXT MORNING, WE PACKED UP AND TOOK A HIKE BEFORE WE HAD to go to the airport for the flight back to Juneau. The walk along Bartlett Bay was just as amazing the second time. Great blue herons stalked everywhere in the very low tidal waters, graceful as Egyptian carvings; we spotted the eagles again, and even the large triangle fin of an orca in the distance.

Mike and I split up, because he was still hoping to spot a bear to photograph, and I wanted nothing to do with that idea. He found a trail and went back through the forest while I continued along the beach, the chill gray stones and broken clamshells crunching beneath my boots.

It was lonely and magnificent. I climbed a barnacle-covered boulder to look around, and ahead of me, a whale suddenly leapt up out of the water, mouth agape in what we'd decided to call a "feeding breech." The creature was so close that I gasped and almost toppled off the rock.

Before coming to Alaska, I'd never seen a humpback with its mouth open. Humpbacks exhibit entirely different behaviors in Hawaii—competing to mate, calving, caring for newborns. Feeding is a completely different sight. Rising from the depths, water streams out of the buff-colored lining of baleen filling the enormous cave of the whale's mouth, contrasting with its long, narrow, pale pink tongue. The way they looked coming up from the depths reminded me of the giant sand worms emerging from the desert in the 1990s cult sci-fi movie *Dune*.

The eagle pair we'd seen yesterday came over to check me out, flying around close, dogfighting in midair just above me, lighting on trees ahead of me.

Feeling the solitude, I started clapping to make noise (recommended so the bears can leave if they hear you); then, I broke into song as I walked.

My voice carried across the still water of the bay, and it sounded almost as good as singing in the shower. Hymns and choruses bubbled up from the memory banks—*Swing Low, Sweet Chariot,*

Amazing Grace, Majesty, All Hail King Jesus, You Are Mighty—rich Christian oldies from my years of worshiping. I sang all the way back to the lodge, my heart swelling with gratitude and joy to be having this experience.

Walking up the now-familiar trail to the lodge, I glanced at my phone and saw that it was Sunday. I'd just been to church, and was spiritually filled.

~

THE PLANE BACK TO JUNEAU WAS AN EIGHT-SEATER THIS TIME, AND having flown on the tiny Piper before, it felt roomy. Our two pilots took a different course, this time through the mountains, flying so close to them that it seemed the wings would brush the trees, gray stone, and dazzling snowy summits as the sun finally came out. Mike and I grinned at each other with delight. The Cessna exited the mountains into jaw-dropping views of ocean and lakes, with boats running like zippers across their smooth blue-green surfaces.

Juneau was shiny and warm this time around. We picked up our vehicle and drove around looking for a laundromat, but it was Sunday, and the two we found were closed. Giving up on clean clothes, we took the famous tram above Juneau to the Timberline Restaurant on top of the ridge above the town and had an unexpectedly delicious lunch. Mike consumed the all-you-can-eat Dungeness crab special, and I devoured a bison steak salad. The steak was pungently flavored and the greens crisp, but it was nothing compared to Mike's festival of fresh cracked crab, dipped in butter and washed down with dark ale.

After that, bulging a bit at the seams, we toddled around the mellow loop hike at the top of the mountain, making that pilgrimage to see more snowcapped peaks and sinuous waterways with the overweight folks from the cruise ships parked at Juneau's immense docks below.

We were camping at Mendenhall again that night and needed a few things, so we pulled into the Walmart.

The Juneau, Alaska, Walmart parking lot had a flock of giant ravens that hung out there, hoping for handouts. The ravens sat on the shopping carts and guarded the trash cans, begging for scraps— or more like threatening to take out an eye if they weren't fed. They were huge and spooky, and made Hitchcock's *The Birds* seem lightweight.

We pulled in beside a beat-up convertible red Mustang. A giant wolfdog sitting inside it about took Mike's head off through the car's open window when he tried to open the van's door. He ended up exiting on my side.

Juneau's Walmart was the most fully equipped store I've ever seen. A full food section, with organic produce and self-checkout, was laid out beside the biggest, most comprehensive sporting goods/camping/fishing/survival section I could imagine: scores of knives, all sorts of ammo and weapons, special whistles, water puri- fiers, tents, nets, and worm blowers all the way down to first aid kits you could carry in your shoe. Walking the aisles, I detected a fashion trend of women in yoga pants and knee-high rubber boots, along with men whose beards began at their eyebrows.

A Native American woman, possibly Tlingit since this was their tribal area, was very helpful, personally walking us around the store to find all of the obscure items we needed to round out our road trip supplies.

"We're out of bear spray," she told me regretfully, scanning the bar code of the spray's empty shelf into the handheld gadget she carried like a gunslinger. "But I can direct you to the bear bells and air horns." I noted her small frame, long black hair, interesting tattoos, and stocky build; she was beautiful in a way I'd never encountered before. My background growing up in Hawaii sensitized me to being white in an indigenous culture's territory, and I was especially grateful for her kindness and generosity.

We ended up buying one each of the anti-bear gadgets, along with a pack of hot dogs, lettuce, yogurt, fire-starter chunks and lighter fluid, and a supply of junk food for when we were driving again.

I was still full from the bison salad and objected when Mike picked up the hot dogs. "Seriously, honey. You just ate three pounds of fresh crab."

"Yeah, but I love a good fire-roasted hot dog," he said.

We were camping at the same site beneath Mendenhall Glacier that we'd been at before, and we bought some firewood alongside the road from a kid and his family that were chopping up seasoned pine and selling it in bundles to pay for his soccer trip.

We pulled into the park with panache, having been there before, but were taken aback to find our assigned campsite roped off with yellow caution tape, and a big sign posted in front of it: *"WARNING: THIS CAMPSITE SUBJECT TO FLOODING. Be prepared to evacuate when alerted."*

The formerly low lake in front of blue-white Mendenhall Glacier was now filled to the brim. The warm temperatures were having an effect on the glacier. We were tired by then and kind of cranky and had to track down the camp host who'd gone fishing to ask for a different campsite. His nice wife tried to help us, but couldn't give us a new spot without making sure it wasn't reserved, and her husband had the phone app that would check the computer.

Mike was able to get some phone reception, go to the park's website, and find a different campsite on high ground and reserve it as a different solution. We were installed, with a fire going, safely ten feet above "sea level," when the camp host finally got back and verified that all was well.

"Yeah, sorry about that," he said. "We can't just reassign you; we don't really manage this place. People don't know it, but this flooding happens every year. Melt begins deep inside the glacier and it fills up in a big pocket of water. Then suddenly the front part of the ice that held it in gives way, and the water gushes out and fills the lake and it overflows. Last year, your former campsite ended up five feet under water."

We were very glad to be on high ground in our dry new site with its own bear-proof bin. By eight p.m., when Mike brought out the hot dogs, nothing in the world smelled or tasted better than those plain, crispy dogs, stuck on a pine branch and cooked over the fire.

Yesterday: five-course, five-star, chef prepared, locally sourced gourmet meal.

Today: beef dog on a stick, seasoned by hunger and the chill outdoors.

CHAPTER FORTY-ONE
MENDENHALL AND BEAR COUNTRY

The beaver was back near our campsite in Mendenhall Campground, crunching his water reeds. He looked like a fat water-going marmot to me, and he let us get very close before he slapped his tail on the water like a pistol shot and dove under. It was a very effective defensive tactic—I was taking a movie of him and almost dropped my phone into the pond at the explosive crack of sound.

We spent a snuggly night in the van, listening to the patter, alternating with the roar of rain on the roof. The fact that it was raining was fine. We'd been able to have one really sunny day in Juneau, and we were leaving early for the ferry to Haines.

"Why are we going to Haines, again? And where is it, exactly?" I asked Mike, sitting up the next morning and rubbing my eyes.

"It's farther north into Alaska, and we're going there because that's where the road through the mountains into British Columbia begins," Mike said patiently. "Take the umbrella to the bathroom and do your morning thing, and by the time you get back, I'll be packed up."

I was still profoundly unwilling to get out of the sleeping bag with the chill rain pounding gloomily down on the van. "You're such a gentleman," I said. "Which means you want me out of the way while you pack up the van the way you like it."

"Exactly," he said. "Here's the umbrella."

I trekked down to the bathrooms in pajamas and boots, grateful for the umbrella sluicing water everywhere but on me. Sure enough, by the time I'd schlepped back through the puddles, Mike had packed, and the van was turned on and warmed up.

At five a.m., we found coffee and tea at a drive-through kiosk in Juneau, a great invention if there ever was one, and began the next leg of our journey as we lined up for the ferry to Haines. We had been able to see Juneau on one of the prettiest days of the year so far, and now we were saying goodbye at the perfect time.

Getting on the ferry was interesting. Several hours ahead of when the boat was scheduled to depart, they organized the cars into lanes according to their destination. Then, they loaded everyone on in the order they were getting off, pointed outward so they could drive right out of the ferry. Thus, we were parked in the line for Haines for two hours, sipping our beverages, and listening to several more audiobook chapters of *Twisted Vine*.

Mike and I were totally sucked into the story, and I could hardly remember that I'd written the book. Hearing the audiobooks voice-acted was weird for me —sometimes I'd get a glimmer that I knew what came next, but mostly it was a take-me-away kind of experience, with Sara Malia Hatfield's rich, dramatic reading, and perfect for whiling away the time.

Though my print books were self-published, my agent had sold the audiobook rights to Audible for production, and that advance had paid for a new roof and solar panels for our house on Maui. Not only that, Audible had listened to me when I insisted that we needed a voice actress "from Hawaii" because the Hawaiian words and pidgin dialect were so difficult to master for anyone not from the Islands. I was delighted with Sara's "local girl" pidgin and flaw-less Hawaiian pronunciation throughout the Paradise Crime

Mysteries, and we'd even become friends and met in person at the Hawaii Book and Music Festival when I was a featured speaker.

"Being able to voice-act Lei and her friends is such a joy," Sara had said. "I absolutely love being able to represent Hawaii's people through these books." Sara even looked a lot like Lei: a pretty, mixed Hawaiian-Asian with an athletic build and a few freckles here and there.

Mike had booked us a berth again, even though the ferry ride was only around six hours. We fell into our little bunk beds and napped to recover from our early departure, took showers, and then had an incredibly yummy buffet lunch in the nearly deserted formal dining room. This ferry, the *Columbia*, was newer and nicer than the mighty but somewhat worn *Matanuska*.

There was nothing much worth seeing outside because of the rain and fog. The dim shapes of yet more pine-covered mountains loomed and disappeared in the distance as indistinguishable, forbidding dark masses. We were going still farther north once we reached Haines, driving into the Yukon and some of the most remote parts of the whole country.

We'd be camping with the possibility of bears around us for days to come—and no internet or phone service since we were reentering Canada.

I didn't let myself think about the vastness but I felt it, outside the confines of the ferry, pressing on the back of my mind and tickling along my nerves.

~

THE BEST WAY TO GET TO KNOW THE "REAL" RESIDENTS OF ANY TOWN is to go to the laundromat. We found one on the outskirts of Haines, a rugged-but-cute outpost of a fishing-oriented village full of older folks, that offered art galleries alternating with sporting goods and hardware stores, peppered here and there with greasy spoon cafés.

The laundromat featured coin-operated showers and many

chiding little signs on notecards: "Check that your load is done!!" and "Absolutely no shoes in the shower area!!"

Once the clothes were loaded, I spotted the cutest little hen on the sidewalk. Small, brightly spotted in black-and-white, and curious, she trotted right up to me, hoping for a handout. I'm fond of chickens, and I took her picture.

"What an adorable little chicken," I told Mike. "I don't think I've seen any on this trip, and we have so many running around at home." Indeed, the loose chickens are downright pesky in Hawaii.

A couple of minutes later, I heard a shout and ran outside. Mike's eyes were huge, and he was struggling to get his camera out to photograph a giant bald eagle that was flapping and jumping around on the ground right next to our parked van.

"The eagle tried to grab the chicken!" Mike exclaimed "He missed it on the dive, but he chased it along the ground. The chicken was dodging like crazy, and it barely got away by hiding under the house!"

The eagle, looking disgruntled, hopped up onto the top of a nearby street sign, rearranging its feathers grumpily.

Now I knew why we hadn't seen any loose chickens on the whole trip.

THE FOUR HUNDRED KILOMETERS OF ROAD FROM HAINES, ALASKA, TO Whitehorse in the Yukon was supposed to be one of the most beautiful routes in the world. Mike had told me this, but as with many of the planning points of the trip, I hadn't absorbed it.

Not being involved in the planning helped with my travel anxiety, and also played to Mike's strengths as a person who needed control, enjoyed visualizing a pattern and plan, and found a useful role for himself through shopping for supplies and tickets and making the arrangements. My job was to pay for everything with my book royalties when the credit card bills rolled in, and I enjoyed that heartily as well. Overall, that division of labor had been a beneficial strategy for both of us.

We were passing through the area at the wrong time of year to witness the annual mass invasion of bald eagles as they fished the spawning beds of the famous Chilkat River, but on the plus side, no one else was there at all. I counted about six cars all day as we drove a wide, well-maintained highway bordered by purple loosestrife, Alaskan fireweed, lupines, daisies, and asters, with aspens shimmering in the background.

We braked for a pair of wild trumpeter swans feeding among the reeds in a quiet area of the river, as unlikely in their snowy splendor as winged horses.

After a few hours, we left Alaska and were greeted by the nicest Canadian border guard. He asked us where we were from, and when we said Hawaii, he grinned, gave us a map, and said, "You're in for a treat, but get gas whenever you can and slow down when you see orange flags on the side of the highway. That means there's a bad patch in the asphalt, and it'll levitate you right off the road."

We thanked him, and reentered British Columbia.

We rose in elevation from the border crossing into the majesty of hills whose green velvet shoulders were studded with yellow daisy buttons. Lone prairie dogs stood perfectly still on the side of the road like little signposts, but whenever we slowed to get a closer look at them, they'd pop into their burrows. As we drove higher still, the trees disappeared. The mountains thrust jagged peaks veined with snow and trimmed in feather boas of trailing cloud, high into the thin air.

Streams threaded through alpine meadows set off by purple, yellow, and white explosions of wildflower blooms, and as we drove around a bend in one of those meadows, we saw a bear.

Not just any bear, but a grizzly bear, as big as a rhino and just as dangerous. The bear, thin and shaggy from winter, was pawing at the ground near one of the streams as we pulled over onto the shoulder of the road to get a look at it.

Mike went into a frenzy of excitement, jumping out of the van and grabbing his camera, determined to get a good shot. "First good bear sighting of the whole trip!" he chortled.

The bear was perhaps a quarter of a mile away, so I was fine with this: I could sit in the van, Mike could get his bear pictures, and we'd both be safe.

I rolled down my window, rested my elbow on the frame, and eyeballed the beast.

The bear sat, lifted his snout, and sniffed the air. Then he got up and ambled in our direction, pausing to dig or chew a bit of vegetation. His coat was golden and shaggy on his head and back, and he had the crested hump on his shoulders characteristic of a grizzly, or "brown bear," as they are being renamed to reduce fear of the species (which is not working, in my opinion).

The bear moved in an oddly graceful, panther-like way, and I tried to think of good similes for his size. A sofa? A refrigerator? A small Jeep?

Mike's excitement increased as the bear came closer. He got out the Rhino Chaser, trying to stabilize the giant lens without the monopod, as the bear sat down on his buttocks and scratched himself. Then it stood up, walked a few steps, and squatted. "He's pooping!" Mike yelled.

"That's going to be a great shot," I teased. "It'll go viral for sure."

The bear left his poop pile and ambled in our direction. He zigged, and then he zagged, never looking directly at us, just occasionally lifting his nose and scenting the air.

He came closer and closer, never appearing to hurry or be aware of us.

I began to get agitated as the bear progressed nearer. We were parked on the edge of the highway, which was elevated about ten feet, giving a great vantage point for the photography. Directly below the road grew a belt of tall bushes and thick vegetation.

"Big Boy smells our saltwater taffy," I said. We also had apples and cheese and a box of fudge. "We're like Yogi the Bear's picnic basket."

Indeed, he seemed to smell us, lifting his head ever so casually to sniff, then ambling closer, pawing the ground here and there, but coming on steadily.

"Here's how you hunt humans," I said, continuing my nervous narration. "You pretend you don't know they're fascinated with you, standing beside their metal lunch pail on wheels, full of goodies. You sidle along, stop and scratch as they go crazy with their little clicking thing, and you can get closer and closer . . ."

Mike needed to get something out of the camera case. He went around to the other side of the van from the bear, opened the door, and rummaged in the case.

"We need to go," I said loudly. The bear had reached the bushy scree beside the highway below us and disappeared. "We need to go now."

"Just one more shot." *Photographers always say that. It should be on Mike's tombstone—and at this rate, it might well be!* Mike came around the side of the van and looked around. "Where'd he go?"

"I'm going without you if you don't get in the van now!" I yelled, rolling up my window and moving toward the driver's seat. "He's directly below us in the bushes, and he's coming our way! Get in the freakin' car!"

Finally Mike got in, fired up the van, and we pulled away, watching for the bear in the rearview mirror until we hit a curve and the scene disappeared.

"I can't believe you were making such a fuss!" Mike said. "That was an incredible sighting."

"And I can't believe you didn't realize that bear was coming for us from the beginning!" I yelled. The outburst from each of us as we got underway was the closest we'd come to a fight on the trip—but we escaped in our picnic basket on wheels.

CHAPTER FORTY-TWO
WHITEHORSE, YUKON

After the bear encounter, we drove on toward the nearest hamlet, a dip-in the-road called Haines Junction. We had been planning to stay there overnight, but the three motels at the edge of town were either full, too scary-looking, or both, so we pressed on toward Whitehorse.

I was enamored of the name. "Whitehorse." I kept saying it aloud. "Whitehorse, Whitehorse. I like the way it sounds." Mike rolled his eyes, but thirty-plus years after marrying me, he was used to how I often fall in love with certain words and repeat them or work them into sentences. *Whitehorse!* It sounded so romantically rugged: "Whitehorse, Yukon. I've been there!"

I planned to get a T-shirt with the town's name on it. Maybe two.

Just outside of Whitehorse, we spotted a band of wild horses trotting by the side of the road, paints and Appaloosas, fat and sassy. Which probably meant they weren't really wild, but they *were* loose, with no fences anywhere, and they eyeballed us with suspicion.

I pointed at a pale, freckled mare standing off by herself. "I've just seen a white horse outside of Whitehorse."

Mike snorted. "My honey is easily entertained."

"Hey, that's a once-in-a-lifetime event." I yawned. "Promise me that our next stop is a soft bed."

The first motel we reached in Whitehorse was a Days Inn with musty hallways filled with the gray road dust of the area and a parking lot jammed with big rigs. We fell into unconsciousness at eleven p.m. with the assistance of the blackout curtains.

The next morning, the Whitehorse Cultural Center was having a festival, and it was filled with First Nations folks in clusters, groups, and seminars, decked out in varying degrees of native dress. We wandered through the exhibits and crafts. Mike looked closely at the canoes, which are higher and wider than Hawaiian canoes, but also made from a single tree.

"No outrigger," Mike said. "Probably didn't need one because they had bigger trees to work with."

"Or the water's calmer than in Hawaii," I said.

"That too."

I got my T-shirts (two of them!) emblazoned with *Whitehorse*, and we left the colorful town regretfully.

We drove on for hours of trees and valleys and streams until we passed two men waving frantically, standing beside a huge black truck pulled over on the side of the road with one of those giant steel trailers hitched to it.

I was apprehensive about helping these strangers, my crime-writer mind providing many worst-case scenarios, but the man hailing us was red-faced and hearty, and a tad stout. He was also wearing a T-shirt with a maple leaf on it that proclaimed, **CANADA, *eh?***

We opened the side door of the van to pick up our first hitchhiker.

"Oh, thank God. I promise I'm not a serial killer," exclaimed the man, whose name was Kent. A fountain of information flowed from him as Mike moved the camping gear and he crawled inside the van to sit on our mattress in back.

Kent was a contractor. He and his workman, who was staying

behind with the truck, were delivering materials to a job site when the truck broke down. He had no cell service and needed to get to the nearest outpost of civilization to make some phone calls. Hearing that we were from Hawaii, he told us he'd been going to Kauai for decades to stay at a timeshare condo that his family owned. He told us about his seven grandkids and how he'd built his business from the ground up and on and on as we drove.

We dropped Kent at a gas station/store so decrepit that we were worried for him, but he told us he'd be fine. We wished him the best and refused his offer to fill our tank.

Our next stop turned out to be the most "local color" restaurant we'd yet stopped at on the route: a tiny store and café manned by a large flannel-shirted man missing his front teeth. He had a Canadian accent so broad that we had to ask for everything to be repeated (or perhaps it was just the missing teeth that made him unintelligible). In any case, he fixed me a sixteen-dollar chef salad, made with much industriousness in the nearby kitchen. The result was a mere handful of iceberg lettuce buried under four equidistant mounds of chopped lunch meat of different kinds. A single cherry tomato graced the center, and the masterpiece was accompanied by a squeeze bottle of creamy bacon dressing.

"This could be why my pants are getting tight," I whispered to Mike. "Man-salad."

Mike hadn't bothered to try to order anything "health food," and his burger looked delicious.

In the corner of the deli/store was an impressive array of progun bumper stickers, everything from *"We don't call 911"* (with a picture of a gun pointed at the reader) to *"Gun Control Means Holding It Two-Handed"* (with illustration).

I tried to take a picture of the rack of stickers without being obvious. People appeared to love their guns passionately in the Yukon.

The distance between Whitehorse and where we finally fetched up, in the grubby oil town of Fort St. John, B.C., was eight hundred and fifty-seven point five miles—our longest drive day yet. We used close to fifty gallons of fuel and drove for twenty hours over roads that varied from smooth and wide to bumpy, narrow, steep, or covered with slippery mud and gravel—and all of them virtually empty. "The worst thing about Canada is the crowds," I deadpanned.

The next day, we "took it easy" and drove for only ten hours. Stiff and tired, we pulled up among reveling Canadians (it was Canada Day, similar to our Fourth of July) with their happy, noisy children at a campground where Mike had made a reservation. We climbed out of the van, looked around, got attacked by deerflies and disappointed by the muddy lake and screaming kids, got back into the van, and drove to a nearby Holiday Inn.

We were both ready for some creature comforts. Mike reveled in watching TV while I swam laps in the basement pool, delighted to be able to just wiggle my body, and then we both took showers and enjoyed the Wi-Fi and catching up with friends and family.

Most of the many miles we'd driven were glorious. They'd begun with a sweeping vista of smoke-tinted, graduated shades of blue hills outside of Whitehorse, covered with the dark green of pines and spruce once we reached them. The ribbon of gray road had the wide, treeless shoulders typical in Canada, maintained by each of the provinces. The cleared belt of shoulder before the dense forest began was filled with grasses and flowers, and that was why, we speculated, we were able to see all the wildlife we spotted. They came out of the forest to graze, forage, and hunt.

The first endangered wood bison we saw was alone, resting half-buried in a sunny sand patch at the edge of the road, chewing his cud as casual as could be. Further along, we met a whole herd of the massive creatures. Something about them, shaggy and indifferent, chewing and switching flies, felt ancient, as if they were relics left over from a more primitive season of the earth.

The bison calves were light-colored, fuzzy as lambs, and just as cute. We watched one baby nursing. His mother got tired of his antics and sat down, effectively removing the teat. The calf relentlessly head-butted and bugged her to nurse some more, nudging and bucking and pushing on her. The cow's long-suffering expression was priceless.

We pulled over so that Mike could take pictures of a small, plump black bear eating clover in a roadside field, totally cute and not scary at all. We even spotted a fox, trotting along through the grass verge with a prairie dog in its mouth.

The best thing about the long days of driving was the unspooling of the road, the green, flowered shoulders, and the deep sky with its three-dimensional clouds. Tiny cotton ball poufs, fluffy cumulus mounds, veiled traceries of reversing herringbone brushstrokes, coruscated fans, and swirls of vapor made a cinematic backdrop for the natural beauty in the foreground.

"I feel like we're not really moving. This scenery just keeps flowing by, never changing," Mike finally said. Even he was feeling the vastness of this country.

"That's exactly how I felt on the ferry," I replied.

The next day was another mega driving day as we tried to reach Jasper National Park, our destination.

We talked about what was working on the trip and what wasn't.

This many long days of driving in a row, without any hikes or sweet destinations to break it up, wasn't working. We were both tired of being stuck in the car except for brief stops to take a picture, stretch our legs, or sample scary cuisine at a truck stop.

"Well, we've proved that the world is a pretty big place," Mike said, as we looped down into yet another stunning valley, cleft by a rippling stream and bordered by cottonwoods and aspen punctuated by the dark note of pines.

"And we've settled the question of whether or not there are enough trees in Canada," I replied, gesturing to more rolling hills covered in conifers of various shades.

We also passed fields of canola, hay, and alfalfa, rich and groomed as a good clip on a show dog. Further along, heavy road work slowed our pace as we made our way through the gouging and reshaping of entire hillsides, and eventually we got back into more trees.

We passed a coal mine and its accompanying energy plant, every bit as darkly dramatic as I'd read about in stories, but the thing was tidier than I'd been led to expect. The whole side of a mountain had been pulled down into various piles of rubble, and on the floor of the valley a vast, shiny black mountain of coal was being backhoed into trucks. The power plant part of the operation boasted a lot of pipes and metal buildings, sprouting power lines like a big, ugly chia pet.

We ran into trouble in the village of Grande Cache, the only food/gas place for eighty-six km in any direction. After a surprisingly wonderful lunch at a restaurant filled with old men playing cards (and no one else), Mike went to the register to pay and discovered he was missing his credit card. He'd forgotten it several hundred miles back in one of the gas pumps. He called, and the gas station confirmed it was there and cut it up. Then he called our lovely Bank of America to report it—and got an automated response that canceled *both* of our charge cards immediately.

This was not what he'd intended, of course, and it took us a hundred kilometers or so to calm down from the ensuing frustration.

Fortunately, though we no longer had a joint card to charge the trip on, we both had our own personal cards. We were still going to be able to get through the trip, but having our joint card disappear so quickly and finally was upsetting. Things seemed on a downward trend as we finally, after twelve exhausting hours on the road, rolled into the Sunwapta Falls Rocky Mountain Lodge in Jasper National Park around ten p.m.

In spite of months-earlier reservations, the place was booked, and we were put in a tiny, dim room next to the lodge's roaring electrical generator. Mike tried to get us a different room, but none were available. The room was so depressing, on top of being overly expensive, that I was close to tears from fatigue and disappointment. We dropped our bags and fled out into the beautiful evening, which was still light and lovely. If you ever find yourself in the area, I advise avoiding room 19A at the Sunwapta Falls Rocky Mountain Lodge in Jasper, if you can!

"I'm just so tired of being in the van," I sniffled as Mike drove along, looking for a good spot to shoot the sunset.

"Me, too. But we can't do anything about it, so let's just enjoy the beauty." We'd alternated saying that to each other on this trip; this time it was Mike's turn.

Jasper National Park was big. *Very big.* Huge, with trees and mountains and streams and lakes, like all of the countryside we'd just been passing through, but more concentrated. Like Canyonlands, it would take days to explore its riches.

We pulled into a tiny parking lot beside a rushing, powerful milky-green river as the sun, at last giving up its hold on the sky at ten-thirty p.m., began its final pyrotechnics.

There, hidden among trees, was parked an older camper, and seated in folding chairs by the river was a couple about our age, watching the far-off mountain peaks lit by gold and the sunset's gentle path across the water.

Mike set up his camera on a tripod to take a picture of the sunset on the river, but I felt bad disturbing the couple's solitude, and struck out on a path through the woods along the river to pull myself together.

"Be here now," I told myself sternly, looking at the long flare of sunset rays striking the snow-laden crags. The song of the river filled my ears, and there was nothing but nature all around me. *Which meant bears.* But I kept a good eye out, and after getting my frazzled nerves under control, I headed back to perch with Mike on a picnic table next to the other couple.

"Do you want us to move? Are we in your picture?" the man asked. He looked energetic and fit, a man of action, and his companion did too. Both were dressed in Columbia hiking gear. Many of the Canadians we'd met had been older and stout, or large families traveling in boisterous packs. At every park there were also the highly fit athletes, toting mountain bikes, wearing Lycra and running shoes, or with bodies draped in climbing gear.

This couple reminded me of us—athletically inclined, but comfortably padded by middle age.

"No, no, of course not," Mike said. "You're good." We were both surprised at this offer to move. *We were the ones invading their space.*

Mike was taking a time-lapse, which didn't require attention every minute, and he put an arm around me and gave me a squeeze.

"Are you okay?" he whispered in my ear. "I could tell you needed some alone time."

"I did, but I'm okay now."

I'd worked on myself to let go of expectations and enter into *now*. Expectations are the number one reason for unhappiness. Contentment is a choice, and joy comes from gratitude. I was thankful to be here, to have this experience, and to understand these things. Returning to them brought peace.

WORKING WITH KIDS HAD TAUGHT ME TO BE IN THE MOMENT, AND that even when some moments were ugly, there would always be brighter ones just around the corner. Sammy, a kindergartener, was someone who embodied this.

Sammy kept touching other kids inappropriately. Three different times, as a result of those incidents, his teacher referred him to me, and we went over a cheerfully illustrated coloring book called *Good Touch/Bad Touch*, with the aim of educating him about appropriateness.

Sammy had never disclosed anything during our previous sessions. I reached the page with children stepping on toes, children touching inappropriately, children pulling hair, children conking each other on the noggin. I asked, "Has anyone touched you bad, Sammy?"

"Yes," he said. He reminded me of a Rhode Island Red chick, sturdy and brown, with round cheeks and a fuzzy buzz haircut. "My babysitter touches me bad. Him and another boy."

When he told me what they did to him, I froze.

A part of me wished—oh, wished so much—that I didn't have to hear this story. I was trained for it; but like being an EMT at a roadside disaster, you can never be trained well enough.

I did what I had to: got names, descriptions of the abuse that I carefully noted down in his own words, when it began ("a long time ago") and when it ended ("November 23") and how often it happened in between ("a lot of times, I can't remember").

I turned a page of the coloring book, and Sammy saw the part of the book where a kid yells "NO!" and runs away, the suggested strategy for dealing with "bad touch."

He pointed at the page with the first real emotion I'd seen: betrayal narrowed his eyes and tightened his mouth into an unfamiliar angry expression. "I yelled 'no'! I tried to run away. But they were bigger than me. They caught me."

"It wasn't your fault," I said, for the first time of what I knew would probably be often. "You did what you could, and you came and told me. That was the right thing to do." Even as I said it, I felt sick about how Sammy's already unstable world, living with a single mom who worked all the time, would be turned upside-down by what we would unleash today.

The distinctness of the date stood out to me, as a kindergartener's sense of time is usually fluid. "November 23," I frowned. "It's February now. That was a while ago. How do you know the exact day so well?"

"November 23 is my birthday," he said. "That day, Mom told them to stop."

My stomach lurched; I swallowed and carried on. "So your mom knows. Do those boys still babysit you?"

"Yes." Sammy turned his eyes longingly to the pirate ship and other play therapy toys in the corner of my office. "Can I play with the pirate ship now?"

"Of course," I said, and followed him over to the carpet. I sat on a nearby beanbag, observing aloud as we do in play therapy, while Sammy acted out an elaborate battle where one under equipped soldier took on a massive ship full of pirates and gloriously slaughtered them using his superpowers.

It appeared to comfort him to believe such things were possible.

I sat numbly on the beanbag, my brain ticking through next steps: tell my principal. Call the police. Get interviewed by the Sexual Assault team. Share my notes and observations with them and the Child Welfare social worker. Then carry on with meetings, and other students, and private practice therapy after my school shift was done.

I just wanted to go home, hide in my bed, and cry. Would this day never end? For me? For Sammy?

I could feel the strange stiffness of my face: my eyes were wide and strained, like I'd looked into the sun a little too long. My mouth was dry, and my lips stuck to my teeth. My stomach churned. I hoped Sammy didn't notice.

He didn't. He had fully entered into his play. Sammy lifted the pirate ship manned by his hero, making motorboat noises, and putt-putted it all around the room.

"You're driving the ship," I observed aloud. "You're in charge."

Sammy pointed to the action figures he'd thrown off the ship. "They're getting eaten by sharks."

"Serves 'em right," I said, and he stomped on the two figures for good measure, looking to see what I thought of that.

I clapped my hands.

None of that was textbook play therapy, but I couldn't help myself—and Sammy's grin with a missing front tooth made my heart lift and my stomach settle.

Yes, this was bad—but it would eventually be better. Sammy was strong and resilient, and he would heal. He was beginning to, right now, by telling his truth and being supported.

He bent over to set the ship down, and the waistband of his shorts bagged open—he wasn't wearing underwear.

I couldn't bear it—that was one vulnerability too many. I stood up. "Come with me, Sammy."

I took him to the Keiki Cupboard closet, a cabinet where the nonprofit I'd helped found provided academic supplies and other necessities for kids in need.

We filled a new backpack with school supplies. He especially liked the toothbrush and a tube of sparkly bubblegum-flavored toothpaste; and I gave him an unopened package of brand-new underpants. Sammy hugged the backpack to his chest like it was Christmas.

I walked him to the bathroom and waited outside while he put the underwear on. I felt marginally better that he was now physically covered, though at this point that was largely symbolic.

Sammy hugged me goodbye when I took him to the cafeteria to rejoin the other students, already at lunch. "Thanks Aunty," he said, the way Hawaiian kids do. I'd told him to call me Ms. Toby, but he never remembered.

"You're welcome, Sammy." I dropped to his level and ruffled the tender bristles of his short hair, gazing into those round, innocent brown eyes. "You did the right thing telling me. Never forget that. You're a good kid."

Sammy would wonder if he'd done the right thing when the shitstorm broke over his head after school; but right now, he nodded and bounced off, excited to show his classmates his new school supplies.

I left to make my calls.

I made the call to police, I told my principal, I informed Sammy's teacher, and I shared my notes with the uniformed cops who arrived. I wrote a complete statement for the eventual trip to court.

The investigators told me that Sammy would be taken directly after school to be interviewed at the Friends of the Children's Justice Center in a child-friendly environment, by trained interviewers. One more time after talking to me, he'd have to tell his story—and that time, it would be videotaped.

His mother would likely be mandated some parenting classes for allowing the babysitter to continue to have access to Sammy, and hopefully, the 20-year-old pedophile and his friend would have their careers molesting kids cut short.

I hoped all of that would work out; but in any case, I'd be there with my pirate ship to help Sammy heal, and I had confidence that he would. Sammy defined resilience to me with his happy occupation of each moment, with his gratitude for a new toothbrush and sparkly toothpaste.

~

SOMEONE ASKED ME ONCE WHAT MIKE AND I HAD TALKED ABOUT ON this road trip, and how we'd passed so much time in each other's company.

A lot of the time, we didn't talk at all. Long stretches went by in comfortable silence as we daydreamed or listened to blues, jazz, or oldies rock, which we both liked. He drove; I stared out the window and made up stories.

Other times, something we saw or experienced would spark a thought or an idea, and we'd go deep, reviewing our lives together, the paths taken and not taken, how the kids were doing, what we wished for them. We'd plan our next trip or build castles in the air for our old age. We'd talk about God, and about our friends. We shared thoughts about our artistic work and got ideas and feedback from each other. A lot of the reason I enjoyed road trips was because Mike and I became almost symbiotic, anticipating each other's needs and moods, finishing each other's sentences.

We weren't like that at home. There, we functioned more like kids playing side by side in two different sandboxes.

The Canadian man in the camp chair asked us suddenly, "Would you like some tea?"

"We'd love that." Mike correctly interpreted my thoughts and mood. Usually I'm not that social, but today I needed some sort of positive encounter with other humans.

The man gestured us over to join his wife at the fire, and we chatted while he went into the camper, where he brewed a big pot of Red Rose tea. He returned with the tea in thermal cups, and we had a lovely visit hearing about their travels.

"Weekends are when we can get away in the camper to explore our beautiful backyard," the wife said. "We're from Hinton—it's only an hour away."

We told some of the saga of our trip so far and didn't leave their campfire until late, our spirits refreshed by their kindness, tea, and hospitality.

On the way back to the lodge, we both remarked on how lovely Canadians were, in general. "It's amazing the way that couple reached out to us. If it had been us, sitting there on the riverbank with our fire, we'd have resented the intrusion of other people," I said. We looked at each other, a little ashamed.

We'd passed a big billboard in one of the B.C. towns: *Courtesy Matters.* At the time, we had both commented on how that sign might be vandalized if it were in the United States! But politeness is important; it's a form of kindness and often segues into compassion and assistance rather than friction. Courtesy can create an environment of harmony, and become a group norm. I wished we had a lot more harmony in the USA, and I resolved to keep a little of that spirit alive in my heart.

CHAPTER FORTY-THREE
JASPER NATIONAL PARK

Day eighteen of our trip dawned in room 19A with the roar of the generator going 24/7. I slept in with the help of my earplugs and blackout curtains as Mike sneaked out for his morning mission of exploring, fishing, and possibly taking a photography boat tour on one of the lakes.

Frankly, I didn't care what he did. I just wanted to be in one place for a while.

After I finally woke up, I went into the lobby to get away from the generator's noise. When I asked about a quiet place to write, Jessica, the young lady at the desk, bilingual and gracious in both English and French, showed me to a deserted dining room.

"Is that room you're in okay?" Jessica asked, looking concerned, as she brought me a cup of tea. She must have known 19A was not a favorite.

"No, but the receptionist last night told us nothing else was available," I said.

"Well, some people have checked out. Let me get you into something better."

"Thank you so much!"

While she worked on that, I hiked through the woods below

Sumwapta Falls. The Falls were part of the same rushing, glacier melt river we'd sat by for sunset last night. The river funneled through a narrow canyon chute, and the roar and chaos of the water drowned out everything else in the vicinity.

I walked several kilometers through the empty forest, singing and clapping my hands to ward off any lurking bears. It felt good to really stretch my legs, work up a sweat, and be by myself in nature.

When I returned, Jessica showed me to a much bigger, quieter room. Mike found me moving our stuff into it. "Good job, honey!"

"We have to thank Jessica in the lounge. She cared enough to ask how we were doing with the generator noise."

"She must be Canadian," Mike said.

"Sure is." I grinned.

We took a drive out toward a trail we'd planned to hike, but it was much farther away than we'd thought. The sun was high at one p.m. when we spotted a white mountain goat napping on some cliffs, and pulled over to take her picture.

The goat, her sharp black horns a point of contrast against her white coat and dark eyes, was sitting regally on a ledge overlooking a small pond the color of emeralds. We didn't realize she was sheltering a tiny, snowy kid beside her until she stood up. I stared and stared at the enchanting scene, hoping to impress it so deeply on my memory I'd never forget it.

A funny thing happens in Jasper National Park when someone pulls over to the side of the road. All of the other tourists follow suit, cameras in hand, a gleam in their eye, trying to see what you've pulled over to get a look at—before they even know what it is.

Many of them have what I call "Disneyland syndrome": *We're on vacation, nothing bad can happen, we don't need to do basic safety.* They stop in the middle of the road, leave their car doors hanging open, and don't even put their flashers on. People vacationing in Hawaii do this also, to their peril.

Mike and I used our flashers, pulled well off the road, and always looked both ways.

I also disliked the way fellow tourists in the park jostled to get close to the animals. These animals are wild, and we should treat them that way. The parks aren't zoos; no fences separate us from them, and we were in *their* home, not ours. Bad enough that we were in visual range, let alone crowding close with our rude gadgets, loud voices, and outstretched, sticky hands.

After the mountain goat sighting, we found a hike called the Valley of Five Lakes. According to the signpost, the hike was moderately strenuous. Mike had a one-day fishing license and was determined to use it, so he carried his pole, along with his camera and a little water in the daypack.

At first, passing hot and sweaty returning hikers on the trail, I worried that we were going to go a long way and find nothing but dried-up swampy mosquito ponds.

I needn't have worried.

The Five Lakes were laid out like a necklace of turquoise beads, brightly colored and crystal clear. As the day grew hot, Mike cast into every pool and caught a small trout in one of the feeder streams. People were swimming in the gorgeous water, and if I'd known we could do that and worn my suit, the hike would have been perfect. We made do with splashing ourselves and I filled my billed cap with water, poured it over my head, and put it on wet, my favorite trick for hot hiking.

My initial assessment of Jasper National Park as huge was correct. The Park, established in 1907, encompasses a substantial wilderness area of four thousand, two hundred square miles of Alberta province, defined by glaciers, lakes, and peaks like eleven-thousand-foot-high Mount Edith Cavell. The Icefields Parkway, a road from the town of Jasper, passes subalpine forest and the immense Columbia Icefield (which we would see on our way out of the Park). Native wildlife included elk, moose, bighorn sheep, and bears.

Back at the room in the late afternoon, we both fell into the coma-like nap of the sun stroked and overtired, waking up in time for a gourmet dinner at the lodge's dining room.

By then I'd revised my first impression of the lodge. The staff were polite young people, the new room we'd been moved to was very good, and the restaurant's food was locally sourced. We both went for "local color" choices: I had the Hunter's Pot Pie, with elk, bison and rabbit in a wine sauce with onions and phyllo crust. Mike had a freshly caught seasoned trout, since his had been too small to keep.

After another spectacular sunset, this time viewed over a nearby lake, we made a fire in the room's wood burning stove and truly relaxed. Jasper National Park got a ten from us.

CHAPTER FORTY-FOUR
NATURAL BEAUTY AND CROWDS

Morning in Jasper dawned much chillier than it had been the last few days, considering we were edging into summer. Mike returned early from his sunrise shoot, lit a fire in our comfy new room, and climbed back into bed to wake me up my favorite way. After that auspicious start to the day, we took a quick stroll to the Falls, and then got on the road for Lake Louise and Banff.

As with many aspects of the trip, we didn't really know what we were getting into until we arrived—a deliberate choice on my part, and sometimes on Mike's because the trip was simply too long and involved for him to have researched every aspect of it.

There were huge glacier and ice plains on the way out of Jasper that we didn't know about (the Columbia Icefield), and they were dramatic and unique. Walking out on the glacial ice was a real possibility, and perambulating the Skywalk, a cantilevered structure of Plexiglas built out over a canyon, looked amazing. We hadn't planned for that, though, so we regretfully passed on after some photo ops.

I'd advise other visitors that if you do pass through that part of Jasper National Park to definitely take the hour or two needed to park in the designated area and take a shuttle bus back to the

Skywalk and explore it—or, trek out on the glacier/ice field, if you've brought proper gear.

Lake Louise, which Mike kept telling me was a major Canadian attraction, turned out to be mobbed. I mean, really, truly crowded, more so than any other places we'd been on the entire trip. We lined up with the other vehicles and crept along for close to an hour through parking lots filled with tourists rendered grumpy and hazardous by attempts to find nonexistent parking spots.

"Let's have a crazy expensive lunch at the big hotel up there and get valet parking," I said, pointing to the monolithically huge Fairmont Chateau Lake Louise, perched on a nearby knoll. I combed my hair and put on lipstick so I wouldn't look quite so Camping Woman, and we parked in the roomy garage of the huge, classy hotel. Parking problem solved!

We ate an amazing lunch out on the terrace overlooking the lake, which was truly spectacular, with snowcapped mountains and a glacier providing a backdrop for water the color of Peruvian opals. People canoed and paddle-wheeled around on the lake's calm surface, and the gardens surrounding it were perfectly groomed and flowering.

We were dive-bombed during lunch by some very sharp-beaked, aggressive birds ominously called "nutcrackers," and Mike tried to get a shot of the showy magpies flying around, chattering melodically. I was entertained by people watching the very international crowd on the terrace. We sat between a Sikh family (guessing by their Indian looks and the men and boys' black turbans) and an Israeli family (wearing yarmulkes and speaking Hebrew). Nearby, a Chinese family took a lot of pictures.

A very high-end wedding was taking place right in front of the hotel as we sipped our iced tea. Everyone at the ceremony was formally dressed. Mike took a photo of a cluster of Mennonite ladies watching the wedding in apparent fascination, grouped together in a curious, out-of-time gaggle in their long, monochromatic dresses and delicate white caps.

Lake Louise was very pretty, but not any prettier than a dozen totally empty lakes we passed along the way, and we were unprepared for the difficulty of finding parking and then a long trek to activities. Canoeing on the lake and walking around it looked nice, but why fight the crowds? Canada has so much room and so much beauty that you could find a more remote turquoise lake and have it all to yourself.

After that highly interesting and stimulating experience, we were supposed to go to Banff National Park to camp. We retrieved our van, got underway, and soon were overwhelmed by crowds again in the tourist trap of Banff town itself.

A storm appeared to be gathering over the area we speculated our campsite reservations were in, so we took a small, local route out of the area. Turning off zooming Highway 90 that heads to Calgary, we promptly got lost on some back roads. Lady Google was offline, the map we had was too big and general, and it was coming up on five p.m. on a small, winding forest road with nowhere to camp in sight. "Let's just continue on to Glacier National Park," Mike said.

I agreed, discouraged by our experience so far. I took the wheel once we were safely on the way and drove us on scenic Route 93 through the mountains out of Banff, heading in the general direction of Montana and Glacier National Park, experiencing normal Canada traffic levels (i.e., another car every five or ten minutes). Mike sat with his camera in his lap and looked for wildlife from the windows.

Even though we were paying close attention, we almost crashed into several other cars when a bighorn sheep doe decided to leap off a cliff and into the road—and lead her sisters, and their two lambs, across the highway.

Mike jumped out of the van as I wrangled it to the side of the road, managing to avoid the bighorns. He ended up chasing the frightened, confused sheep back onto the safe side of the road instead of photographing them, as they continued to mill about in traffic until he got them safely across. Later, we learned that bighorn sheep migrated through this area every summer—thus explaining the herd in the road.

We drove past the hot springs that the town of Radium Hot Springs was named for and could see that the large pool was crowded with bathers. The water was a bizarre color, even brighter aqua than most of the other alpine lakes in this area (and that was saying something). The word "radium" put me off from trying the springs, but upon reading more, it was apparent that no biohazard was involved, just unique minerals that colored the water.

Too tired to fight any more crowds than we'd dealt with already at Lake Louise and Banff, we were hoping to nab a room and call it a night. We pulled into the Apple Tree Inn, a roadside operation in Radium Hot Springs, run by a Luddite with frazzled blonde hair and a weary smile. "I refuse to run this place off the internet," she said, handing me a heavy, old-fashioned brass key. "All the other motels are booked up online and every day they're calling me to take the overflow from their booking mess-ups. Besides, there would be nowhere for people like *you* to go."

"Amen to that," I said. "We're so glad you take walk-ins!" I liked the heavy heft of the key in my hand and the dull gold shine of the round brass door tag. Once inside, the room had everything necessary and we passed out, grateful we'd made it to a comfy place to sleep.

Travel often reduces experiences to a deep satisfaction when physical needs are met; and yet we still seek these challenges. Maybe we aren't designed to always be comfortable.

We found a laundromat the next morning after Mike bagged some shots of bighorn sheep rams clambering on a nearby hill, and I caught up on my journaling. While the clothes were washing, we had breakfast at a restaurant called The Melting Pot.

As often happens for me, there were no non-egg choices on the menu. The waiter steered me to the meatloaf-and-egg special. "I'll bring extra toast instead of eggs," he promised.

When breakfast was ready, the waiter returned, bearing a plate with a slab of meatloaf atop a mountain of shaved potatoes, surrounded by EIGHT slices of heavily buttered toast—a hilarious sight.

I tried to only eat the meatloaf for calorie-counting's sake, but ended up munching down several slices of toast with blueberry jam as well. Mike, in the meantime, had a smoked salmon, feta cheese, and asparagus omelet that he said was one of the best breakfasts he'd had on the trip.

I had found maintaining my careful diet and daily yoga routine challenging as we traveled, and I often ended up eating odd combinations to avoid my trigger foods. Occasionally I'd try to sneak in a cup of coffee or a bite of egg; the rash immediately punished me. At

345

least I was able to write almost every day, and that helped me process and integrate the experiences we were having. Reviewing my journals, it was clear that I'd come a long way in letting go of the therapy work experiences that had haunted me, and with each new mile and vista, I was embracing my new life as a writer more.

Fueled up, with a bag of freshly laundered clothes, we left Radium Hot Springs and rolled through the remainder of British Columbia, heading for the Montana border.

The country in that area was warm and dry: rolling golden fields of grazing land peppered by pines of various kinds. Goatsbeard, daisies, and bachelor's button lined the somewhat battered roads.

Lured by a *"Fresh Cherries!"* sign, we pulled over to a working farm and drove down a graveled road toward the outbuildings. The acreage on either side was heavily planted with a variety of spectacular tiger lilies, as well as corn, tomatoes, cabbages, and beans. We pulled into a potholed dirt area behind some barns and parked, looking for where the cherries might be.

A bakery room was set up in one of the barns, lined with fragrant loaves of bread, racks of pies, and bins of rolls. The produce room beside it held caches of blueberries, cherries, beets, snap peas, kale, and more. We were tempted by the homemade strawberry rhubarb pies, but couldn't figure out how we'd deal with one in the van, so contented ourselves with a bag each of cherries and blueberries.

"Your flowers are so amazing," I gushed to the older woman swathed in a denim apron we'd roused from the kitchen of the bakery area to ring us up.

She tried to smile, but she had the exhausted look of years of getting up at four-thirty in the morning around her eyes. "They're pretty. We do something with them when we have time," she said. "But we don't have time this year."

"You mean they'll all go to waste?" I was horrified.

She shrugged. "Nothing ever goes to waste on a farm."

All those tiger lilies falling to rot broke my heart a little.

Glancing around, I saw her husband, toothless and overall-clad, toting a big sack of vegetables in from a golf cart. Out in the field, bent over in the sun, a couple of Hispanic-looking folks were working. So far out in a depressed-looking countryside, with no young people to help out and no gourmet farm-to-table restaurant to benefit from its bounty, the place looked like it took a lot of struggle to keep going, and the two food showrooms couldn't possibly support it.

As we drove away, I rested my chin on my hand and stared out the window, daydreaming solutions to help turn the farm's fortunes around as the miles rolled by. Most of my ideas revolved around creating opportunities through social media and internet-related sales, or possibly retreats for rich Calgary folks who wanted to experience farm life. It wasn't my problem to solve, of course, but I wished it were. I cared about the place from the moment I saw its lovely bounty and the farm woman's tired face. A part of me was drawn to that kind of life—the routines, the gardens, the animals—and I resolved to include more of that kind of setting in my books.

We crossed the border into the United States at Roosville, Montana, behind one other car. We entered the U.S.A. with no fanfare from the Canadian side, brusquely questioned by a poker-faced border guard—and then passed literally miles of cars lined up in the "Enter Canada" lane on the other side.

The traffic looked like a mass exodus to escape the zombie apocalypse. Miles of cars, vans, SUVs, Winnebagos, and fifth wheels stacked with every kind of boat, jet ski, quad, and bike, were all fleeing the United States.

"Do they know something we don't?" Mike exclaimed. We stopped in the middle of the road to allow an RV towing a jet ski to turn around into our lane to get out of the endless queue.

Perhaps these were all Canadians returning home after a long weekend, or United States folks running away to Canada over the Fourth of July holiday. Whatever the reason, the disparity was overwhelming, and we were glad to be in the "Enter the U.S.A." line this time.

Montana looked much like British Columbia, only the roads were rougher and we saw lots more roadkill—a deer, a squirrel, and bird or two, whereas we'd seen none at all on the other side of the border. The trash cans at the rest stops, always pristine and empty in B.C., were overflowing with refuse in the U.S.

We finally rolled into Glacier National Park around four, tired and holding onto carefully cultivated low expectations. Established in 1910, Glacier National Park is a fifteen hundred and eighty-three-square-mile wilderness area in Montana's Rocky Mountains, with glacier-carved peaks and valleys running up to the Canadian border. It was crossed by a famous route, the mountainous Going-to-the-Sun Road, and featured similar wildlife to Jasper National Park, though only a third the size.

"We made it all the way to Glacier National Park!" I told Mike.

"It's some kind of accomplishment," he agreed. Our route from Haines, Alaska, to where we were, with side trips, had covered close to two thousand miles.

Beguiled by no need for expensive fishing licenses in that location, we stopped every mile or so along a verdant green highway rolling through the woods to fish in pristine, sparkling Avalanche Creek. We didn't get anything, but the joy of standing so close to the singing water, listening to the birds, and watching the sun strike the tops of mountain peaks renewed our energy and excitement.

Coming back from one of these fishing pullouts, I returned to the van and set my pole in the open back hatch. Warm from the exertion of casting and hiking along the river, Mike had shed his jacket and was wearing only his T-shirt. He'd gone ahead of the van to take a photo of the road, a sinuous curve through the trees accented by a sunlit mountain at the end. The composition was perfect—the wild of nature all around, but the open road leading ahead and then out of sight. It seemed a perfect metaphor for our journey through this part of our lives; and in fact, out of all the many wonderful choices of images from our trip, it became the one I chose for the cover of this book.

Noticing that Mike's pole was already stowed, I put mine away, then shut the back hatch of the van and walked to the passenger door and pulled. The thing was locked. "Shit," I whispered, feeling a prickle of alarm at the back of my neck.

I walked around, checking. All of the doors were locked. My heart rate soared and sweat popped out of my pores. "Oh, no." The only thing I dislike more than running out of gas is getting locked out of the car.

The sun disappeared behind a snowcapped mountain, and it was suddenly very chilly—*but Mike probably had the keys.*

"Mike!" I called. "Come unlock the car, please, I'm getting cold."

Mike slowly stood up from where he'd been kneeling beside the road, camera in hand. The stark expression on his face told me what I didn't want to hear.

CHAPTER FORTY-SIX
GLACIER NATIONAL PARK, MONTANA

"Why did you close the hatch?" Mike exclaimed. "The keys were in my jacket! And now the jacket's locked in the back."

"The back hatch was open, so I thought the rest of the doors were open. And you never put the keys in your jacket," I said. "You always keep them in your pants pocket."

"Not this time," he said glumly.

The two of us circled the van, now shut up tight as a turtle in its shell. We ran through the conversation again, said a few bad words to no one in particular, then agreed it was a mutual accident. A situation like this would have resulted in Words Being Exchanged and Much Blaming and Shaming when we were younger. Thirty-plus years later, we knew that kind of thing didn't help.

"Now what?" It hadn't taken five minutes for the cold roaring down from the snow-topped mountains to raise the hairs on Mike's bare arms, as we tried our cell phones to call for help—but there was *No Service*.

Fortunately, cars were coming along beside our pullout fairly often. We waited for the next park shuttle bus and flagged it down with waving arms. Thankfully, they pulled right over and called the rangers, then left us there, self-conscious and embarrassed but no longer worried (much) about dying of hypothermia.

Mike refused to take my awesome Viking jacket from me, but accepted the weird thermal hoodie I'd been wearing underneath it. The hoodie fit him as tight as a sausage casing.

"It looks good on you," I said. "Not girlie at all." I squeezed his arm muscles to cheer him up. I was proud of us. We hadn't lost our tempers or been mean to each other. We'd focused on solving the problem.

Mike passed the time while we waited scrolling through the photos he'd taken on his camera and editing out the bad ones, and I read a book on my phone app. The story was so engrossing that I sat on the ground behind a boulder out of the wind to concentrate, and I was so into it I didn't realize that the ranger had finally arrived until I heard Mike talking to someone out by the road.

The ranger, a tall, kindly man, stuck a rubber wedge device inside the front door of the van, pumped it up with a handheld bladder, then inserted a long, bent metal prod into the car and pressed the Unlock button. *Presto!*

"I bet you didn't think breaking into cars was going to be in your job description when you applied for the Park Service," Mike said, grinning.

"I quickly discovered it's one of my main functions." The ranger packed up his fascinating bag of tools.

We got on the road again with many thanks to our rescuer, thrilled that the semi-disastrous problem had been relatively easy to solve, but I sagged in the front seat from an overdose of too much stimulation.

"Let's just get to the cabin where we have reservations." I refused to get out of the car again as we drove from the valley floor into the most stunning section of road we'd yet come across—and that's saying something, because we'd feasted our eyes on almost three weeks of outrageous beauty.

But Going-to-the-Sun-Road is just that—a winding ribbon

leading through the mountains that seems to show glimpses of heaven.

Glacier National Park had an immediacy to it, an in-your-face drama that elicited gasps from us around every corner, similar to Arches or Yosemite. Named for the radical carving action of the glaciers that inhabited the area and gouged open the peaks and valleys here, the park didn't allow for fatigue or ennui, especially at sunset.

Going-to-the-Sun-Road was narrow and perilous, hugging the side of striated granite cliffs like a goat trail, boulders bulging from its walls and water trickling down its cliffs. No RVs could fit on it, and it was nice to have left those vehicles' bulky company behind as we crept along the spectacular thruway.

It was after seven p.m. by then, and the light was sharp, slanting in from the west in the beginning of a lengthy sunset. Clouds snagged on razor-sharp peaks, downy wisps backlit by sunset. Snow in the highest areas gleamed like veins of marble, and I smelled the chill, elemental scent of stones and heard the roaring gush of melted ice.

Waterfalls poured around and beneath every gully, covering an entire mountain alongside us in a lengthy section of route called the Weeping Wall. Every time we came around a corner, I was close to the edge of a vastness that sucked at me. Looking out into it felt like an act of faith. The beauty was so acute that it felt like pain, making my teeth ache and my eyes water. Even driving slowly, there was no way to take it all in; I clung to the door handle as if it were a life preserver.

We finally made it through the exquisite twenty-eight miles and turned into the driveway leading to Rising Sun Motor Inn and Cabins. Checking in, we were astonished to find a really good restaurant, after having resigned ourselves to a dinner of beef jerky and potato chips, the only snacks we had left in the car. Two Dog Flats Grill featured local, natural gourmet food, and we each had a delicious, reasonably priced meal—local trout over whole wheat pasta primavera and beans, corn muffin, pulled pork, vegetables, chicken, and a steak. The whole bill, including wine, came to sixty dollars, which felt like a giveaway after Alaska's and Canada's high prices.

Our tiny cabin was adorable and cozy with a powerful heater and good beds. Our low expectations and gratitude had been rewarded.

"Thank you, God," we both said, closing our eyes on another amazing day.

~

I WOKE FROM THE DEEP, REFRESHING SLEEP THAT TIREDNESS, A CHILLY room, and thick blankets bring on, feeling as grateful as I had when falling asleep. The twenty-first day of our road trip, location Glacier National Park, Montana, dawned crisply cold and filled with bird-song that reverberated off the stony bluffs surrounding our eight-thousand-foot elevation.

Mike was long gone, chasing the sunrise, and I was eager to get outside, too.

I dressed carefully for the walk I'd planned down to nearby St. Mary Lake, knowing it was the coldest outside that we'd yet encountered. On went my special hiking socks, thick stretchy pants, a long-sleeved shirt, the weird thermal hoodie of a thousand uses, the green fleece tube they called a "buff" that I'd bought in Lillooet but hadn't worn yet, my old gloves with the fingers cut off for typing, and of course my Viking jacket.

I stepped outside the cabin into light as pure as gold dust that filled the thin, clear air; visibility was so incredible that I could pick out the colorful details in nearby cliffs and gorges. Unfamiliar birds filled the area with music as I walked briskly down the road, watching tiny clouds hovering above the forest like exhaled breath, swirling around the flanks of the spires and crenellations of dark, upthrust crags.

With all of the drama of the mountains and plummeting waterfalls, it would be easy to miss the incredible variety of wildflowers in Glacier National Park. Rocket daisies, bachelor's button, black-eyed Susans, statice, buttercups, ferns, and everywhere, five-petaled wild pink roses—all of these rioted along the roads and massed in meadows filled with hopping, chirping wood tits and bouncy ground squirrels.

I walked to the dock where we planned to take one of the boat tours across St. Mary Lake. I enjoyed the perfect reflections of the nearby mountain in the turquoise water, the quaint old-fashioned launch adding a timeless note. I had the same reverent feeling I'd had on the edge of the ocean, escorted by whales and bald eagles when I'd walked the beach in Alaska singing hymns.

I took myself to breakfast, and as often happened on this trip, Mike read my mind and met me there without even returning to the cottage where I'd left him a note. Breakfast was excellent, and after grabbing a hat for me, the backpack camera carrier for him, and a couple of water bottles, we took off for the boat tour and hike.

This turned out to be a great way to enjoy new views of the park from a unique angle via the charming vintage motor launch. The guide on board told us about the interesting geology of the park.

Glacial upheaval put the oldest rocks on top of mountains and newest at the bottom. The road construction in 1910 killed so many horses and mules pulling loads of rubble and supplies that the area we were passing was named Dead Horse Bluff, because they used to throw the carcasses over the edge to avoid attracting bears to the workers' camps. Another interesting fact was that the park had opened in 1910 with a hundred and fifty glaciers and was down to twenty-five, which will be gone entirely by 2030 at this rate of thaw.

A wingtip of grief brushed over me at this news; no one knows what this kind of change will mean for the park or even for us as humans—but the signs are not encouraging.

We were supposed to hike with the ranger in a group once the boat docked, but I could tell that Mike was restless after having to sit through the guide's speechifying. He'd gone out into the open bow of the boat, where the infomercial talk didn't carry. As we neared the drop-off point and trailhead, the captain mentioned that we didn't have to stay with the ranger, we could hike by ourselves as long as we were back at the dock by one p.m.

When Mike finally returned to our seat, I whispered, "We can do the hike by ourselves. We don't have to stay with the group. Let's hop off and hurry out in front of the crowd."

"I love you," Mike said, and hugged me.

So we hurried off the boat and up the trail to beat the group, so we could stop and take pictures, listen to silence and birdsong, and yes, miss out on an educational opportunity. We exchanged that for a chance to experience the hike unfiltered by another's interpretation.

The trail was fairly level and gloriously massed with flowers, an inviting path of possibilities with views of the lake around every turn. By walking more quickly than the nature-talk folks, we were able to reach two crashing, aqua waterfalls instead of just one. The water was the magnificent hue caused by minerals carried by glacial runoff, particles too tiny to sink that colored the water aqua in sunlight.

We spotted a black bear fording the river on our way back to the motor launch, which gave everyone a thrill, and an even bigger thrill came later in the day, when we took Going-to-the-Sun Road to the Logan Pass Visitor Center for a little afternoon hike around the mountain peaks nearby.

We walked the short path around the center's clutch of buildings, trying to get a shot of a herd of male bighorn sheep on the nearby butte. They were so far away that they looked like ants on the side of the mountain. Since our encounter with the herd of does outside of Radium Hot Springs, we'd learned that these sheep foraged in same-sex herds unless it was mating time.

We were heading back toward the van and the parking lot when suddenly one of the bighorn rams trotted out of a nearby stand of trees, directly toward us.

Mike plunked down the Rhino Chaser on its support monopod and began shooting.

Cars screeched to a halt as the bighorn crossed the road. A stampede of people from the Visitor Center milled toward him as he trotted through the grass verge toward the parking lot, still heading toward us. I froze, waiting to see what he would do, hardly breathing.

Up close, the ram was the size of a small pony, with a glossy buff hide and delicate legs. He smelled musky and powerful, and snorted breaths through narrow nostrils. His eyes were golden brown, with that eerie sideways goat pupil, and he looked at me contemptuously as I gaped at him, too surprised to fumble for my camera as others had the presence of mind to do. His demeanor was casual but haughty as he moseyed along the perimeter of the parking lot. His giant horns reminded me of huge nautilus shells curling back from his head, crownlike and heavy, and yet clearly just a part of him.

Four feet from me was a waist-high barrier made of logs defining the parking lot. The ram paused, looking at the cars in the lot and the milling, exclaiming crowd, and then bounced over the barrier with no apparent effort or even what you could call a jump —it was more like he simply levitated over it and continued down the sidewalk, testicles the size of footballs swaying, regal as an emperor.

He'd passed so close to me that I could have touched him.

A young, pink-cheeked volunteer in a ranger outfit had stopped beside me, assessing the situation, and I asked, "What the heck is he doing?"

"Looking for antifreeze in the parking lot," she said. "This herd is so used to people that they come over here all the time, looking for salt."

As if to lend credence to this, the herd of five rams we'd been trying so hard to get a photo of had come down from the butte. They galloped back and forth beside the highway, performing for the crowd and looking over at the parking lot where their brother was still roaming, lowering his head periodically to sniff the asphalt. None of them were as bold as the biggest ram, who was now clip-clopping between the parked cars.

"Yeah, they even follow people into the bushes because they've learned when people are going into the bushes, they're peeing. They lick up the pee to get the minerals and salt in it."

"Ew," I said. "I thought antifreeze and urine were poisonous."

"In large amounts, yes. But these animals are voracious when it comes to salt and minerals, and they'll do anything to get them."

Finally, the big ram seemed to tire of his quest. He pranced back across the street to join the others, and they trotted off into the forest.

"Where are the females?" I asked.

"The males have their herd, and the ewes and babies are in another herd. We don't see the females in this area."

I thanked her for the information.

Excitement over at last, we drove back to St. Mary Lake, where we threw some lures, went to the restaurant and had another great dinner, and then retired to our cottage for writing and photo editing.

"I wish we had more time here," I told Mike. "A whole week, even."

"This is the first time you've said that, and I agree," Mike said. "Jasper was so big and spread out, it was hard to get a sense of it.

Banff we never saw at all. Glacier Bay in Alaska was mostly the water. But this park is kind of like Yosemite. It's all close enough to really enjoy."

Regretfully, we spent time plotting the next day's course out of the park toward Washington State, where we were meeting our grown kids for four days at a cottage in the San Juan Islands, the perfect end to a great road trip—or so we hoped.

CHAPTER FORTY-SEVEN
GLACIER NATIONAL PARK TO WASHINGTON STATE AND THE SAN JUAN ISLANDS

We awoke to approaching thunderstorms in Glacier National Park on day twenty-two of our trip. We had a long way to drive, but we prolonged the journey out of the park along the thirty miles of Going-to-the-Sun Road by stopping to take vista shots of the deep indigo morning, the cloud kerchiefs, and the rain-washed brightness of the roadside flowers.

The threatening thunderheads had busted open and it was pouring by the time we got to the Trail of the Cedars walk on the floor of the West Glacier valley, a place I'd wanted to hike before we left. We contented ourselves with grabbing an all-you-can eat salad bar brunch at the lodge down in the valley and a couple of souvenir mugs instead.

Speaking of souvenirs, I like to collect magnets from places we visit because I see them often on the fridge, and they're fun reminders of a trip. Plus, they don't take much money or space in suitcases. Be careful, of course, to store the magnets away from anything techie like phones, computers, or cameras.

Today's goal was to get as close as possible to Anacortes Ferry Terminal on the Washington coast, from which we would depart for the San Juan Islands, so we drove from Montana through a corner of Idaho and into Washington State. All day, the skies were a flat and impenetrable lid of smoke from fires burning on this side of the country.

That particulate matter in the air made for a long, dramatic sunset we drank in at a roadside pullout overlooking the huge, calm Columbia River meandering through arid, rocky banks outside a hamlet called Vantage in Washington. There was no food or lodging in Vantage, though, so we spent the night at a Days Inn in Ellensburg, a personality-free truck stop and college town.

Within just a day of driving, the cool green forests and jagged mountains of Glacier were only an achingly lovely memory.

WE BLEW OUT OF THE DAYS INN IN ELLENSBURG WITH ITS INEDIBLE breakfast (nothing but carbs and a few sad, bruised apples) and got on the road for Anacortes. Desert surrounded us, somewhere in the middle of Washington: rolling hills peppered with rocks, golden stubbly dried grasses, and the occasional minty-green accent of sagebrush. Vultures whirled overhead, and the Columbia River appeared and disappeared alongside us.

Many, many giant big rigs rattled past us on the highway, making me so nervous and jumpy that I had to listen to the self-hypnosis relaxation recording I'd made before the trip, putting my therapy practice into personal use. I should have listened to the recording when I was freaking out with anxiety on the ferry to Alaska, but I'd forgotten I had it on my phone.

The recording worked like a charm, making me sleepy, even, so that when we stopped for gas, I bought an energy drink—the healthiest one I could find in the limited selection, with "vitamins, taurine, and 20% real fruit juice." I'd resorted to buying these hideous concoctions as a last resort caffeine boost since becoming a tea drinker.

I'd learned to like tea, but it simply didn't have the caffeine kick that coffee does. The situation was better in Canada because they were set up for tea drinkers. Every Canadian restaurant had little metal teapots, at least, and some even had delightful "Brown Betty" ceramic teapots, which was one of the things I was beginning to enjoy most about tea. They had good quality flavors, too, so I was able to indulge in English Breakfast or chai, my favorites. Canadians even served the beverage as if it were coffee, with a waiter coming around with a carafe of tea in one hand (orange pekoe Red Rose, the Canadian default brand to our U.S. Lipton) and a pot of coffee in the other. I was never made to feel a second-class citizen when I ordered tea in Canada.

That situation immediately changed when we entered the coffee-drinking USA. As an example, I sat beside an English couple the morning I had breakfast alone in the Two Dog Flats café in Glacier National Park. Servers came by repeatedly with coffee pots, prompt and courteous, but when the three of us said, "We're waiting for hot water for tea," they passed on. Our overwhelmed waitress finally trotted back with a single mug of semi-hot water and a Lipton tea bag on a saucer for each of us.

We exchanged sympathetic looks, and the English couple, clearly in the know, took out their own high-grade packets of Earl Grey while I squished the Lipton bag in the mug with a spoon, hoping to get more juice out of it.

This kind of thing almost never works to get me the high-octane caffeine hit I crave in the morning. For one thing, the water has to be super-hot, a degree or two off boiling, for tea to release its full flavor properly. In general, I steep my tea longer and make it stronger, a throwback to my coffee addiction.

Developing allergy conditions has opened my eyes to a whole segment of the population (and it seems to be growing) who have food sensitivities and can't just eat whatever traditional food we've decided as a culture is what a meal or beverage should be.

This whole aside brought me back to the moment at the gas station when I had to buy a gruesome energy drink, having been unable to get the tepid water and tiny Styrofoam cup at the Days Inn to steep the Lipton tea bag to anything like effective morning strength.

"What is that?" Mike's brows flew up at the sight of the black can with its terrifying logo and *SUGAR FREE ENERGY BLAST!* emblazoned on the side. "My health foodie is drinking *that*?"

"A last resort." I gagged down a couple of sips, all I could manage to swallow of a drink that tasted like melted saccharine Jolly Rancher candies—but even a couple of sips were enough for my eyes to finally open.

We eventually left the desert and rolled into what I'd expected Washington State to be like: green mountains and wooded hills. We blundered into the morning commute traffic to Seattle, confirming that we never want to be part of that rat race again, and skirted the city, ending up in Marysville, a pleasant small town an hour from Anacortes.

Mike washed the crusted-on Canadian mud off the van at a truck wash, while I did a major shop at Safeway. I was stocking up for the stretch of days we'd have at one location—a cabin on the ocean at Lopez Island, one of the smaller of the San Juans. I had made a meal plan and a lengthy list, because our two young adult children were joining us there and we'd be cooking in the vacation rental.

Wandering the aisles with a shopping cart for the first time in three weeks and buying enough food for an army—or the Neal family, on vacation—was pure joy to me. Much as I'd come to love being an empty nester and my adventures with Mike, I loved just as much when we'd get together as a family and I got to be a mom again, even if it was only for a few days.

Chores completed, we tried to get on the twelve o'clock ferry to the San Juans, but didn't make the standby cutoff and thus had four hours to kill in Anacortes.

This bald sentence covers a three-hour stretch of optimistically arriving and buying tickets, getting in the proper lane to get on board, waiting in the car with the windows down and the motor off, and then talking and looking around and playing with our phones for an hour. It covers the moment when the massive ferry docked and the boarding began, foot and bike traffic streaming onto the ship as cars rolled down the metal grate. It covers the three cars ahead of us that rolled forward onto the dock, taillights saucily flashing, and the moment when the pudgy woman wearing a pair of pink plastic sunglasses and a bright yellow, reflective-tape-trimmed vest, lowered the boom on our hopes by setting an orange road cone down in the lane right in front of our vehicle.

"Next boat is the five-ten p.m.," she said. She handed us a ticket to mark our place for the next ferry. "Sorry."

We regrouped with an effort and pulled out of the lane to make the best of the situation. Anacortes was a colorful mix of cute cafés, shops, and hard-boiled local boat/fisherman culture. Mike loved the Marine Supply and Hardware store on the main street, a mix of real-man spools of rope, chain, anchors, tools—with antiques and funky recycled parts for every possible fix-it need. There were several art galleries that showcased a strong art community as well. By the time we'd walked around the good-sized forest park in the middle of town, Mike and I felt a bubbling excitement: we hadn't even made it to Lopez yet, but sensed we were close to somewhere that was going to be very special to us.

The ferry ride, when it finally happened, was wonderful. We drove the van onto the monster boat, squeezed out between the cars to trek up onto the deck, and parked ourselves on the foremost point of the ferry to scan for orcas and other wildlife as we traversed smooth green water between numerous forested islands. The forty-five minutes to Lopez flew by as I felt everything that was the best of British Columbia and Alaska come together for me: open sky, smooth rich green water, cool air, a sense of wilderness, but with connectivity at all times—we had three bars of phone reception!

I was predisposed to fall in love with the San Juans before we even got there because I was an island girl, through and through. I'd also heard stories of how great the islands were from my parents, who visited a lot in the 1990s after Hurricane Iniki hit Kauai and devastated their community. They were enamored with the place and even thought about relocating there, and I'd seen enough pictures to know I'd love it too.

Lopez Island was the perfect combination of quiet, rolling farmland, thick, wild forest, and cute but unpretentious tiny town. We happened upon a great fine dining restaurant right after debarking the ferry, where we ate outside and enjoyed watching the boats entering and exiting Fisherman's Bay at sunset. Driving along flower-trimmed, mellow roads where friendly people waved because end to end, the island was only fifteen miles long, I pronounced myself in heaven before we even got to our cottage.

Renting the cottage sight unseen for a week had been a real act of faith. It was the only place Mike could find at high season in the San Juans for under a thousand dollars a week, not being particular about which island we were on. The cottage looked okay in the photos, but on the trip we'd learned that the secret to happiness was to have high appreciation and low expectations.

That's what we had when we finally turned down a graveled drive to find that the cottage was . . . well, amazing. It had a modern kitchen, was clean and updated, and was even equipped with a romantic gas stove in the living room. Two large bedrooms and bathrooms would give us and the kids plenty of space and privacy, and it had satellite TV and speedy Wi-Fi, not to mention a view of nearby Hunter Bay framed by trees off a large deck.

"You're never going to want to leave," Mike said, and he was right.

~

TAWNY AND CALEB FLEW OUT FROM THEIR RESPECTIVE HOMES IN California to Seattle, rented a car together, and took the ferry to join us at our remote oceanfront cottage. At their age, with their busy lives, Mike and I were honored that they still wanted to spend time with us.

The first night, we recapped stories from the trip while toasting marshmallows on the deck. The kids were thrilled by the sight of a pair of bald eagles that liked to perch on a tree nearby in the evening, and even though we'd seen many on the trip, these majestic birds were still awe-inspiring up close.

The second day, the four of us took a walk out onto the sparely beautiful, wind-carved bluffs of Iceberg Point, unexpectedly expansive and grand. Lichen in pale green and orange bloomed across dappled gray rocks, and there was a view all the way to Canada, which wasn't far, about seven thousand feet, it turns out. Being together—the banter, the stories—made it a joy to share time with our children, not yet encumbered by spouses, and we didn't take it for granted.

Adventure can be tricky. Sometimes an activity that starts out as a pleasant, optional entertainment can pivot into something painful or even life threatening—but that's what makes adventure worth having: risk that can season an experience into reward.

I had occasion to remember this when we split up after our morning hike. Tawny and I took a walk along the raft of pebbles off of Fisherman's Bay Road on the public beach, then went into the tiny town to cruise the bookstore and stop at a café for tea and coffee. We talked about love, career paths, creativity, and moving to new homes, and returned for a blissful afternoon of reading together in the living room with the fire going. Mike and Caleb, cut from the same action/hunter cloth, spent their afternoon renting kayaks and fishing.

The next day we broke into the opposite constellation, with Tawny and Mike going to Orcas Island on the ferry together and taking a whale watch tour while Caleb and I went hiking.

Caleb and I decided to check out a corner of the island called Watmough Bay, where we found the pristine little gem of water unexpectedly crowded with Saturday afternoon picnickers and a few brave souls even leaping off the rocks and landing, with shrieks of agony, in the lovely but frigid water.

Crowd avoidance being a Neal trait, Caleb spotted a zigzagging trail that climbed to the top of Watmough Head, a spectacular bluff. "Let's get a view from above, Mom. That looks like a fun hike."

A fun hike to him, at a physically fit twenty-seven, looked like a daunting mountain to me at fifty with joint issues, but I didn't want to disappoint him. We'd paused on the path toward the water and glanced at a map of the area; I vaguely remembered seeing that there was a trail that appeared to be a loop from the top of the Head back to the parking lot.

"Sure, why not?" I still liked to take any challenge I was presented with. We set off with nothing but our phones and the car keys in my pocket.

The climb up the Head was almost vertical in places, and went on a good while past my comfort level. I kept thinking we must almost be at the top, but we weren't. I worked my way up from one rock to the next, grabbing roots, reaching for smooth red manzanita trunks to cling to, hauling myself higher each time. About halfway up, I began worrying about the descent, because my knees and hip had been bothering me, especially when going downhill. Caleb was a gentleman and paused often for me to catch my breath. He even asked if I wanted to turn back.

"No, I want to see what's at the top," I said.

"And that's how humans have been finding things since the dawn of time," Caleb said.

The view from the top of Watmough Head bluff was totally worth the exertion to get there—a vista of complicated clouds, emerald bay, and calm ocean, with a tufted blanket of trees stretching off in every direction.

We reveled in the endorphins released by serious exertion as we sat on the edge of a great egg-shaped boulder looking into the heights and depths, enjoying a slight cool breeze and the bond of having done something challenging together.

I felt the vastness, but in a good way, and took some photos.

"I think I saw that the trail was a loop," I said, the sweat having dried on my brow but not wanting to retrace my steps down the precipitous trail. "Let's find our way back to the car by taking the loop."

We hiked inland in good spirits. Glossy-leaved, waist-high bushes and ferns provided an understory filled with chirping birds as dim afternoon sunshine filtered through a conifer forest. The trail seemed well-trafficked, with soft dirt underfoot and gentle rolling ups and downs, a nice change from our climbing ascent. Caleb bounded ahead, then returned to talk as I trudged along. We bantered and discussed movies we liked and the state of modern relationships.

After a good long while of walking, the forest began to take on a sameness, and we'd been walking much longer than I thought we should have.

"Seems like we should be circling back to the main road by now,"

Caleb said, reading my mind. "Let me run ahead and see what I can see."

"Okay."

Caleb shot down the path, clearly eager to make sure we were on the right route. He soon returned. "I don't think this is going in the right direction, Mom. We should go back."

"No, I'm sure I saw that the trail was a loop," I insisted, reluctant to admit defeat, and still more reluctant to clamber down the extremely steep trail we'd come up, especially after adding several miles of hike to the equation. The 'sunk cost principle' was at work: The longer a certain path is traveled, the harder it is to admit you were wrong and turn back.

I'd only thought of that as a metaphor, but now I was experiencing it literally.

By the time the trail had forked three times with no signage, and the light through the forest canopy overhead was getting dim, we were worried.

I felt disembodied and highly anxious as I experienced an emotional transformation: the woods, at first pretty and green, chittering with carefree wildlife, began to assume a frightening monotony, an impenetrable depth. Every turn in the path looked like every other turn, and none of it was taking us where we wanted to go.

My heart sped up. I told myself to relax—there was no danger here, no bears on this island—but, still, the feeling of being "lost" gnawed at me, and it wasn't a good feeling.

At six p.m., we were facing a fourth fork in the trail when I finally took out my phone to try to see if Google Maps would work and give us some clue where the road was.

Eventually the GPS, by some miracle, found us. It was an eerie experience to look down at the pulsing blue dot on the lit phone screen in the dim forest light and see no trails, no roads, and the outline of the coast a long way off. Somehow, we'd walked inland along the Head's ridge, meandered to and fro, and gone a good way into a large forest. We were nowhere near an exit of any kind.

I revised my casual attitude toward Lopez Island, which had seemed almost too tame and domesticated until this moment.

"I feel dizzy." Nausea rose up to tighten my throat. My phone in my hand and my feet both seemed a long way off. I was in danger of fainting.

Caleb threw a burly arm around me in a hug and helped me sit down on a stump. I smelled the fright on him too. It affected him differently, giving him a jolt of adrenaline.

"Just rest, Mom. Wait right here and I'll scout ahead." He galloped off down the trail, clearly experiencing a burst of energy that had to be burned off physically.

I sat at that crossroads of the path alone, trying not to shriek, "Don't leave me here!"

This was every scary movie where stupid people wandered into the wilderness with no map, no compass, no water, and were slain, eaten, or both.

But we weren't going to die. There were no bears, cougars, or headhunters on Lopez Island. I bent over at the waist, put my head between my knees, and used it to think.

Yes, we were lost.

But not truly lost, because we knew our way back. The lefts we'd taken at the forks would just have to be rights. We'd have to hike all the way back to the bluff and back down the cliff we'd come up. It sucked, but it would have to be done.

Caleb returned at a run.

I stood up. He put both arms around me and hugged me again, a big hard squeeze. I tried not to cling.

"We're going to be okay, Mom, but we have to go back the way we came," he said firmly. He'd calmed himself down, too, and come to the same conclusion I had. "I want to get started now, so we don't run out of light." Worry for me showed in the tight corners of crystal-blue eyes just like his father's.

Caleb felt responsible for me.

This was the first time we'd been in a situation where our roles were reversed—or at least equal. I wanted to make him as proud of me as I was of him, and I rose to that challenge with a burst of energy. "Let's just take our time. There's no emergency here, and I can hike a long way, farther than you think I can," I said. "Call me 'Iron Mom.'"

"Good one." He patted my shoulder. "Let's do this."

So back we went. Caleb paused to hug me periodically for encouragement. We had another bad moment when I thought we'd only had three forks where we needed to take rights but Caleb remembered four. Finally, uncomfortable with thirst neither of us would admit, we reached the bluff again and looked out over a dimming sunset. Thank God it didn't get dark until after nine p.m. this far north!

"I'm going to write about this," I said, heady with relief to be on familiar ground. "Let's take a 'back-here-again' selfie." We did, bantering a little once more, and then, using a sturdy stick, Caleb in front of me to break my fall if I went down, we slowly climbed down the precipitous bluff I'd tried to avoid.

At the car, we found one small bottle of water and drained it. We made a pact that neither of us would ever again have the hubris to take off on an unknown hike without a map, compass, and water.

Dinner at the cottage was lively as Caleb and I told our tale. Mike shook his head, Tawny laughed, and we looked at photos of the orcas Mike and Tawny had seen on their boat tour.

The San Juan Islands are a beautiful place—but they're a little wild, too, and we love them for it.

CHAPTER FORTY-EIGHT
OLYMPIC NATIONAL PARK, WASHINGTON

We left for Olympic National Park and cut our time at the cabin short on Lopez Island for two reasons: 1) to distract me from getting too sad over saying goodbye to the kids, who needed to return to their lives two days before us, and 2) to have more time to explore Olympic National Park, which is six hundred and fifty-five thousand acres of magnificent and varied wilderness.

We packed up and waited in the alarmingly long line for the return ferry from Lopez Island to Anacortes with our faithful van parked behind Caleb and Tawny's bright red rental.

The locals were prepared for the Sunday afternoon waiting lineup that wound a half-mile along the road from the dock. They took spots in line and cracked open beers, sat in lawn chairs, and whiled away the time gossiping and playing cards, while the four of us (and the rest of the non-islanders) paced around, trying to use cell phones that weren't working.

"I can tell waiting for the ferry is a real part of living here," Mike said. "When does the next Paradise Crime audiobook come out?" Unfortunately, we'd listened to our last one a ferry-wait ago.

We all ended up making it to Anacortes in time for the kids to catch their flights from Seattle. We hugged them goodbye on the pavement outside the Anacortes Fire Department, where we'd pulled over to gift them some of our camping gear, since we couldn't take it all back to Hawaii.

Bittersweet emotion silenced me as we drove away from that last hug. A certain relief, on the one hand, because things were back to our familiar long silences and gentler speed, but also the severing—a low-level grief that has haunted me ever since that affectionate, adventurous boy and bright, brave girl moved out; an amputated sense of something missing, which I've learned, reluctantly, to live with.

THE CHANNEL CROSSING FROM COUPEVILLE TO PORT TOWNSEND ON the Olympic Peninsula was the roughest we'd yet encountered. Heavy swirling rivers of current moved beneath wind-ruffled steely waters and dense fog engulfed us, but the ferry plowed on unperturbed. This was one ride where I avoided the deck and enjoyed watching the sea spray through the thick viewing windows while sipping a hot cup of tea.

We disembarked the ferry in Port Townsend after that rough ride, with an hour's drive to reach where we planned to stay the night. We stopped for seafood at a restaurant, and by the time we pulled into Port Angeles, Washington, we were too tired for any further exploration.

Port Angeles is the gateway to Olympic National Park, and we nabbed a room at a Days Inn that I spotted from the highway. (I'd picked Days Inns three times on the trip as a good compromise between the tawdriness of a Super 8 and the expense of a Holiday Inn.)

The next morning Mike woke me. "It's looking rainy and overcast." He'd already been into Olympic National Park, scouting around. "Let's go up to Hurricane Ridge and see what we can see."

"Hurricane Ridge is one of the highest points in the park that you can reach by car." I scanned a brochure and summarized aloud from it as we drove. "Olympic National Park covers several microclimates, from the top of the Olympic Mountains to old-growth rain forests in the Hoh. Mt. Olympus is popular with climbers, and hiking and backpacking trails cut through the park's lush forests and along its Pacific coastline, apparently." I closed the brochure and looked at Mike. "It's another big one: fourteen hundred and forty-two square miles—but right now, I can't see anything."

The mountain was completely socked in with clouds so heavy that they clung to the car as rain, and as we drove up toward Hurricane Ridge, we could hardly see beyond the yellow glare of our headlights. We wound higher and higher, traversing seventeen miles from the park gate, disappointed by the foglike conditions. "I bet this is how people feel a lot of times going up Haleakalā," I commented, thinking of our beloved volcano, often hidden in clouds.

Near the top, the mist began breaking up, unraveling like so much carded wool into skeins and swatches, spinning and lifting in the light wind. I gasped at the deep-cleft valleys we were skirting, as the belly dance of teasing cloud veils accompanied us all the way to the summit.

The top was a spank of cool air so clear that every blade and twig seemed limned in light. Hurricane Ridge swept away below us, a golden velvet meadow trimmed in a million yellow daisy flares pierced by purple fireweed. A harrier hawk hovered and plunged, glorious as he did so.

The cloud drama was an orchestra: rolling uphill trumpet salutes, great billowing bass notes, timpani-thin shreds. Mike and I both set up cameras for time-lapses and were conferring about the best angles when a bearded young ranger approached us. "Are you Tawny's parents?" he asked.

"Indeed we are," I said, belatedly remembering our daughter telling me that a friend of hers from college was a ranger here. She'd texted him that we'd be coming through the park, but it was pure coincidence that he'd passed by and recognized us from her photos.

Ranger Tyler was official in his green uniform with a shiny gold NPS badge, and he recommended three major parts of the park: here on the Ridge, the beach, and the rain forest. Fortunately, we had outings planned to all three areas.

We ate some breakfast at the Visitor Center and took in Tyler's entertaining official ranger talk about bears. He told a personal story of a bear encounter and showed us a black bear skull with its highly developed nasal passages, educating us on the bear's role as an important part of the food chain. The bear is a top consumer and distributor of fish/ocean by-products, and even a pollinator and seed spreader through all the berries and vegetation it eats (and seeds it poops out all over its habitat).

The talk helped me be a little less afraid of bears, and I was glad to have met such an enthusiastic and capable young man who has chosen a life of service in the National Parks.

We went back down the mountain reluctantly, taking in the beaches along the way as we headed for the rain forest. The fog at Rialto Beach kept us from seeing the famous rock spires that are so often photographed, but I got a good picture of a totem pine, raising its skeleton arms above the silky gray stones of the beach.

We were saddened to find that the famous Hoh Rain Forest was dry. Not just a little dry, but *really* dry. The swamps were nothing but mud holding the footprints of elk gone foraging. The lush moss the Hoh was known for hung in brittle brown beards from the trees. Salmonberries had dried on the bushes, and dust rose from the well-traveled trails to lie like pollen on the fern skeletons surrounding the paths. The streams were so low that watercress lay dying above the waterline, and the creek beds held nothing but stones.

"We haven't had rain in thirty-eight days," one of the ladies at a snack shop outside the forest told me. "It's unprecedented for this area."

Still, the magic of the rain forest remained, captured in arches of dappled green light and dizzyingly tall, big-leaf maples shrouded in flags of moss. Mike took a picture of me sitting in a stump alcove that felt like a fairy queen's throne, as incredibly tiny birds sang their hearts out all around me, and I breathed in the loam and the chemistry of the biosphere. Walking along I felt myself as nothing but a dandelion seed, blowing by briefly and for that time, a part of things.

At the end of our hike through the Hoh, a knot of sightseers drew our attention.

A pair of spotted owls, a variety neither of us had seen before, were sitting on a branch high in a moss-draped tree, and as mosquitoes circled us in a humming swarm, Mike got as close as he could, capturing the owls' curious looks at us and their darting, Egyptian-dance-like head movements. They cuddled and preened, entirely the most adorable creatures we'd seen in the parks so far.

"That was the cherry on the cake of a perfect day," I said as we drove to Kalaloch Lodge, a wonderful old hotel directly on the park's beach and still inside its boundaries. We ate dinner in the lodge's dining room and went to sleep on pure white, deliciously silky cotton bedding, the sound of the sea in our ears.

∽

I WALKED DOWN TO KALALOCH BEACH IN THE MORNING. THE handout from the hotel had predicted an extra-low tide, along with its dire warning: *Beware Killer Logs!* Apparently, the giant driftwood trees all over the beach, currently stacked like dinosaur bones, roll up in the surf and inevitably squash a few people every year.

This was an unexpectedly jarring note, but I wasn't worried about being crushed because the tide was out as I set out across fine gray sand that seemed to go on forever, an ocean of grains from white to black and everything in between. Water runneled from above and below the wide tidal swath of beach into crinkled patterns similar to the surface of a brain. Seagulls moved in shapes like schools of fish, rising as one, circling, descending, flowing back and forth, and landing once again. I ran into their midst, and as they rose around me I flew with them, arms outstretched, laughing out loud with joy.

Thousands of small crab shell molts crunched underfoot, and the fine, silty sand blew around them in a mournful way, covering and uncovering their fragile calcium-deposit carapaces. A river that ran from the direction of the lodge carved an arc pattern across the sand, bold as a scimitar stroke, and following its path was a bald eagle.

He gave that harsh cry they do, a croak followed by a whistle—but the eagle was still a grand sight as he followed the stream, his yellow beak a rapier, his white head and tail catching the light.

Breakfast at the Kalaloch Lodge was exceptional. They had a yogurt and granola parfait that was perfect for my food issues, and the tea situation was as good as Canada, with a full thermos of hot water, a selection of teas, and a little pot of cream and sugar. I was in heaven, and so was Mike with his bacon omelet.

Just driving through Olympic National Park is worth doing. The park is spectacular, from views at Hurricane Ridge to the moss of the Hoh rimmed by stunning, empty Kalaloch beach. The road through the park is mile after mile of flowers, ferns, and trees, and everywhere plays the drumbeat of woodpeckers and birdsong, especially in spring.

We explored the nearby Quinault Lake area, taking in side trails at Maple Grove and an old homestead, enchanting in the mossy woods, and then hiked the North Fork of the Quinault River for a couple of miles.

The river had been reduced by drought to a sparkling turquoise creek that Mike was determined to fish. With my new, less-fearful-of-bears attitude, I thoroughly enjoyed a level trail imbued with light sifting down through magnificent old-growth trees, painting the ferns and berry bushes below in watercolor shades.

As a treat for our very last night on the trip, we rented a cottage all by itself with a bank of windows facing the panorama of Kalaloch Beach.

A little sun-struck and tired from hiking, Mike and I sat in Adirondack chairs on the little deck and watched the longest sunset we'd yet seen, a spectacle that ran like a Las Vegas light show from eight-thirty p.m. until ten p.m., when at last darkness fell and the sun bade us a reluctant goodbye.

"Guess it's over," Mike said. "What a month it's been."

I reached for his hand. "Until next time." We went inside and closed the curtains.

EPILOGUE

A week after our trip, I was ushered into the same examination room for my physical where I'd seen my doctor on the visit that inspired our trip. Slipping into the paper gown that would more easily permit the indignities soon to follow, I gazed around the room and thought of all that was similar to, and different from, the last time I'd been here three years ago.

My blood pressure was down. My lungs were operating at one hundred percent capacity. I'd lost twenty-five pounds. My skin rash had cleared up. My blood lab results were great, and according to my EKG and stress test, I had the "heart of a twenty-five-year-old."

I was filled with energy since I'd left my stressful mental health jobs and had gone into writing full-time. Although there were times when I missed my former career, I didn't miss the heartbreak of it; and I'd come to believe that I could still do good in the world through my writing.

Mike's health results were similar, and our relationship was stronger than ever.

As I slid my butt up onto the tissue-covered table, I spotted the newest calendar on the wall.

July was open to Crater Lake National Park in Oregon. Hyper saturated in cheap-print color, a giant volcano cone filled with azure water seemed to call to me. "I haven't seen you yet," I told Crater Lake. "But I will."

The doctor entered, reviewing my labs and intake information. I distinctly remembered puzzling with her over my rash: the multitudinous referrals and office visits, the tears I'd shed in this very room over my eroded physical and emotional state.

"This is amazing." She looked at me with a grin. "I hardly ever get to see these kinds of results with someone your age. You must have been on a real health journey since I saw you last."

"It's been a journey, all right," I said. "And I think Crater Lake might be next."

We have two ways you can affordably enjoy Mike's photographs from the trips written about in the book—a monthly calendar or a magazine he designed with quotes from *Open Road*!
Magazine: tobyneal.net/MNORbk
Calendar: tobyneal.net/MNcal

Sign up for a newsletter to be notified about my next memoir: tobyneal.net/TWNnf

If you haven't read my first memoir, *Freckled: A Memoir of Growing Up Wild in Hawaii*, turn the page for a sneak peek.

SNEAK PEEK
FRECKLED: A MEMOIR OF GROWING UP WILD IN HAWAII

Age: 4, Rocky Point, Oahu, 1969

Sand. Big yellow mountains of sand. So much, and a long way, a giant tabby cat napping in the sun. Mom's holding my hand, and I'm naked because we're going swimming when we get to the bottom of the long wooden stairs leading away from our house.

I drop to my knees and dig into the big smooth grains, wriggling my body deep in to feel it all over, sinking in delicious warmth because the sun is hot on my head. When I push my arms into the sand and they come up, my skin is the same color. My freckles look like the beach. This always makes me happy.

The sand feels different as the day changes. Morning, it's gray, cool, and the air is blue. The mynah birds talk, and the ghost crabs are out running on skitter legs over the beach. The coconut tree next to my window makes a sound like clapping when the wind first comes up; it's cheering that we have a new day. And when the day ends, the sand is orange, warm, and soft when we sit on it and watch the sun go down.

I love having no clothes on. I can feel everything better that way.

I feel a shivery-good sensation in my legs. I come up out of the sand and walk out of the way by the *naupaka* bush and squat to pee.

"You always do that," Mom says, and I laugh, because what else would I do when I get that feeling?

The ocean is the color of the stones in Mom's silver bracelet as she reaches to take my hand. Her skin is hot and brown and smells like coconut oil, and I want to lick it as we walk down to the water, slow because her belly is so big now with my brother or sister inside —*hapai* it's called.

Mom wades in, and the cold water hits us. I squeal and cling. She laughs some more, sinking down so it covers us, prying me off to hold me by both hands.

"*Opihi*," she says, and she means the little round pointed shells that stick on the rocks. Sometimes we pry them off with a screwdriver and eat them. They taste like rubbery seaweed.

She holds my hands. "Kick! Kick!" she commands.

I kick, the feeling of the water sliding over my skin like the silky blanket I sleep with. I kick and kick and she swirls me through the water, and then puts one hand on my tummy and says, "Now rainbow your hands," and I do, making the paddling rainbow motions she's showed me before, and suddenly her hand is gone and I'm swimming! And I see the yellow beach, our little blue house, the coconut tree beside it, and the windows that watch the ocean.

Then I'm sinking. I gasp for breath, and I paddle harder, but I'm under now, my eyes stinging, but still open to see the waves ahead hitting the white foamy sand and my breath held, tight and burning, until Mom's hand comes and lifts me back up.

I cough and cough. The water stings inside my chest, much more than the pool or the bath. I'm mad that I sank and surprised that I can't swim yet. I was sure I could!

"Again!" I say when I'm done coughing.

"You never give up, my sassy bug. You're going to get this. I know you are." We start over with kicking, and rainbow arms, then she lets me go and I sink . . . but this time I know it's going to work.

I hold my breath and keep my eyes open while I kick and rainbow. Underneath I see fish—shiny *aholehole* and green-striped *manini*, and the black rocks on the bottom that make this place called Rocky Point.

I like it under the water. I feel like I can fly, and this time my kicking and rainbow arms bring me back up by myself. I blow out my breath, drops spray off my lips, and I grin big even though my face is barely out of the water.

"You did it!" Mom catches me, and I cling around her giant belly, and the belly pushes back at me. I push back at it, and it's like we're talking. I can't wait to meet who's in there. Mom laughs. "The baby's excited too. You're just going to get better and better at this." She lets me ride on her back as she swims, holding onto the strap of her crocheted top. My legs trail behind, and sometimes touch her, a silky feeling.

Pop's watching from the top of the stairs. He is big and tall, and the sun shines on his blond hair. He has his camera out. He takes pictures a lot, and he's looking to see if there's any surf, because he takes mostly surf pictures. There's no surf today, and I can tell he's grumpy by the way his mouth makes a line—so do his eyebrows. He's usually grumpy when there's no surf or he drank a lot the night before, and I want to cheer him up.

Maybe he will be happy that I swam. I wave to him from the water. "I swam! I swam!"

Pop nods, enough so I know he heard me. I should have known that wouldn't cheer him up, but I can't think of anything else.

I drop to roll in the sand again when we get out, because it's warm and feels so good.

Mom hoses us off outside the house, and she chases me with the cold water as I squeak and laugh. We go back out to the beach, and I help her dig a hole in the sand for her belly to go in. She puts her towel over the hole and lies down with a sigh. "Untie my top, will you?"

I pull the cord of her top so there's no tan line on her back; I burrow into the sand beside her and feel it's warm fingers all over my skin.

Pop comes down the stairs. "She really did it this time?" He sits beside us in that way all the surfers do, with his knees up and arms looped around them. His eyes look a little red, how they get after he's been smoking a doobie. *Good.* He's not as grumpy when he's had a joint.

"You know Toby never gives up." I hear the smile in Mom's voice. I lie next to her and rub a piece of her long, chocolate-colored hair between my fingers and suck my thumb, happy.

At preschool I heard the ladies talking about ESP. There are two kinds of ESP: the kind where you hear other people's thoughts, and the kind where people can make other people do what they want just with their thoughts.

I always listen to grownups so I can know things— "Elephant ears" Mom calls me. Grandma Gigi, Pop's mom, believes in ESP too. "I can tell when you're thinking about me, so that's when I call," Gigi says. She does usually call when we need something, and I love when her packages come in the mail, even though Pop grumbles that I'm getting spoiled.

I want to have the make-people-do-stuff kind of ESP.

We're at dinner, and the sun has gone down behind the ocean. I can hear the surf outside; it's coming up bigger with a shushing sound.

"Should be good tomorrow," Pop says, sipping his beer. Because my dad's a surfer, we always pay attention to what the surf is doing and the weather conditions. There's "onshore," which means the wind is in my face off the ocean and that's bad for surf—I don't really know why. Then there's "offshore," which is best to make the waves good, and "Konas," which means the wind is light and from the side.

Mom is sitting between Pop and me. Her tummy is super big, almost touching the table, and she's wearing her favorite blue muumuu that she sewed herself. There are some oven-baked fries, special because they are not *goodforyou*, and fish Pop caught, and Mom's salad with bean sprouts. We have white plates with a flower border, a milk bottle filled with daisies, Mom's favorite flower, and everything is pretty and good.

Even after he smoked today, Pop was still grumpy. I can see how he's feeling like a black cloud over his head. Bad things can happen when I make him mad, and I do that a lot because I'm noisy and too bouncy. I'm always trying to get him to like me and see that I'm smart and can do things as good as a boy. Because I was supposed to be a boy and be named James Theodore the Third.

Mom and Pop didn't know what to call me when I was a girl, so they named me Toby after the redheaded boy who runs away to the circus in a movie Mom watched at the hospital. I have no middle name because "when you're old enough, you can choose your own middle name." This worries me. How do I pick the right name? I wish I could just be named James Theodore the Third, even if I am a redheaded girl.

Maybe I can make Pop do something with ESP.

PICK UP THE KETCHUP, I think. *PICK UP THE KETCHUP. PICK UP THE KETCHUP.*

Pop looks up at me. His green eyes have red around them. The overhead light shines on his curling blond hair, going thin at the top. I stare at him, my lips moving, as I think as hard as I can—*PICK UP THE KETCHUP.*

"What are you looking at?" His voice is a low thunder sound. He narrows his eyes. I don't look away or answer. He's going to *PICK UP THE KETCHUP* any second now. I just know it!

"Stop staring at me." Pop gets louder and seems to swell.

I can tell how mad he's getting, but I stare until my eyes hurt because I can feel it almost working—he's going to hear me any minute now. I don't blink. I want to be scary: eyes wide, mouth tight, staring hard as I think *PICK UP THE KETCHUP.* I will make him do what I want!

"I said stop looking at me, disrespectful little brat!" He stands up and his chair flies back and lands on the linoleum with a thud. He's *enormous.*

My mom makes fluttery noises, but it's too late. Roaring something I don't hear, he comes around the table and whips me off the chair by my hair. I crash onto the floor and hold onto my head and use my legs to hold myself up, trying to keep from being dragged— it hurts so bad, as he hauls me down the hall, but I won't cry. I'm stubborn like that. I'm not afraid of pain.

I'm still thinking, *PICK UP THE KETCHUP.* Like it's going to save me. Like he can hear me.

But he doesn't.

He drags me all the way into my little white bedroom, sits on my bed, and throws me over his knees, lifting my cotton dress. He spanks me hard, and it goes on and on.

Tears start against my will. I wriggle and bite my lips and finally scream—a loud shriek because I'm so angry and sad that ESP didn't work; the spanking hurts, and he hates me more than ever now.

The scream's what he's been trying to get out of me, though, because he's done with the spanking. He throws me onto the bed. I bounce, and my head smacks the wall.

I lay there stunned. *I guess I don't have ESP.*

He slams my door so hard it shakes the walls of the little old house.

He rages at Mom outside my bedroom. "Goddamn spooky kid, staring at me like that. I can tell what she's doing; she's trying to get inside my head! Goddamn it, you better straighten her out . . ."

Mom argues with him. I feel bad for her because I hear her crying as he yells about how bratty I am, what a pain in the ass, why did we have a kid in the first place, and now we're having another one.

I put the covers over my head and suck my thumb, rubbing the silky edge of my blankie and thinking about my favorite story. Aladdin can ride a carpet like it was a floating car, and he has a genie in a magic lamp. I wish I could ride a carpet to get away, and if I got three wishes, the first would be that Pop would be nicer.

Mom reads to me every night, and I can't wait to be able to read to myself. Miss K at preschool says I'm almost ready—sometimes I can even read the books Mom has read to me the most because I remember what each word was.

Mom sneaks in with my dinner plate after Pop has gone outside with his evening six-pack. She sits on my bed, and it dips toward her. I come out from my nest of covers and rest my hot, angry face against the mound of the baby under her muumuu, and the baby pushes at me. I put my hand on her belly and push back, and it bumps my hand again.

Mom strokes the hair off my face. "You shouldn't irritate him like that."

I know I shouldn't, but I can't help it. Even when I'm being good I irritate him. He's never been happy with me. She knows this, too. I'm pretty sure the real problem is that I wasn't James Theodore the Third. "Would Pop like me if I was a boy?"

Mom jumps a little like maybe the baby kicked her. "Oh, no, honey. You two are just oil and water."

I sit up and eat my dinner, my plate on my knees, and I know a secret. *Maybe I don't have ESP, but I can get into his head. And he can spank me all he wants, but I'm not afraid of him.*

It's almost as good as if he loves me.

~

Continue reading Freckled: tobyneal.net/Frwb

ACKNOWLEDGMENTS

Dear Readers:

Memoir is the form of writing in which you make art out of your life, a process akin to serving up your guts for public consumption: it's not for the faint of heart. Cheryl Strayed said it well: "Making art is not the same as making sense of yourself on the page." That's what I was up against in this book, and for the second time; it was difficult to know how to follow up a story like *Freckled: a Memoir of Growing up Wild in Hawaii*. That narrative was such a unique bit of history, and it had a clear trajectory.

This segment of my life made sense to forge into memoir because I'd already learned that the idea of a "trip to find yourself" resonated with others, as I posted most of these chapters, as they happened, on my blog. Many people dream of the kind of road trip we took, as much a personal journey of transition and change as a tour of the National Parks.

Mike and I saw firsthand that many Americans never visit the parks, public treasures that belong to all of us and that now, more than ever, need our help, support, and advocacy. I hope that through these adventures, you fall a little in love with the legacy that President Woodrow Wilson set in motion on August 25, 1916, in creating the National Park Service. If you're at a turning point of whatever kind in your life, a journey to be renewed by nature couldn't hurt and might even put you in touch with a self that you've lost touch with.

Once again, I owe my editor and dear friend, Holly Robinson, the sincerest thanks for two fearless structural edits of this book. She always pushes me to dig deeper and share more bravely, and I thank her for her clear eye and fearless red pen.

I want to acknowledge and remember Sean King, lava guide extraordinaire, who took Mike out on the lava on the day he lost his gear to the ocean. Sean was killed in 2018 while guiding some visitors out on the lava when the group was ambushed by poisonous gases interacting with a rain squall. He made sure his group escaped before succumbing. We were blessed to have known him.

Thanks also to Mike, not only for the gorgeous photographs, but for putting up with being married to a writer who, in the middle of any given activity, gets a gleam in her eye and says, "This will make a great scene!" and feverishly jots it down on a Post-it, a napkin, or her phone.

Mahalos to my wonderful agent, Laurie McLean, and our fabulous book development team: Angie Lail, and Dorothy Zemach, who copyedited. Another thank you goes to Emily Irwin, for crafting a unique and visually gripping cover from Mike's photos. And a special thank you shout-out goes to my business manager, Jamie Davis, for all she does to support me and my writing and make everything we do, the best it can be. You rock, lady!

And finally, a big THANK YOU to Mom and Pop, for raising me in such a way that I learned to deeply love and experience nature. May your lessons be passed on to others through this book.

And dear readers, until our next adventure together, I'll be writing!

Much aloha,

Toby Neal

~

We have two ways you can affordably enjoy Mike's photographs from the trips written about in the book—a monthly calendar or a magazine he designed with quotes from *Open Road*!
Magazine: tobyneal.net/MNORbk
Calendar: tobyneal.net/MNcal

~

Sign up for a newsletter to be notified about my next memoir:
tobyneal.net/TWNnf

BOOK CLUB QUESTIONS

1. Toby becomes inspired to plan a month-long trip after seeing a photo calendar on her doctor's wall. Think about the pieces of art in your home (photos, pictures, even knick-knacks on the shelves). What do they look like? Do they represent places or people you know, or experiences you'd like to have, or feelings—or something else?

2. Toby mentions that although she and Mike had lived quite near Haleakalā for many years, they had never hiked into the crater before. Why, do you think? What are the famous sights near you? Where would you take visitors? Are there any famous sights near you that you haven't visited yet?

3. Mike and Toby are both artists—Mike a photographer and wood-worker, Toby a writer. Is there anything that Mike can accomplish or show through his art that Toby cannot (or cannot easily)? Is there anything Toby can accomplish or show through her art that Mike cannot (or cannot easily)? What are some differences between a scene 'described' by a photograph, a painting, by prose, and by poetry? Even though Mike takes professional-quality photos, Toby

still takes her own photos, even of the same scenes. Why, do you think?

4. Toby says one thing that impressed her about Mike when they first met was that he had the courage of his convictions; she gives the example of him not being embarrassed about demonstrating his faith. What examples from the book show that Mike would have seen a similar quality in Toby?

5. Toby discloses that before she got married, she had hoped to fashion for herself a "normal" adult life. Looking back from the perspective of *Open Road*, talk about some ways in which Toby's life seems "normal" (whatever that is!) and some ways in which it doesn't.

Toby struggles with her decision to leave her counseling career to become a full-time writer, at one point wondering if she might be able to continue to help people through her writing. What are some ways in which books help people? Have you ever been helped by a book?

6. For the two road trips in *Open Road*, Mike does most of the planning, although even so, not every step is completely planned. What are some advantages and disadvantages to planning a trip in advance? and to not planning a trip in advance? Do you consider yourself more of a planner or someone who takes things as they come?

7. Throughout *Open Road*, Toby discusses her writing—her fiction, her journal, her poetry, and her earlier memoir. Why might a writer want to explore these different modes?

8. Have you visited any of the of the national parks described in *Open Road*? Have you visited any other national parks? Talk about

your experiences and impressions. Which of the parks in *Open Road* would you choose to visit, if you had the opportunity?

Toby had some specific goals to accomplish when she set out on the two trips that make up *Open Road*. Do you think she accomplished those things? What might be her motivation for wanting to take another long trip?

A trip or journey is a common metaphor for life. Why, do you think? Do you see your own life as a journey? Talk about some ways in which the comparison fits, and some ways in which it doesn't. Why is this book called *Open Road*?

9. Have you read any of Toby's fiction? Her first memoir, *Freckled*? What did you think of her other work? What draws you to one genre over another?

TOBY'S BOOKSHELF

PARADISE CRIME SERIES

Paradise Crime Mysteries
Blood Orchids

Torch Ginger

Black Jasmine

Broken Ferns

Twisted Vine

Shattered Palms

Dark Lava

Fire Beach

Rip Tides

Bone Hook

Red Rain

Bitter Feast

Razor Rocks

Wrong Turn

Shark Cove

Coming 2021

Paradise Crime Mysteries Novella
Clipped Wings

Paradise Crime Mystery
Special Agent Marcella Scott
Stolen in Paradise

Paradise Crime Suspense Mysteries
Unsound

Paradise Crime Thrillers
Wired In
Wired Rogue
Wired Hard
Wired Dark
Wired Dawn
Wired Justice
Wired Secret
Wired Fear
Wired Courage
Wired Truth
Wired Ghost
Wired Strong
Wired Revenge
Coming 2021

ROMANCES
Toby Jane

The Somewhere Series
Somewhere on St. Thomas
Somewhere in the City
Somewhere in California

The Somewhere Series
Secret Billionaire Romance
Somewhere in Wine Country
Somewhere in Montana
Date TBA
Somewhere in San Francisco
Date TBA

A Second Chance Hawaii Romance
Somewhere on Maui

Co-Authored Romance Thrillers
The Scorch Series
Scorch Road
Cinder Road
Smoke Road
Burnt Road
Flame Road
Smolder Road

YOUNG ADULT

Standalone
Island Fire

NONFICTION
TW Neal

Memoir
Freckled
Open Road

CONNECT WITH TOBY

Facebook: tobyneal.net/TNfb
BookBub: tobyneal.net/TNbb
Instagram: tobyneal.net/TNin
Twitter: tobyneal.net/TNtw
Pinterest: tobyneal.net/TNpin

Join the TW Neal newsletter to learn about new nonfiction titles as they are available: tobyneal.net/TWNnf

Join my Facebook Group,
Friends Who Like Toby Neal Books, for special giveaways and perks:
tobyneal.net/TNFriends

Made in the USA
Columbia, SC
13 July 2021

41793428R00245